Service Providers

ASPs, ISPs, MSPs, and WSPs

A Wiley Tech Brief

Service Providers
ASPs, ISPs, MSPs, and WSPs

A Wiley Tech Brief

Joseph R. Matthews
Mary Helen Gillespie

Wiley Computer Publishing

John Wiley & Sons, Inc.
NEW YORK • CHICHESTER • WEINHEIM • BRISBANE • SINGAPORE • TORONTO

Publisher: Robert Ipsen
Editor: Margaret Eldridge
Developmental Editor: Adaobi Obi
Managing Editor: Micheline Frederick
Text Design & Composition: Benchmark Productions, Inc.

This book is printed on acid-free paper. ♾

Published by John Wiley & Sons, Inc.

Published simultaneously in Canada.

Library of Congress Cataloging-in-Publication Data:

ISBN 0-471-41818-8 (pbk. : alk. paper)

Printed in the United States of America.

10 9 8 7 6 5 4 3 2 1

To Martha Enid Matthews,

she epitomizes excellence
as a service provider
at the Information Desk
in the Carlsbad (California) City Library

Wiley Tech Brief Series

Other books in the series:

Ray Rischpater, *Internet Appliances.* 0471-44111-2

Debra Cameron, *Optical Networking*. 0471-44638-9

Tom Austin, *PKI.* 0471-35380-9

Steve Mann and Scott Sbihli, *The Wireless Application Protocol (WAP).* 0471-39992-2

Ray Rischpater, *Palm Enterprise Applications.* 0471-39379-7

Chetan Sharma, *Wireless Internet Enterprise*. 0471-39382-7

Traver Gruen-Kennedy, *Application Service Providers.* 0471-39491-2

Jon Graff, *Cryptography and E-Commerce.* 0471-40574-4

William Ruh, Francis Maginnis, and William Brown, *Enterprise Application Integration.* 0471-37641-8

Contents

Introduction

This book is a guide to Internet-enabled services from a technology and business perspective. While the landscape of technology-related services is ever changing, several have emerged as key players in the service provider market—Internet service providers (ISPs), application service providers (ASPs), wireless service providers (WSPs), management service providers (MSPs), and other xSPs. These service providers allow businesses to outsource Internet, software, and other technology needs ranging from email and faxes to enterprise resource planning (ERP) and customer relationship management (CRM) in an easy, cost-effective, and efficient manner. Alternatives to in-house technology can serve to tighten internal control over the total cost of project ownership while creating a managed, secure, customer-centric infrastructure.

This book will point out commonalties, highlight enabling technologies, and develop guidelines for strategic partnerships between various service offerings. Trust is a critical selling point in convincing management of any business or organization to transfer important in-house data to an outside provider. The decision makers must be certain that a service provider can demonstrate that its infrastructure is better, faster, and cheaper than one the organization can produce internally. To win the business, the service provider must provide professional staffing, first-rate equipment, and proven procedures, in addition to computer processing and network capacity. To keep the business, it must under-promise and consistently over-deliver.

Security has been cited in some groups as managers' number one concern when it comes to outsourced technology. As risks can never be eliminated entirely, it is up to service providers to address all potential points of failure and to their customers to decide how much risk is acceptable. This includes physical threats such as fire or theft and technological risks like a system breech by hackers. This book will help managers evaluate these risks and determine if the mitigation strategies will reduce the risk to acceptable levels.

A *customer* is an organization (business, institution, government, etc.) that subscribes to services offered by the service provider. A *service provider* is an Internet-enabled business that offers an outsourcing alternative to customers for some or all of their business functions. An *end user* is a person like you or me at a desktop who must call the help desk when some system or software is nonfunctional. A *vendor* provides a piece of software, hardware, or system, without the ongoing relationship offered by a service provider.

Successful service providers must help their customers to equip internal teams and external partners with cutting-edge tools that reach customers with a seamless continuity and competitive advantage. A few years ago, many of these service providers did not exist. A year from now, who knows? But the service providers that survive and thrive will be the ones that go beyond the terms of their service level agreements with customers. They will act as strategic partners instead of outsourced vendors, embrace a passion for innovation and forward thinking, and volunteer to help create global best practices and industry standards.

Overview of the Book and Technology

Customers demand their technology to be *high-speed*, *highly available*, *scalable*, and *far-reaching*, but organizations often lack the internal resources to provide these cutting-edge technology solutions. This creates increasing demand for third-party sources of reliable, trustworthy information on technology-based business decisions leveraging the Internet. Many industry observers forecast that the market for a variety of service provider offerings will grow exponentially and exceed $100 billion in the next five years.

The generally accepted wisdom about handling strategic functions internally and outsourcing the rest is easily torn apart after just a quick look at what should be the most strategic functions in any company: those that affect customer relationships directly—sales, marketing, and customer service. Yet companies routinely outsource any or all of these activities. Independent distributors or commission-only sales people handle sales; companies use ad agencies for some or all of the marketing activities; and there are a number of call centers that handle everything from telemarketing to technical front-line software support. Thus, to date, strategy and outsourcing have had no correlation.

Benefits of outsourcing applications include the following:

- Enabling information technology resources within a company to focus on more strategic projects

- Lowering up-front costs for implementation of business applications, which usually lowers the overall cost of ownership
- Creating a more predictable cost model
- Facilitating reduced implementation time for applications, which results in more rapid access to the desired business functionality

Technology-related business models are complex and demand significant planning to integrate all of the required processes. As IT managers begin their requirements analysis for a new software project, they inevitably ask themselves: "Do we build an application ourselves, purchase a third-party software product, or partner with a service provider?" Partnering has become a general requirement in today's business environment, demanding the seamless integration of processes and the unity of service-level commitments. To convince a potential customer to transfer important data, the service provider must be able to demonstrate to the customer that it has professional, first-rate facilities.

Managers should expect their technology outsourcing partners to deliver the following:

- Integrated and proactive processes for system, application, network, and service level agreement monitoring management and reporting
- 24/7 call center support
- Full data backup
- Off-site storage of backup media and disaster recovery
- Web-based, self-provisioning account management (adds, changes, and so on) and support
- Regular, professional maintenance and upgrades of all application software and server hardware

How This Book Is Organized

Readers should have a basic familiarity with the Internet and Web-enabled technologies such as email as well as a comfort level with team building and customer relationship management concepts.

Chapter 1 provides a discussion of the factors that favor the rapid expansion of the service provider marketplace as well as a general overview of the service provider industry.

Chapter 2 discusses the various Internet-related technologies that are enabling the exploding use of the Internet and some of the innovative uses of the Internet that benefit businesses and organizations.

Chapter 3 discusses Internet service providers, perhaps the most familiar of the service provider models. ISPs maintain networks linked to the Internet via high-speed dedicated communication lines. An ISP offers the use of its system to companies and individuals, which, for a fee or through advertising support, are able to connect to the Internet via modems or maintain Web sites or Web servers that Internet users can access. The ISP model ranges from mammoth enterprises like AOL to small mom-and-pop companies with local ISP access.

Chapter 4 focuses on application service providers, which aim to allow businesses to outsource their software needs via an Internet browser in an easy, cost-effective, and efficient way. ASPs manage and deliver application capabilities to multiple users from a data center across a wide area network. The ASP community has carved out an emerging marketplace where the software and telecommunications industries converge with critical information management tools.

Chapter 5 examines wireless service providers. WSPs allow Internet access that involves sending and receiving specific information such as personalized news and email via technology such as Wireless Application Protocol (WAP), Bluetooth, and Voice XML.

Chapter 6 concentrates on management service providers, which deliver IT infrastructure management services over a network to multiple customers on a subscription basis. An MSP can provide security or network management, which is not an application but a best-practices method, and the technology resources enabling it. The MSP helps allow an IT staff to focus on a higher level of development for its business organization to be more competitive. The MSP takes on the role of handling the day-to-day operational tasks, providing the IT staff with the information to make business decisions.

Chapter 7 outlines the offerings from a plethora of other service providers. In this chapter we focus principally on four groups of xSPs: hosting service providers, infrastructure service providers, Internet telephony service providers, and content service providers.

Chapter 8 provides information about the importance of service level agreements. An SLA defines the responsibilities of a service provider and the users of that service. It also identifies and defines the service offering as well as the supported products, measurement criteria, reporting criteria, and quality standards for the service. Dispute avoidance and resolution techniques are discussed so that when conflicts arise, the parties can avoid costly and lengthy court hearings.

Chapter 9 discusses a number of concerns businesses have raised about using an xSP, principally security and system availability issues.

Chapter 10 discusses the options for choosing a service provider. Several checklists are provided to assist the reader in selecting a specific type of service provider.

The authors have attempted to minimize the amount of jargon found in this book, but some use of acronyms is almost inevitable. A glossary is provided so that readers who are unfamiliar with all of the jargon they are likely to encounter when considering use of a service provider will be able to quickly understand the terminology. An appendix also provides information about additional resources for various xSPs.

Who Should Read This Book

This book is ideal for senior- and middle-level managers in marketing, sales, finance, and human resources departments. The goal: higher sales, better marketing tools, up-to-date HR records, and tighter supply chain controls through the outsourcing of technology functions that improve an organization's ability to plan and execute strategies focused on core competencies.

There will be instances when a business or organization will want to own software, maintaining direct control. The total ownership model will be the best solution for some, while other organizations will continue to outsource certain areas like accounting and back-end office support. But for many organizations, the costs of ramping up and running a new application are going to outweigh the pleasures of ownership.

Nothing new here. Think about paychecks. Thousands of companies for decades have outsourced payroll functions to service companies like ADP with nary an ounce of guilt or a second thought. In the payroll business, organizations didn't, and still don't, want to chuck time, money, and bodies down a big black hole building a state-of-the-art payroll system.

Now, extend this train of thought to the new economy and do the math. Management teams who are building cutting-edge, in-house email systems are not building cutting-edge deliverables to bring to market.

Every IT department is tremendously overburdened right now—even those immune to the skilled labor shortage who are operating fully staffed. The internal IT teams can't begin to support all the projects and programs driven by the competitive demand for technological innovation and initiatives from the legal, procurement, or marketing departments, never mind develop them. Although a number of companies will consider using a service provider only to outsource noncore business functions, it is also true that some organizations have no qualms at all about outsourcing important core business activities to a service provider. While it is possible to outsource non-IT related functions, like market research, office services (printing, presentation development, and Web-based distribution), and many others, a discussion of these latter options is outside the bounds of this book.

"The ability to get IT involvement in a project is very, very difficult, yet the need is crucial. And getting more crucial as competitive trends increase," says Paul D. Mann, CEO of Informative Inc., a California-based ASP that provides online performance measurements by surveying customers and employees for Fortune 1000 companies like Cisco Systems, Nortel, and 3Com. Those companies certainly have the internal resources to do their own market research. But they use Informative's real-time Web channels because, as Mann says, "it's not in their best interests with the rapid pace of change to support and upgrade" internal market research technologies. "I like to tell our clients that we are virtually the department down the hall," Mann says.

Note that pricing models are still immature in the service provider marketplace; however, with a bit of effort it is possible to do some comparison shopping. Managers should do a cost-benefit analysis that measures labor and capital costs along with the actual costs of hardware and software. The savings also come from an accounting perspective. Leases or rentals are entered over time as business expenses whereas actual purchases of software are recorded at the point of sale as a one-time, and usually huge, capital expenditure.

What is created when a service provider is used effectively is an internal technology team that is able to enhance products and improve time-to-market and customer relationships.

If you are considering a service provider, just think about how many bodies you won't need to recruit in this cut-throat hiring environment. Many organizations outsource noncore operations to companies whose own core competencies, enhanced by economies of scale, are faster and cheaper than any internal team. That allocates, in theory, more funding to staff marketing, sales, manufacturing, and the other business lines.

Summary

Decision makers at organizations seeking external technology options to manage traditional internal functions and customer channels should not find the relative newness of the service provider industry a deterrent to its use. This book will help you to develop the processes and hire the people to create service provider partnerships that supersede your company's standards of excellence and take advantage of the lower costs resulting from technological economies of scale.

For those involved in the service provider industry there is an enormous opportunity to partner with other xSPs so that each company is able to extend its offerings to different market segments. In order to do so it is important to recognize that the partner organizations but most importantly for the customer of the xSP.

CHAPTER 1

Overview of Service Providers

Existing Internet-based technologies continue to evolve and new technologies are continuing to be introduced, seemingly on a weekly basis, despite the dramatic dot-com fallout. In today's competitive global marketplace, businesses of all sizes—from home-based ventures to Fortune 100 enterprise leaders—are turning their primary focus away from the traditional model of creating and delivering products and services to a targeted audience. Instead, organizations increasingly view customer relationships as the key strategic tool to success.

Intellectual capital and technology are the main drivers of this business model, which demands 24/7 access to all resources. Boundaries and borders are eroded, as the Internet becomes The Network of Choice for more and more businesses and organizations that now rent software over the Web rather than buy shrink-wrapped packages. Interoperability is the "inter-" of the Internet, and increasingly software is being developed for a net-centric view of the world.

Internet-enabled technology has become the latest tech commodity, prompting organizations to rely even more on their intellectual assets to affect competitive advantage. To maintain that edge, decision makers hesitant to invest significant capital in ever-changing technology applications choose to outsource the organization's technology needs. These service providers, whose product can range from a simple email package to a universal end-to-end-solution, promise to provide and safeguard their customers' data as if it were their own. Ideally, these service provider offerings interact seamlessly with desktops, servers, and other computers to sculpt an invisible channel where information flows freely, quickly, and efficiently.

According to some analysts, worldwide spending on IT outsourcing will top $100 billion by 2005, starting from a base point of some $46 billion in 2000. Outsourcing is nothing new to the network and system sides of information technology management. What is new, and what is revolutionizing the vendor-client relationship in IT, is the outsourcing of application and database layers by maximizing and leveraging Internet connections. The result: technical, organizational and financial touch points that impact the value chain of the entire organization.

The main benefit of outsourcing, which will be repeated many times throughout this book, is the liberation of the internal IT staff to spend less time on keeping less critical applications running and more time developing new and innovative IT solutions that reflect the organization's core competencies. By leveraging the current in-house IT staff in a more effective manner, organizations can expect, in theory, to reap increased efficiencies and economies of scale.

Neither partners nor vendors, service providers create a new level of relationships for managers across all lines of business. Within the organizations, executives who formerly relied on the rigid rules of vendor contracts now find themselves managing a service agreement often promising more intangible benefits than actual return on investments. For service providers, creating the correct set of individual customer expectations with mass-produced technology is a delicate juggling act demanding considerably more face time with end users than ever before.

Managing in Turbulent Times

Clearly, the rather quick downturn in the economy is causing all organizations to take a fresh look at their situation. As resources dwindle across the board, management faces higher risks to the company's reputation, operations, and security, especially regarding key financial and customer service strategies.

And despite a legacy of consistent best practices driven by profits, growth, and regulatory guidance, many businesses and organizations are confronting organizational chaos. This is not the time to ignore mission statements, strategic goals, and project implementation plans. It is the time to reassess the core competencies of the business unit, quantify its value in this new paradigm, and determine whether any task or process could be more efficiently outsourced.

The effective cross-organizational relationships that have driven successful team projects over the last five years must be protected and fostered. And the value of each individual's past, present, and future contribution is assessed. These tasks, hampered by bottom-line demands for profitable or at least break-even numbers, are daunting.

We all know the right mix of qualitative and quantitative tools to help reach the best plan of action for layoffs, reductions in force, or other shutdowns. Metrics and matrixes, though, often tend to address solutions to the current failures. They help us dig out of the mess we are currently in, and they end once the digging stops. These immediate solutions tend to exclude factors that may enable or lead the newly retrofitted organization to its next set of goals.

And this is very, very important to remember as the pink slips start to fly: The current strategies have already failed. They are useless save for their educational and historic value. It is the future strategic plans and their subsequent implementation that must succeed and, indeed, may not fail.

So how can managers effectively link their organization's cultures to these new visions?

First, assess the *human capital*. What is the value of an organization's employees? Does their experience and collective wisdom make a meaningful difference? This goes beyond body count and back-end systems. Who are the most valuable team members? They are the talented individuals who are leaders as well as players and, most importantly, willing and able to share their expertise. No hoarding, no back stabbing, no limited disclosures.

It is not really fair to look at numbers and quotas to determine these levels of success. Adjustments must be factored for extenuating circumstances like the nascent Internet-driven technologies that stormed the U.S. workplace over the last five years. Example: The business-to-consumer (B2C) market in a pure-play Web-enabled channel that is not viable for most companies. We all know this now. But for those that experimented, tested and tried it, there was a huge learning curve whose end result found employees invested in learning, adapting, and using emerging technologies. End results: business management tools that help them do their job more easily, faster, and more cheaply. Individuals who lamented in 1997 that they were afraid of computers are not only excelling in the use of technology in their daily professional lives but using it in their personal lives as well to connect with family, friends, and special interests.

Managers need not only to practice but to excel at this ability to share and expand intellectual capital. This requires scrupulous acceptance and encouragement of innovation, plus the freedom to work without fear-driven directives.

This brings us to our second point: *communications*. A truly successful organization has very little internal information muzzled in a "need-to-know-only" directive. Questions pop up, answers are found, and there is an open, expansive sense of verbal engagement. Employees, mindful of competitive and regulatory boundaries, have access to all educational, training, and developmental material necessary to their jobs. Communication flows easily in all directions—horizontally and vertically—regardless of the emotions they might raise. People don't want to base their professional lives on rumors that live for weeks or months. They want, and expect, the facts, no matter how ugly. But once words like "layoffs" and "buyouts" start to become part of the everyday vocabulary, they crowd out the effective work language. Managers and employees alike must be able to voice as well to criticize the truth as they may see it and be respected for its intention as well as its content. The days of the yes-ing ourselves into compliant numbness are officially over.

Hence, our third point: *experience*. It is extremely common to find an employee under 45 with a total work experience of nearly 20 years. But it is not as common to find employees under 30 with the same relative scope or depth of experience. About six months ago, right when this current new economic meltdown was just starting to sizzle, the pundits started heralding the Return of the Suits to the dot-com arena. The experts applauded the replacement of those smart-aleck whiz kids that dropped out of Stanford and Harvard MBA programs before they mastered a ROI spreadsheet to start these dot-com dreams juiced by millions of VC funds. The applause, however, was a tad tardy. It was appropriately too late.

The goals of the massive corporate restructuring we now see must not correct the past, but create the future. To achieve those goals, management must assess its current human capital resources and find innovative ways to leverage and maximize its technology-enriched workplace teams.

Trends Affecting the Service Provider Market

A number of trends are affecting businesses and other organizations. These trends can be broadly grouped into four categories: economic trends, technical trends, business trends, and value-added trends; they are shown in Figure 1.1.

Economic Trends

There are three key economic trends:

Increasing competition. Businesses and organizations find themselves facing an increasing amount of competition due to the pressures of globalization and the ready availability of information via the Internet. Some organizations are willing to reengineer themselves in order to capture a greater share of the marketplace and dot-com companies are splintering barriers to competition.

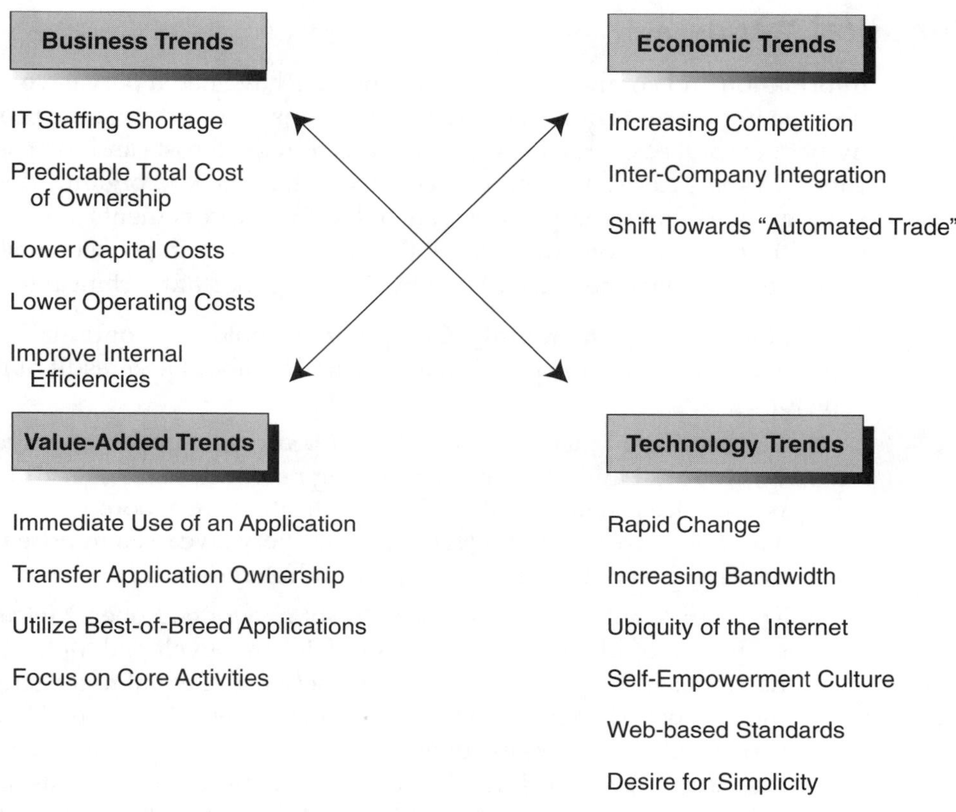

Figure 1.1 Trends affecting the xSP marketplace.

To counter this increased competition, some organizations are asking themselves, What is it about our products or services that is really essential? How do we really add value? Once these critical activities are known, then these organizations are shedding responsibility for the nonessential activities or functions by outsourcing those activities or functions.

Intercompany integration. Organizations are moving not only to integrate their own systems but also to integrate with the systems from other companies, especially suppliers and customers using an Extranet. A lot of this intercompany integration is using XML to tie these disparate systems together.

Shift toward "automated trade." Software is becoming smarter to allow it to stand in the middle of transactions—in place of employees. Automated trade takes place in many forms, including business-to-business (B2B) and business-to-consumers (B2C) portals.

Technical Trends

Information and communications technologies have had a pervasive and positive impact on businesses and organizations by improving the productivity of employees, allowing organizations to reduce costs and increase revenues. In some cases, information technology has allowed organizations to redesign workflows and processes such that the improvements are orders-of-magnitude better—some would call this revolutionary improvements! Such improvements have been facilitated by several important technical trends:

Technology is changing rapidly. Computer technology is continually undergoing change. This consistent change has come about as a result of these factors:

- ➢ The significant increases in computer processing power as expressed by Moore's Law (computer processing power doubles every 18 months while price is held constant). The implications of Moore's Law suggest a tenfold increase in processing power every 5 years, a hundredfold increase every 10 years, and a thousandfold every 15!
- ➢ The significant increases in the value of networks. Robert Metcalfe, originator of Ethernet and founder of 3Com, developed Metcalfe's Law, which states that the value of a network is equal to the square of the number of nodes. Thus, as a network grows, the value of being connected to it grows exponentially, while the cost per user remains the same or even declines. Double the number of participants and the value to *each participant* is doubled, and the total value of the *network* is increased fourfold.
- ➢ The introduction of new classes of computers—mainframe computers, minicomputers, then the personal computer, and most recently the personal digital assistant.
- ➢ A constant decline in price per megabyte (MB) of disk space over time.
- ➢ A change in computer architecture—from mainframe and minicomputer-based systems linking networks of dumb terminals, to client/server-based systems with a graphical user interface workstation sitting on the desktop; to a Web-centric network with servers accessible to a broad range of users using a Web browser.
- ➢ New "killer software applications," for example, email. Approximately 10 billion emails were sent every *day* during 2000.
- ➢ A new user interface, which over time has moved us from character-based displays, to the Windows-based graphical user interface, and the World Wide Web graphical interface.

Bandwidth. Network infrastructure technology advances have been occurring at an increasing pace for the last several years. Gilder's Law, proposed by technology author George Gilder, states that available bandwidth triples every 12 months while costs decline—primarily due to fiber optics. As a result it becomes more feasible to access applications residing on public networks (as opposed to residing in-house on a set of servers).

The ubiquity of the Internet. The growth of the Internet is well known to most people. Factors leading to this growth include improved reliability of the network and security of transactions. More than half of all American homes now have Internet access, as do a majority of businesses, local governments, libraries, nonprofit organizations, and more. The Internet has had and will continue to have an enormous impact on individuals within organizations as well as on the life of consumers.

Self-empowerment culture. The Internet has significantly changed the way in which people acquire, share, and exchange information.

The ready availability of information about products and services means that the rules are changing about how people conduct business and buy and sell products and services. People are now very concerned about convenience and immediacy. Examples include Web sites that provide comparative shopping options, sites that gather complaints about a company's products or service, business-to-consumer (B2C) portals (for example, Amazon and Yahoo!, among others), and business-to-business (B2B) portals (for example, Dell Computer, Federal Express, and Cisco Systems, among others).

Illustrating the power of these changes are the following theses from *The Cluetrain Manifesto* (Locke et al. 2000):

- Markets are conversations.
- Conversations among human beings sound human.
- The Internet is enabling conversations among human beings that were simply not possible in the era of the mass media.
- Hyperlinks subvert hierarchy.
- These networked conversations are enabling powerful new forms of social organization and knowledge exchange to emerge.
- Markets are getting smarter, more informed, more organized.

Web-based standards. Web–based standards are generally adopted in a fairly short time frame due to the efforts of the W3C. Short for *World Wide Web Consortium,* the W3C is an international consortium of companies and organizations involved with the Internet and the Web. The W3C was founded by Tim Berners-Lee, the original architect of the World Wide Web, to develop open standards so that the Web would evolve in a single direction rather than being splintered among competing factions. The W3C is the chief standards body for HTML and XML.

Once adopted, these standards are then incorporated into a variety of products. Web standards will continue to have a big impact in the marketplace. The most widely adopted and pervasive standard is the Internet Protocol (IP), thanks to the Internet and other related IP networks. TCP adds verification to IP. The amount of IP traffic is expected to grow almost exponentially over the coming few years, as shown in Figure 1.2.

Hypertext transmission protocol (HTTP) aggregates TCP/IP "packets" of information into documents. Hypertext markup language (HTML) formats the HTTP documents into Web pages using the Web browser. Extensible markup language (XML) formats these documents into a wider set of self-describing files. The interesting thing about Internet-based digital standards is that they are cumulative, starting with the transportation of data and ending with content.

As a markup language, XML contains data elements and formatting elements that describe what to do with the data. An XML schema describes the structure and meaning of the information within an XML document, and this information is contained in a Document Type Definition (DTD). XML will be particularly helpful in the future because this standard simplifies and lowers the cost of data interchange and publishing in a Web environment.

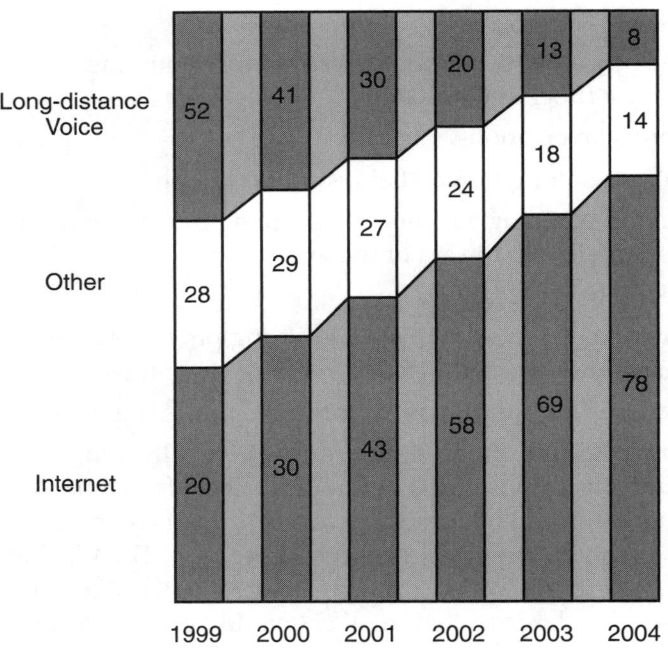

Figure 1.2 IP-Based traffic growth forecast.
Source: adapted from Ewing et al 2001.

Given the widespread adoption of these and other standards, a majority of hardware and software vendors have the assurance that products and services that embrace these Web-based standards will have much greater acceptance in the marketplace. Standards are subject to an increasing rate of return and have a powerful "network" effect: the greater the penetration, the greater the competitive advantage.

Desire for simplicity. End users are looking for simplification and predictability in terms of a user interface to make their daily lives easier and more productive. Currently, computer users face a seemingly bewildering array of applications that have a different look and feel. Even among seemingly similar software applications, a user may need to click in different locations, using different icons or buttons to accomplish the same task. An increasing number of applications are migrating to a Web-based user interface, so the end user is beginning to realize the goal for simplification. The two dominant Web browsers, Microsoft's Internet Explorer and Netscape's Navigator have evolved to provide more ease of use for millions of users.

One of the positive implications of a common Web-based user interface for all applications is that it significantly reduces the amount of training that needs to be provided in order to get staff up and running in a productive manner with a new application.

Business Trends

Information technology does not exist within a vacuum but rather is just one of the many components available to a business that helps get the job done. Other components include the availability (or lack thereof) of qualified, skilled employees, the need to carefully budget for technology projects regardless of the economic up and down cycles, the difficulty in getting IT projects approved when competing against a long list of projects requiring capital and the constant demand to improve operating efficiencies. Thus, there are several important business trends to consider:

IT staffing shortages. A number of surveys have indicated that there is a shortage of some 75,000 computer programmers and more than 300,000 open IT positions in North America (Allen 2000). In addition, as some of the new dot-com companies have begun to grow, they have been providing their programmers and other IT staff with compensation packages that include signing bonuses, high salaries, fringe benefits, and stock options. Thus, it is not surprising for some businesses and local governments, for example, to see entry-level and more experienced IT staff leave for more lucrative opportunities within the IT industry.

Most IT departments are in organizations whose main emphasis is something other than providing IT. As a result, most IT departments usually get enough money to maintain existing applications but not enough for the staff, equipment, and software they would need to develop and implement innovative applications. Having multiple engineers in the same room to assist in resolving a problem is a luxury most IT departments do not experience.

Due to the pressure to cope with a seemingly never-ending list of problems to resolve, it is more than likely that in-house IT staff will be backlogged with performing routine administrative tasks—or example, assigning a new employee access rights and creating an email account, performing system backups, and so forth.

But more significantly, some planned applications simply require an implementation expertise lacking in the existing information technology staff. So, rather than attempting to compete in a very tight labor market, some organizations are turning to outsourcing as a solution.

Predictable total cost of ownership. One of the principal frustrations with most organizations that have an IT department is that a majority of software development projects are canceled after some period of time or the projects are completed but with time and budget overruns. Thus, costs for the IT departments in some organizations are typically not predictable, and in some cases, the IT department becomes a resource sinkhole. In some organizations, top management is coming to the conclusion that the economic costs of maintaining applications and infrastructure have far exceeded the value equation. According to Zona Research (1999), application outsourcing can reduce the total cost of ownership by 50 percent or more.

In organizations that develop their own applications or purchase an application but then make significant modifications to it, customers often demand frequent modifications to the application (the end user says, "Now that I see it, what I really need is ..."). These changes often have a severe disruption to the organization's systems environment.

In addition, a recent study revealed that the recurring costs of providing applications could exceed $10,000 per user, per year. Hardware costs make up less than 15 percent of this total. The remaining 85 percent includes costs of network and communications infrastructure, the cost of personnel required to develop or acquire, maintain, and update applications; and ongoing technical support (Kapoor 1999).

Capital costs. One of the frustrations for many departments within an organization is that they need to get into a capital queue once a project has been approved. Any organization has just so many capital dollars, which must be allocated to a number of competing projects. If there was an option to outsource the provision of a software function, as can be done with a service provider, then the organization need not use capital dollars to receive the benefits associated with a particular application.

Lower operating costs. Outsourcing one or more applications will, in most cases, allow the organization to save money, especially when the costs of the staff needed for the care and maintenance of an application are considered. Given the existing cost structure within an organization, the cost savings may range from 25 percent to more than 50 percent per year. Depending on the size of the organization and what application(s) are being outsourced, the savings in dollar terms may be dramatic.

For example, among the costs that may be eliminated by using a service provider are central site hardware (servers and disk drives), software application licenses, and staff to manage and implement the new application.

Improve internal efficiencies. Whenever an organization selects and installs a new software application, it has the opportunity to examine existing procedures, forms, and workflow to determine what changes should be made in order to maximize the benefits that will be derived from using the software. This can also be done when an organization decides to use a service provider. Increasingly, organizations are realizing that the more paperwork that can be eliminated, the greater the annual savings to an organization.

Value-Added Trends

Use of an xSP allows a business to be more focused and to start receiving benefits sooner. Some organizations that have outsourced using an xSP have discovered that they can derive benefits in a number of ways. There are five trends that influence this area:

Focus on core activities. Any organization can go though a strategic planning process to identify what activities are crucial for the product or service that it provides. Once they are identified, an organization can then decide to outsource the activities that are not core or critical to its long-term success. And one way to outsource is to utilize the services of a service provider.

IT as a competitive weapon. Some organizations are able to conceive of providing a valuable resource by using IT in new and creative ways. Businesses that do so will then find that IT has become a marketplace differentiator.

Immediate use of an application. Utilizing a service provider will allow the customer to begin to use the application almost immediately. No longer must the customer wait for the software to be shipped, load the software on a server, convert and load the database, receive end-user training, and so on. The typical installation process for an enterprise application in a medium to large organization will run from 18 to 24 months. In addition to the initial cost of the software license and purchase of the servers, an organization will usually spend .75 to 2.5 times the initial software license fees in staff and consulting services for installation, customization, and training services. Once signed up with a service provider, the customer can begin to use the application in a matter of a few days to weeks.

Transfer application ownership. Using a service provider, the customer organization effectively transfers the ownership of the software to the service provider because the customer is renting access to the application. Thus, the customer is no longer concerned about managing the annual tasks associated with providing access to an application. Among these tasks are purchasing and installing the central computing equipment, performing backup of the data on a nightly basis, paying for and installing new releases of the software, and providing staff to maintain and operate the central servers.

Utilize best-of-breed applications. Because the service provider typically provides access to the application based on a "number of seats" basis, an organization of any size can become a customer. Thus, even small organizations can now have access to the most functionally rich application at an affordable price, whereas if they were to purchase a traditional software license, it would not be financially possible.

The net effect of all these trends is that there is an increasing opportunity for individuals, small businesses, organizations, and governments to gain access to data and a wide range of application software from a central location. From the user's perspective, applications appear to be installed and running on their own computer or an in-house computer center.

What Is a Service Provider?

Despite the relative "newness" of the service provider marketplace, a plethora of acronyms abounds. Sometimes the whole service provider market is referred to as "xSPs." Due to the breadth and variety of vendor activity, it has become difficult for customers to clearly delineate the core competencies of a particular kind of service provider. The xSP acronym has come to represent a broad range of service providers, offering a variety of services using Internet access, application functionality, and support for business processes. In broad terms, a service provider can be defined as follows:

A service provider manages and delivers access to the Internet or access to Internet-based services or application capabilities to multiple entities from a data center.

Several defining characteristics distinguish a service provider.

It is externally managed. Rather than being located within the organization, the Internet-based service is managed from a central location or distributed locations, owned or under contract to the service provider vendor. Customers access the Internet or Internet-based applications remotely, for instance, over the Internet or via leased lines, which may include T-1 telephone lines or a cable modem.

It offers one-to-many service. The service provider's services are designed to be a one-to-many offering. A service provider typically partners with other IT and/or telecommunication vendors to package standardized offerings (providing for minimal or no customization) to which many organizations will subscribe over a specified contract period. For example, a company might gain access to the Internet using an ISP or utilize an ASP service that provides accounting and human resources.

IT outsourcing and application management services, conversely, are one-to-one offerings, with each solution deployed to meet the unique needs of the customer organization.

It delivers on a service contract. The service provider is the firm that is responsible, in the customer's eyes, for delivering on the contract—ensuring that the contracted service is provided as promised. If a problem arises (e.g., hardware problems with a server), the service provider is responsible for solving the problem, even if other companies provide the actual support. The service provider may warrant accessibility, reliability, and overall performance with a service level agreement (see Chapter 8).

It may provide access to applications. Part of the value of an ASP service is that a business or organization can gain access to a new applications environment—for example, it can replace its old character-based system with a Web-based system. It thus can avoid making up-front investments for the software application's licenses, other third-party software licenses, servers, personnel, and other resources. The ASP, rather than the customer, owns the application software or has a contractual agreement with the application software vendor to license and provide access to the application.

Among the mainstream xSPs that you may have encountered are ISP, MSP, ASP, and BSP as shown in Figure 1.3.

The *Internet service provider* (ISP) provides access to the Internet via dial-up or dedicated lines. Access options range from analog telephone lines, digital telephone lines (e.g., Digital Subscriber Line or DSL), to cable lines using modems. Costs for such services typically range from low to pricey, depending on the speed of the line (bandwidth), whether the connection is a dial-up or a dedicated line that is "always on," and the amount of competition in a given area (e.g., America Online, EarthLink, Netcom, etc.). Most ISP's are too busy providing communication links, IP addresses, email and other basic services to even consider expanding the range of services offered.

A *management service provider* (MSP), community service provider (CSP), managed service provider (MSP), or managed security service provider

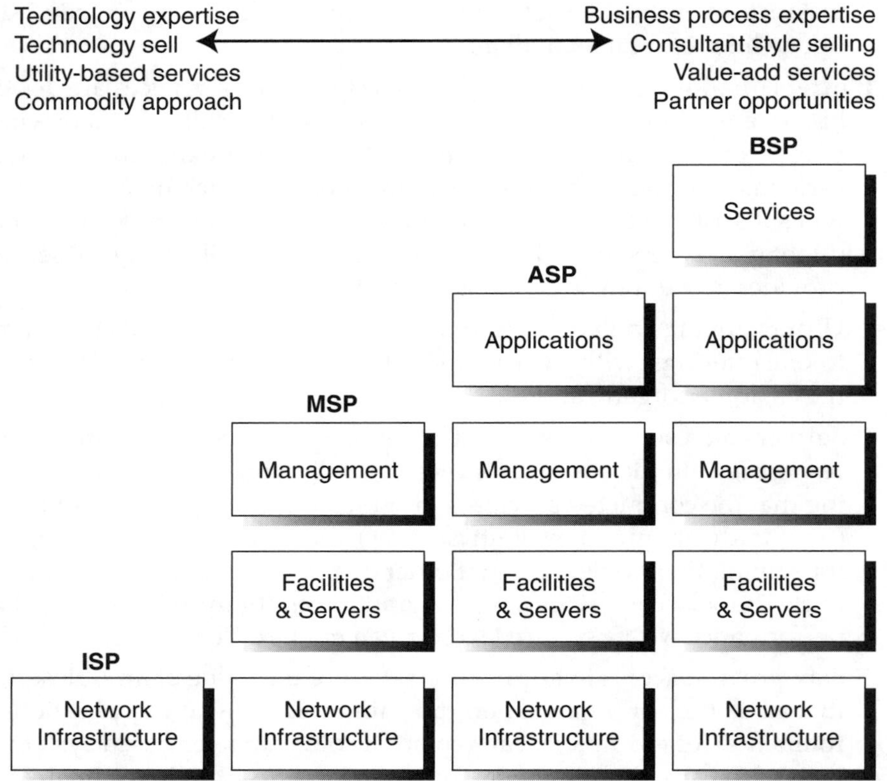

Figure 1.3 Significant xSPs.

(MSSP) will focus primarily on the management of infrastructure issues. For example, they will provide the staff to manage the operation of the servers (e.g., perform system backups), ensure that the application is operational and available for use, provide billing and meter access, provide capacity planning and load balancing, and provide security in addition to providing the physical space to house the servers. Firms that provide this type of service include Qwest, NaviSoft, InteQ, Data Return, siteROCK, SevenSpace, NOCpulse, Loudcloud, Intira, SiteSmith, Telenisus, Avasta, Nuclio, StrataSource, and Totality, among others.

An *application service provider* or ASP, sometimes called an Internet business service (IBS), a managed applications provider (MAP), a commerce service provider (CSP), a content service provider (CSP), a content management service provider (CMSP), an email/messaging service provider (EMSP), a Web analysis service provider (WASP), or a vertical solutions provider (VSP), provides access to one or more software applications to their customers.

Claire Gillan, an analyst at International Data Corporation, in Framingham, Massachusetts, has the unique distinction of having coined the term ASP in 1998. Former Hewlett-Packard Chairman Lew Platt has nicknamed such services as "Apps on Tap." Others have called this approach "apps by-the-drink." An ASP may host its application(s) at its own data center or subcontract this activity with an MSP. Examples of ASP firms include E-Benefits, eALITY, Great Plains Software, ExpensAble, TeleComputing, Broadvision, and Commerce One, among others.

A *business service provider* (BSP) is sometimes called a solutions service provider (SSP), a convergent solutions provider (CSP), a full service provider (FSP), a total service provider (TSP), a rentable applications provider (RAP), a rentable applications integrator (RAI), or an Internet business service provider (IBSP). In addition to an ASP service, this firm provides consulting services so that customers can learn how to change policies and procedures in order that the organization can derive more benefit from the set of applications that is being used. Often, a BSP will provide a suite of services tailored to one industry (e.g., banking, airlines, retail, etc.). One of the ways a BSP will accomplish this is to develop a suite of application programming interfaces or APIs to move data from one application to another in a way that is invisible to the user. Examples of a business service provider include USinternetworking, Breakaway Solutions, and Corio, among others.

A *wireless service provider* (WSP) is also called a wireless application service provider (WASP). A WSP can provide access to a wireless network so that the customer's mobile employees can view real-time information about their customers, current status of the firm's inventory, and so forth. Alternatively, the WASP can provide both the wireless network and access to specific wireless applications.

Another way to view all of these various services is to recognize that they work together to create a solution for a company's problem or need. Specifically, these service providers create an xSP value chain as shown in Figure 1.4.

It is important to understand that a service provider is not an outsourcing firm. Information technology outsourcing firms can be grouped into three categories: application maintenance outsourcing, business process outsourcing and platform IT outsourcing, as shown in Table 1.1.

A variety of outsourcing options have evolved over the last twenty years to better meet the needs of potential customers. Addressing the issues of ownership—ownership of the application software, hardware and IT staff, allows us to differentiate the options as noted on page 17.

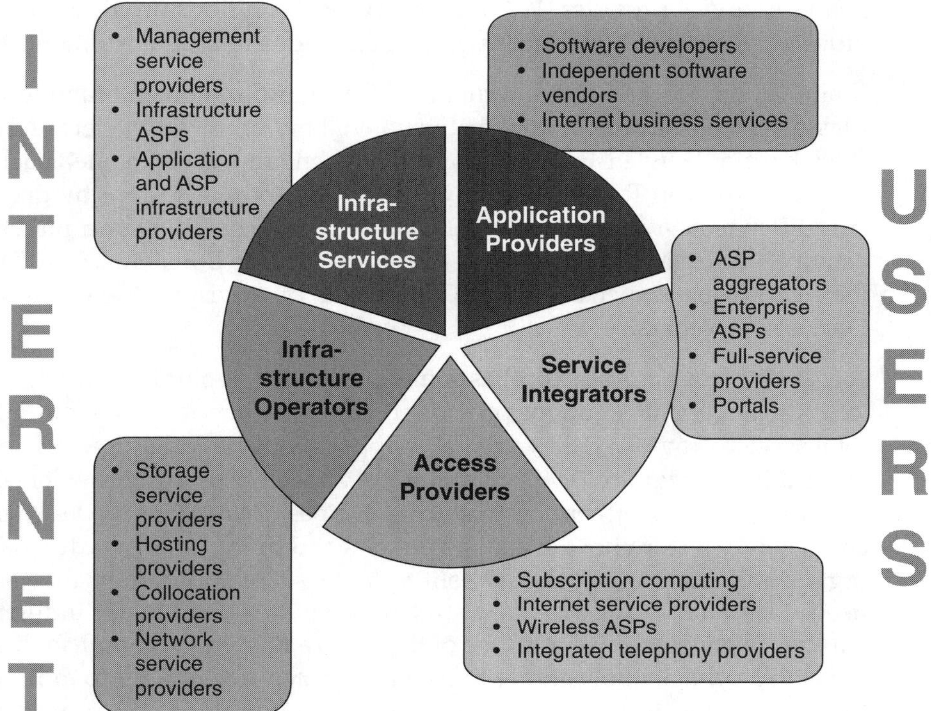

Figure 1.4 xSP value chain.
Source: ASPnews.com

Table 1.1 IT Outsourcing Options

	APPLICATION MAINTENANCE OUTSOURCING	BUSINESS PROCESS OUTSOURCING	PLATFORM IT OUTSOURCING
Ownership of application software	Customer	Provider	Customer
Type of application	Proprietary or package	Package	Proprietary or package
Ownership of hardware	Customer	Provider	Customer
Location of IT assets	Customer or provider	Provider	Customer or provider
Location of IT support	On- or off-site	Off-site	On- or off-site
Sample companies	"Big 5" consulting firms	ADP, Equifax, Ceridian	CSC, EDS, IBM, HP

- *Application maintenance outsourcing* allows an organization to maintain ownership of the applications and yet the third party assumes responsibility for the operation of the computer system.
- *Business process outsourcing* focuses on providing efficient outsourcing solutions for complex but repetitive business processes (e.g., payroll, finance and accounting applications, etc.).
- *Platform IT outsourcing* offers a range of data center services and typically involves a transfer of IT facilities, staff, and/or hardware to the third party.

Businesses and organizations that are considering the use of an xSP do not all move to adopt this outsourcing option at the same point in time. Rather, organizations, because of their own cultures, have different personalities, which is reflected by their willingness to accept risk. As noted by Geoffrey Moore (1999), it is possible to group companies into five basic categories, as shown in Figure 1.5. While there are those "innovators" that are willing to be the guinea pig and experiment with the latest technology, there are others who will wait until much later, the "late majority" and "laggards," before they will implement a technology that by now has become proven. As Moore has noted, there usually is a "chasm" that separates the innovators from the "early adopters" that technology service providers must recognize. The chasm is a period of time that results as the press reports on the experiences of the innovators, both positively and negatively. Once there is a sense in the marketplace that the technology is good, then the market adoption rate will proceed in a more or less orderly manner.

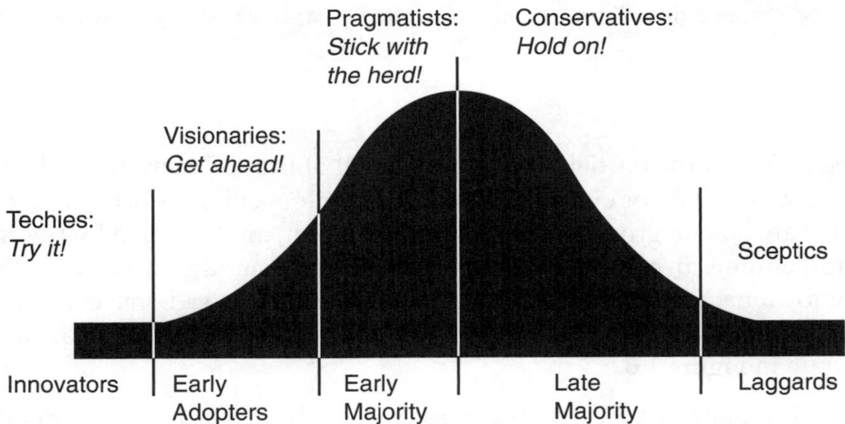

Figure 1.5 Technology adoption life cycle.

SP Case Study: The SSP for an ISP

XYZ Internetworking is the Internet service provider (ISP) arm of XYZ, one of the largest publicly held U.S. telecommunications companies with annual revenues exceeding $23 billion. XYZ offers local and wireless service in 29 states and long distance service and Internet access in all 50 of the United States. XYZ Internetworking is one of the fastest-growing consumer and small business ISPs in the marketplace today. XYZ Internetworking, chartered with providing residential and small and medium business Internet services, boasts an installed base of more than 800,000 dial-up accounts and over 600 nationwide local points of presence. Growth exceeds 20,000 new accounts weekly, due in great part to a series of high-profile OEM agreements that bundle XYZ Internetworking's Internet access onto thousands of PCs shipped daily. New users nationwide can also sign up with XYZ Internetworking for a variety of service packages ranging from $19.95 for basic dial-up service to $29.95 per month for ISDN service. With each option, users get a minimum of one email account, news service, and personal Web space. The core objectives of implementing this architecture are to create a state-of-the-art system that can scale to millions of customers and reduce overall maintenance and operational costs. Anticipating the rapid growth of its service, XYZ Internetworking looked for ways to scale its Windows NT environment up to the millions of customers it plans to secure in the next few years. After a comprehensive assessment and evaluation, XYZ Internetworking decided to outsource its storage needs and selected a storage service provider to supply the massive storage system required to support its ambitious growth plans. Since adding the Storage Service Provider (SSP) to its IT environment, XYZ Internetworking has experienced a 10 percent to 20 percent performance improvement when dealing with large file structures, such as a single directory with 100,000 subdirectories. The SSP storage services have also provided XYZ Internetworking with better than 200 percent more uptime than local disks, and overall system administration costs have been greatly lessened.

Regardless of the particular xSP market, all of the xSP markets are in a constant state of flux or evolution. New competitors enter the scene and older firms are able to grow and remain independent, are absorbed by (merged with) another firm, or don't make it and become another casualty in the dot-bomb arena. The ability of a business to succeed is based on a combination of factors, but overall the marketplace takes on a number of the characteristics shown in Figure 1.6.

The dominant xSPs noted previously will be discussed in greater detail in the following chapters.

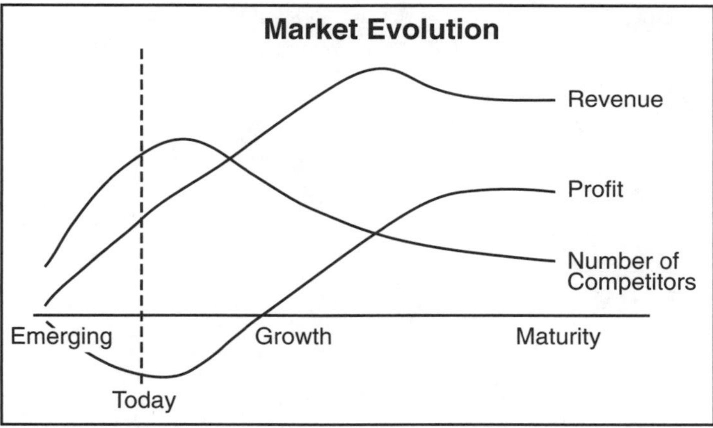

Figure 1.6 Market evolution

Case Study: Multiple Service Providers Equals Multiple Loopholes

You pay a provider for a service, and that service provider delivers, right? That's what David Taylor-Kraus, president of the Atlanta Web design firm Digital Positions, thought until his Verio DSL Internet access went dead because of a line cut. To get the problem fixed, his company would have to call Verio, and Verio would call NorthPoint, the DSL wholesaler that provided the DSL service to Verio. NorthPoint, in turn, would call BellSouth, which owned the line that had been cut. Each step through this multi-layered service would take 12 to 24 hours, Taylor-Kraus feared. In the past you may have had to deal with one or two providers—a local carrier and a long distance carrier—for your network needs. But now the complex network services you buy can rely on four or five or more providers lurking in the background. And as companies put more of their business online and outsource support to application service providers (ASPs) and Web hosters, the situation becomes even more complex, says Laurie McCabe, vice president and service director at Summit Strategies. The days of dealing directly with all your providers are numbered. Users must thoroughly investigate these services before they buy and aggressively pursue fixes when problems arise, experts say. If Taylor-Kraus had it to do over again, he'd buy from a provider that owned all of the elements that made up the offering. "I would absolutely rather buy a service from the primary provider," he says. "They can control the process." In the end, Digital Positions called the third-party installer that put in the original DSL link. That third party coordinated the other providers to get the line back up and running within a day. If Digital Positions didn't have a close relationship with the installer, though, the outage would have lasted far longer, Taylor-Kraus says (Martin, 2001).

CHAPTER 2

Enabling Technologies

What hardware, software, and human resources does it take for the Internet to operate and continue to evolve? In this chapter, we will look at some of the enabling Internet technologies to help you understand how data travels around the Internet.

The Internet, often called the Net, the Information Superhighway or cyberspace, has been variously described as a network of networks or as the world's largest network. The Internet links your computer to computers all around the world that are connected to each other in small groupings called local area networks or LANs (see Figure 2.1). Computers that communicate with each other over the Internet have several features in common:

1. A shared communication software standard.
2. Connections to routable networks.
3. A shared naming system.

Communication Software

Unless there is a consistent way in which data or messages could be moved about any network, then linking of a variety of computers would be impossible. The consistency is achieved because the data adheres to a standard format called a protocol. In the case of the Internet, the underlying communication protocol is called TCP/IP (Transmission Control Protocol/Internet Protocol).

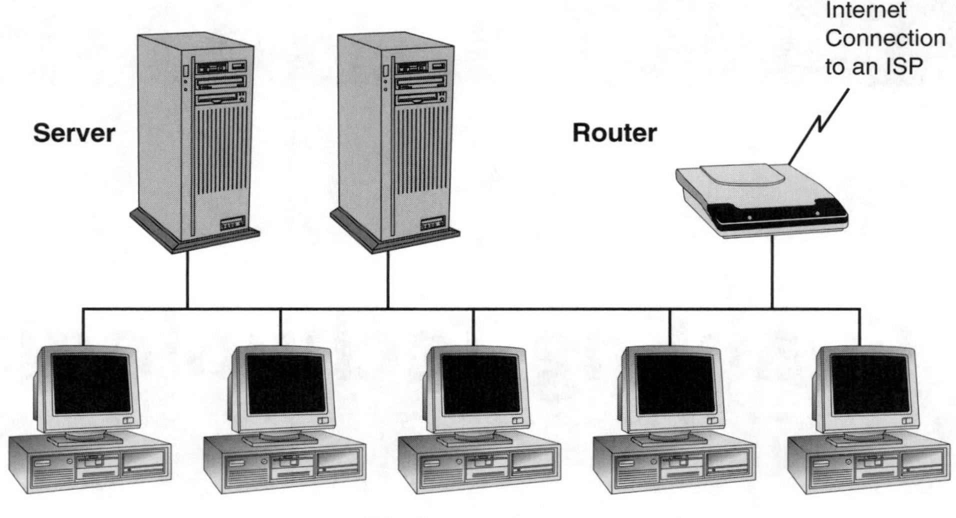

Figure 2.1 Typical local area network.

TCP/IP is the standard computer language of the Internet; if it is not properly installed on your computer you won't be able to connect to the Internet.

Using your computer and TCP/IP software allows you to send and receive email messages, view Web pages, search for information, send and receive files, download audio files—for example, MP3 music files—and so much more.

We'll cover more about TCP/IP later in this chapter when we discuss the importance of various protocols.

Routable Networks

The second common factor for computers on the Internet is that they are connected through routable networks. The distinguishing feature about a routable network is that a message or data can be routed or directed to a designated computer using a specific address or location.

Not too surprising, devices called *routers* perform routing on the Internet. These devices, actually very sophisticated computers that use the TCP/IP communication software, figure out the correct path for a message to take and direct it on the network to its ultimate destination.

As shown in Figure 2.2 in conceptualized form, the Internet is network of networks. Connecting each network is the router. Each device that data must pass through is referred to as a *node* within the network. Notice that there are multiple paths down which a message might be routed and thus multiple paths that a message might take when moving from point A to point G.

Rather than sending an entire message or file from one location to another, the message is broken up into pieces called packets (on the Internet, packets are called datagrams). The packet contains not only the destination address but also some data.

A router is a device that connects any number of LANs. Routers use headers and a forwarding table to determine where packets go, and they use a protocol called ICMP to communicate with each other and configure the best route between any two hosts. ICMP, which stands for Internet Control Message Protocol, is an extension to the Internet Protocol (IP). ICMP supports packets containing error control, and informational messages. Very little filtering of data is done through routers. Routers do not care about the type of data they handle.

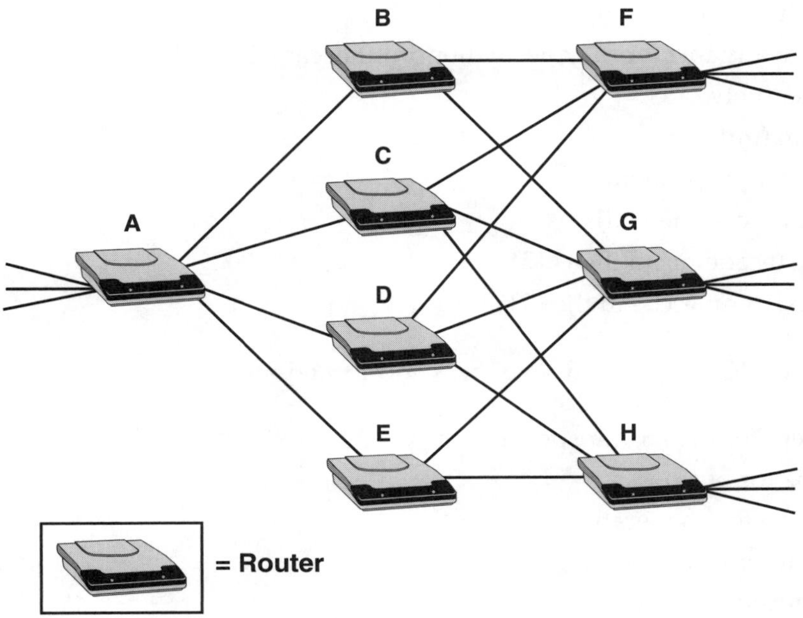

Figure 2.2 Pathways on the Internet.

Shared Naming System

In the early days of the Internet, you needed to know a computer's IP address to locate information stored on the computer. The IP address or IP number might look something like this:

714.213.858.202

This is not an actual IP address because it breaks all of the naming rules with the exception that a real address can have up to 12 digits in groups of 3 (the numbers are actually telephone area codes). Rather than attempting to remember a unique numeric address for each Web site, the developers of the Internet added something called Domain Name System (DNS) as an easier way to access an Internet site. The Domain Name System translates the IP address (714.213.858.202) of a Web site into an easier-to-remember Web site name: www.wiley.com. Another advantage of the DNS approach is that a large Web site might actually have a number of computers to host the complete Web site.

The nonprofit organization Internet Corporation for Assigned Names and Numbers (ICANN) manages the overall control for domain names. Originally the only available top-level domains or domain name suffixes were these:

- .edu (education)
- .org (organization, typically nonprofit organizations)
- .net (network)
- .mil (military)
- .gov (government)
- .com (commercial)
- .ac (academic in the U.K.)
- .co (commercial in the U.K.)

Recently, ICANN added seven new top-level domains:

- .aero for the air transport industry
- .biz for businesses
- .coop for cooperatives
- .info unrestricted use
- .museum for museums
- .name for individuals
- .pro for professionals (for example accountants, lawyers, and physicians)

A number of organizations (Network Solutions and many other competing firms) are now able to assign domain names (the names used for a Web site and email addresses) to companies and organizations that pay a fee for the right to use the name for a period of time. The domain name and the corresponding IP address to which it points are maintained in a large database (similar to a telephone directory).

Each Internet service provider (ISP) has one or more computers that hold a copy of the master DNS database. Updates to this database are transmitted all over the Internet to each of the DNS servers on a regular basis.

TIP

To learn more about domain name registrations and learn what companies are able to handle domain name registrations, go to the ICANN Web site:

http://www.icann.org

Or, alternatively, you can visit a service on the ICANN Web site called WHOIS, which shows you who owns a particular domain name:

http://www.icann.org/whois

Thus, when you type the name of a Web page into your Web browser address window and press Enter, the following things actually happen:

1. You type in www.wiley.com.
2. Your ISP's DNS server checks its database to figure which IP address matches the name you entered.
3. With the IP address in hand (208.215.179.75), not the name you typed, your message is passed on to a router that relays your request to other routers on the Net until the message reaches its final destination.

Web Browser

The Web browser, a software application used to locate and display Web pages, has had a revolutionary impact on the Internet. The two most popular browsers are Microsoft Internet Explorer and Netscape Navigator. These are graphical browsers in that they can display text and graphics (images). In some cases, the browser can also present multimedia information, including audio and video files, though they may require additional software, called plug-ins, to work effectively. Figure 2.3 illustrates a home page as displayed using a Web browser.

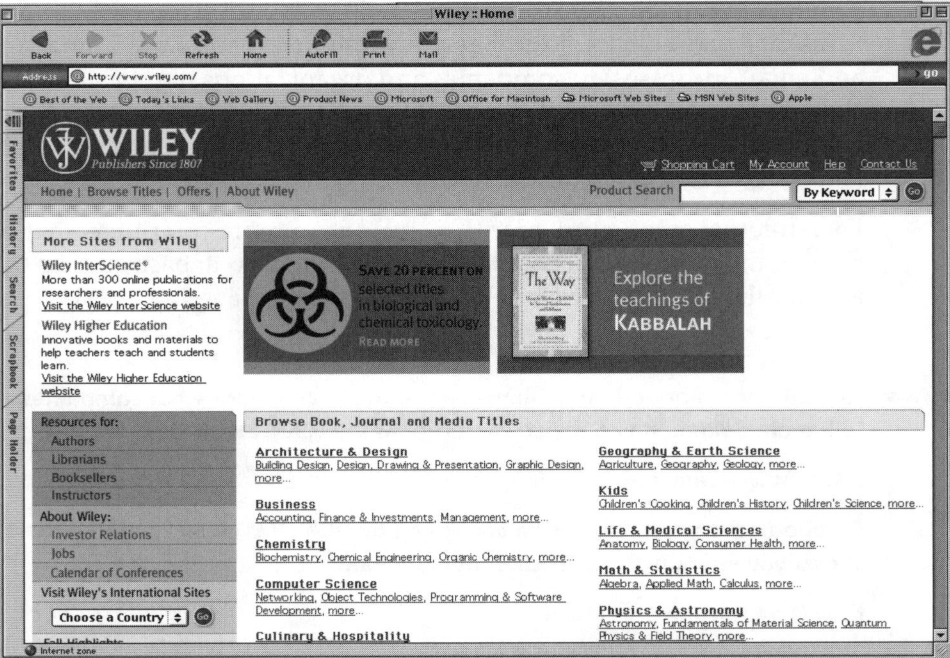

Figure 2.3 Wiley home page as seen from a Web browser.

Protocols

The Internet has always been governed by an open process in which a proposed standard or method is shared with all interested parties. These individuals and organizations then have an opportunity to review the proposed standard and make comments, identify problems, and suggest improvements and enhancements. After a relatively short period of time, usually measured in months, the proposed standard is then voted on and typically approved.

The group governing the Internet is called the Internet Engineering Task Force (IETF) while the group governing the Web is called the World Wide Web Consortium (W3C). The W3C typically meets quarterly in different locations around the world, but a large volume of email messages and discussions revolve around the various proposed Internet-based standards. The W3C, a vendor-neutral organization, promotes interoperability by promoting open (nonproprietary) computer languages and protocols in order to avoid the market fragmentation of the past. According to the W3C, the Web is the universe of network-accessible information available through a number of devices. Web pages can include textual information as well as pictures, sounds, video, File Transfer Protocol (FTP) links for downloading software, and much more.

TIP

To learn what proposals the World Wide Web Consortium is currently considering and discussing, go to:

http://www.w3.org

The more significant protocols and Internet-related standards will be identified and briefly discussed next. Notice that the standards and protocols range from the infrastructure necessary to move messages from one location to another as well as how to move and display the content itself.

Transmission Control Protocol/Internet Protocol (TCP/IP) is a suite of communications protocols used to connect hosts on the Internet. TCP enables two hosts to establish a connection and exchange streams of data. TCP guarantees delivery of data and also guarantees that packets will be delivered in the same order in which they were sent. IP specifies the format of packets, also called *datagrams,* and the addressing scheme. IP by itself is something like the postal system. It allows you to address a package and drop it in the system, but there's no direct link between you and the recipient. TCP/IP, on the other hand, establishes a connection between two hosts so that they can send messages back and forth for a period of time. A new version of the IP standard (IPv6) is being finalized, and this will provide us with 128-bit address space—this would allow everyone on earth to have millions of unique IP addresses.

Point-to-Point Protocol (PPP) is a standard for the transmission of IP packets over serial lines. PPP supports both asynchronous (data can move in both directions) and synchronous (data moves in only one direction) lines. PPP is a multiprotocol transport mechanism that supports TCP/IP as well as IPX and AppleTalk traffic. This protocol is used whenever an individual uses a modem to make a dial-up connection to an ISP. An older protocol, called SLIP (Serial Line Internet Protocol), can handle only TCP/IP traffic; thus SLIP is being used less and less.

Multiprotocol Label Switching (MPLS) integrates information about network links (bandwidth, latency, and utilization) into the IP protocol in order to simplify and improve IP packet exchange. More importantly, it allows some packets (for example, those for audio calls) to take priority. The protocol simplifies routing between Ethernet-based networks and long-haul Internet Protocol networks.

Hypertext Transfer Protocol (HTTP) defines how messages are transmitted and formatted as well as various commands for controlling Web servers and browsers. HTTP is called a stateless protocol because each command is executed independently without any knowledge of what the user has previously done. By allowing Web pages to be displayed graphically, the Web browser brought the Web to life and is what fuels its continuing dramatic expansion.

Uniform Resource Locator (URL) is the name of a Web site—for example, http://www.wiley.com. Optionally, the URL may also be the address of a particular file or area within a Web site—for example, http://www.wiley.com/Corporate/Website/Objects/Subjects/0,9049,16065,00.html. The browser then converts this to an HTTP command to the Web server, directing it to fetch and transmit the requested Web page.

Hypertext Markup Language (HTML) is the authoring language used to create documents on the Web—for example, controlling the placement of text and images and controlling the size of a font, the background color, and so forth. HTML is similar to Standard Generalized Markup Language (SGML) but is designed to accomplish tasks using the Web. Hundreds of tags and attributes are used to format and lay out the information found on a Web page. It should be noted that HTML does not define meaning.

Extensible HTML (XHTML) is a fairly new authoring language that has the potential to write an online application just once and deliver it across multiple platforms—whether wireless or PC-based. Extensible hypertext markup language is HTML rewritten in XML. XHTML marries the best aspects of these two protocols, combining the display capabilities of HTML with the data description function of XML. XHTML will significantly reduce the development and testing time to roll out a new version of an application. The Wireless Application Protocol Forum and Nippon Telegraph and Telephone Corporation (the developer of the popular Japanese DoCoMo wireless i-mode service) back XHTML.

Extensible Markup Language (XML) is a smaller version of the older and more complex SGML but is designed specifically for Web documents. It allows organizations to define, transmit, validate, and interpret data between applications and databases. XML is not a language or a presentation system; rather, it provides structure. Because XML separates the underlying data from how the data is displayed, the data itself can then be more easily organized, programmed, edited, and exchanged between Web sites, applications, and devices. XML and its associated Document Type Definition or DTD will play an important role in the exchange of information between xSPs. In addition to the rules for establishing XML entities there are nine other XML-related standards.

You can find the standards at http://www.w3.org and you can check out http://www.xml.org for discussions related to each of the standards.

XML Schema Definition (XSD) defines a standard way of describing Extensible Markup Language document structures and adding data types to XML data fields. It is anticipated that this standard will facilitate cross-organizational document exchange and verification. This standard will assist e-commerce business exchanges and other loose associations of trading partners possible. Tools for converting XML DTDs (Document Type Definitions) to XSD will assist the exchange of information.

A significant amount of effort is needed to define vocabularies rather than attempting to start off defining transactions. The Organization for the Advancement of Structured Information Standards (OASIS) has cataloged more than 100 standard vocabulary definition projects at its Web site:

http://www.xml.org.

XML Information Set (XIS) is a standard that provides a common reference set for defining abstract objects such as elements within a document.

XML Query provides the capabilities to create queries on collections of XML files that might contain unstructured data—for example, documents and Web pages. The intent is to provide a set of searching capabilities that are comparable to those found with SQL (Structured Query Language) used when searching relational database management systems (RDBMS).

SOAP (Simple Object Access Protocol) is a specification that defines a uniform way of passing XML-encoded data from one application to another. It also defines a way to perform a remote procedure call (RPC) using HTTP as the underlying communication protocol.

UDDI (Universal Description, Discovery, and Integration) provides a standard way for an organization to describe the way in which it provides services and products. UDDI will allow organizations to create a new kind of software called Web services. Web services are self-contained, self-describing, modular applications that can be published, located, and invoked across the Web.

Hardware

By hardware, we mean the physical equipment used by a business or organization, an ISP, the routers, and the millions of Web site hosts used to deliver services. The hardware includes everything from servers to modems at the customer's location.

Connecting to a Network

Connecting to any network, but especially the Internet, can be accomplished using a variety of technologies including dial-up telephone lines, dedicated Digital Subscriber Lines (DSL), dedicated Integrated Services Digital Network (ISDN) lines, cable modem lines, dedicated high-speed telephone lines, fiber optic lines, and microwave access.

Modems

A modem is a device that converts the signals from one medium to another. The original modem, an acronym for modulate-demodulate, converted the digital computer signals into the analog and continuous signal used by the telephone companies. The modem is used in a dial-up mode to connect a computer workstation to a computer system or computer network. The speed of a modem is typically represented as Kbps. Thus, a 56 KB modem is theoretically able to communicate at 56,000 bits per second although the actual performance is usually less depending on the quality of the line.

Other modems include converting digital signals so that they can operate using a coax cable (cable modem), a specific modem for Digital Subscriber Line access (DSL modem), or using radio signals (wireless modems).

A modem may be a physical device separate from the computer device itself, or it may be located internally in the device.

Dial-up Internet Access

Dial-up access to the Internet is provided via an analog modem. These modems, actually specialized microcomputers, are available in many different speeds: 14.4 Kbps (kilobits per second), 28.8 Kbps, 33.6 Kbps, and 56 Kbps (a.k.a. 56K). Note that the actual throughput of a dial-up modem is less than the rated speed because the modem must make a connection using the public, switched telephone network, and the volume of calls and the quality of the connection affect the ultimate speed. A new V.90 modem standard (90 Kbps) has been adopted as the global communications standard by the ITU (International Telecommunication Union), a United Nations agency. Dial-up access is more appropriate for a home-based or small business with few users who do not depend on speed for operational efficiencies. As such, this very inexpensive option is not addressed further.

Digital Subscriber Line

Digital Subscriber Line service delivers high-bandwidth information at rates up to 6.1 megabits per second to small and medium-sized businesses over copper telephone lines, if the customer company is physically close enough to the central telephone office that provides the DSL service. And that's a big *if*. Most DSL service is limited to a radius of 3.5 miles surrounding the telephone company switch location (office).

Why the problems? DSL service requires complex infrastructure and systems to ensure smooth operations for service start-up, repair, and billing—realities that industry experts say the United States DSL providers ignored. As difficulties mounted, so did turnover of support and installation staff, creating skill shortages. DSL service providers must purchase the DSL service from the regional telephone companies and then, in turn, increase the price to their customers. Recently the telephone companies began to offer DSL services directly to the end customer, thereby putting significant financial pressures on the DSL service providers.

When two DLS providers, Covad Communications and Rhythms NetConnections, announced early in 2001 that due to increasing financial pressures both were discontinuing DLS service in some areas, small to midsized businesses had just weeks to find new service providers. Technology research giant the Gartner Group forecast that more providers are likely to follow as competition in the DSL market decreases and prices likely increase. Enterprises that purchased DSL for use in small and home offices will still get value for their investment because these users are predisposed to pay for a better class of service, which still costs less than T-1 leased lines (Girard 2001). Several industry analysts expect that there will be approximately 3 million DSL users in North America by the end of 2001.

Integrated Services Digital Network

ISDN is the high-speed access technology of choice for small and medium-sized businesses. Nothing else is as widely available, economical, or mature. ISDN allows for digital transmission over ordinary telephone lines. Business users who install ISDN adapters instead of their modems can download data very quickly (up to 128 Kbps). ISDN, available in most urban areas, provides end-to-end digital connectivity between your computer and a remote computer or network by using a local telephone line for network connection. Actually, ISDN works over the same two-wire copper lines as existing analog phone lines. Note that it has a line limit of 1,800 cable feet from the nearest switching station.

ISDN gives two 64K-bearer (B) channels and one 16K-delta (D) channel that acts as a controller. You can use one or both B channels for surfing, for speeds of 64K or 128K. Because the lines are digital, there is very little noise, and you're assured of getting a connection at the full speed. Thanks to the two phone lines, and two phone numbers, customers can be online and use the phone at the same time. Practically all consumer ISDN hardware has a port (called a POTS port) for plugging in analog phone equipment (telephones, fax machines, etc.) so that you can use your analog equipment over the digital line. You can even plug your modem into the POTS port for calling services that don't support ISDN.

Your telephone company will install the ISDN line at your site. An ISDN adapter must be installed in place of a modem in both your computer and the remote access server. Note that the costs of ISDN equipment and lines may be higher than standard modems and phone lines. Due to the higher bandwidth of DSL, though, ISDN is becoming a less attractive option for most potential customers.

Phone Lines, Leased Lines

A business or organization can lease a dedicated telephone line, either a copper line or a fiber optic line, to connect to other units of the organization. The higher the bandwidth, the more expensive the monthly charge. The amount of the monthly service charge is also based on the distance the leased line travels from point A to point B. A call to the local telephone company will provide a very specific cost estimate to install the leased line along with the monthly service charges.

The advantage of a leased line is that it is available for use, 24 hours per day, 7 days a week—with no meter to monitor, and charge, for the actual usage of the line. A leased line also bypasses the telephone company switches so that the quality of the line is typically superior to that experienced by using a modem and a dial-up line.

T-1 Lines

With a T-1 connection, a business customer is getting a much faster connection to the Internet. A T-1 connection is designed for medium and large organizations that have more than 16 Internet users or require high-capacity Internet connectivity for office locations. A T-1 line is dedicated, meaning that it is always on and there are no per-minute charges. You do not need to dial in. And with a T-1 line, you can provide dozens of computers with Internet access without modems, telephone lines, and dial-up accounts for each one.

A T-1 provides approximately 1,500 Kbps of bandwidth as compared to a 28.8K modem. Companies that have a LAN (local area network) or organizations that are Internet centric in their business require this level of bandwidth as a minimum baseline.

What this means is that 10 computers can simultaneously access the Internet and each have 150K of bandwidth (5 times what they'd have with 28.8K modems). Given that most access is not simultaneous, you can easily support 100 or more computers with one T-1 line. If you currently have a number of computers in your office, each connected to the Net with a modem, phone line, and dial-up account, a T-1 may actually reduce the amount your company pays for Internet access. Leasing a fractional T-1 line provides access to some portion of a full T-1 line.

A T-1 connection is actually made up of two separate services and equipment. First is your T-1 line, which is the wire (the local loop) that actually connects your site to the network center. The second part of your T-1 is the connection to the Internet. This connection typically provides a business customer with 1.5 megabits per second of bandwidth for a flat fee of $500 to $600 per month.

T-3 Lines

A T-3 line is a dedicated digital communication link provided by a telephone company that offers 44.75 megabits per second of bandwidth, commonly used for carrying traffic to and from private business networks and Internet service providers.

The line actually consists of 672 individual channels, each of which supports 64 Kbps. A T-3 line is sometimes referred to as a DS3 line.

Cable Modem Access

A cable modem allows businesses to hook personal computers and laptops to a local cable TV line and receive data at about 1.5 Mbps. This data rate exceeds that of the prevalent 28.8 and 56 Kbps telephone modems. Cable modems attach to a coaxial cable line to communicate with a cable modem termination system at the office of the local cable TV company. The advantage to cable modem access: Aside from increased speed, it is always on. Always! It eliminates the need for "dial up."

Two options are available for accessing the Internet through a cable network. The first is to use the dial-up telephone services provided by your cable company in conjunction with a modem or ISDN adapter. The second is to use a cable modem, which is much faster than the first option.

When choosing standard dial-up services, a business customer will receive a telephone or ISDN line from its cable company. And that's about all. The business customer then must choose an ISP as well as the Internet connection equipment, such as a modem or an ISDN adapter.

For high-speed access that is almost as fast as a T-1 line, business customers will need a cable modem, which is a device at the subscriber end of a cable that allows a computer to be connected to the Internet through an existing cable network connection. Unlike a dial-up connection, it does not require a phone line.

A cable modem works in a similar manner to a standard modem in that it takes a signal from the computer and converts it for transmission over the cable network. There are two major differences between a cable modem and other modem/ISDN devices. The first is that a cable modem attaches to your computer through an Ethernet network interface card ('NIC'). The second and more significant difference is that the bandwidth available to cable modems is far in excess of that of a dial-up modem or ISDN. A number of industry observers suggested that the number of cable modem users would top 3.4 million by the end of 2000.

The downside? Cable modems connected to the head-end equipment at the cable company approximate the situation of your computer being connected to a LAN hub. This results in having to share the line with other people on your branch of the cable network (perhaps as many as 500 other people). Unless you have some type of file sharing or server active on your computer this will not normally represent any risk or danger. For total peace of mind you can use a firewall product such as the Vicomsoft Internet Gateway (www.vicomsoft.com), which can be configured to ensure that your computer or other computers on your LAN are not at risk.

Microwave Transmission

In lieu of a physical leased line, for example, a company may wish to consider using a microwave connection to an ISP. Using a small antenna typically located on the top of a company's building, the organization is connected to the ISP with the same bandwidth of a T-1 leased line. In most cases, the microwave option is less expensive than leasing a T-1 line from the telephone company, and it provides the nice bonus of being able to add incremental bandwidth as needed without having to add one or more lines (with their attendant installation charges).

Even though microwave transmission is wireless, consider it an invisible wire in the sky, it is actually a point-to-point communication medium rather than a true "anywhere" wireless option.

To find a microwave ISP in your community, do a search on the Web for "wireless Internet communications."

Optical Fiber Connections

It is possible for most businesses and organizations to install an optical fiber link between their building and the Internet. As shown in Table 2.1, available bandwidth varies considerably, depending on the line option that is chosen. Even choosing an option at the low end of the possibilities, the amount of bandwidth is quite large.

Physical Location/Office

The equipment typically required to connect a business or organization to the Internet includes one or more servers and a router. It is assumed that the office has installed a local area network (LAN) so that multiple computer workstations may have access to a shared printer and other shared devices.

Servers

One or more servers probably will be required to accomplish a variety of tasks. For example, there may be a dedicated or shared server to send and receive email messages. The server will store email messages until a specific individual logs onto the LAN; at that time the server will forward the email messages to that individual.

Other servers may be required should the business have an extensive set of Web pages, provide an intranet to their employees, allow selected suppliers and customers to have access to an Extranet, and so forth.

Table 2.1 Optical Fiber Bandwidth Options

OPTION	OPTICAL FIBER BANDWIDTH
OC 1	52 Mbps
OC 3	155 Mbps
OC 12	622 Mbps
OC 48	2.5 Gbps
OC 192	10 Gbps
OC 768	40 Gbps

Routers

A router is a specialized computer that determines the next network point (sometimes called a node) to which a packet should be forwarded toward its destination. The router is connected to at least two networks and decides which way to send each packet based on its current understanding of the state of the networks to which it is connected. Typically a packet will travel through a number of network points with routers before arriving at its final destination.

Human Resources

A local area network, a set of servers, routers, printers, and other technology-related devices and software must all work together to provide access to information within an organization as well as maintain a connection to the Internet. Depending on the amount of equipment and the amount of computer-related equipment and software within a business or organization that must be maintained, the size of the computer support or IT staff can be considerable.

In some cases, a business will need a system administrator to maintain and administer the local area network and ensure that people who work within the organization are able to access the information that is appropriate. Other individuals may be needed to maintain the desktop computers, file servers, printers, and other devices connected to the LAN. In some cases, the introduction of a new version of an operating system, application, or physical device may lead to a cascading effect of problems that will need to be resolved, causing new versions of device drivers to be installed and so forth.

Security

For any kind of service provider as well as for the business or organization, constant attention must be paid to the security of the computer systems. Security concerns are addressed in greater detail in Chapter 9. It should be noted that any organization would certainly be subjected to receiving and coping with a large number of viruses (usually distributed via email) on a monthly basis. In addition, an organization may be the target of various hackers who will attempt to "burrow" their way into the company's computer systems—for fun or for profit.

Web Services

Web services are a new suite of services just becoming visible in the marketplace. Web services are software components that represent business functionality that can be accessed by users—via applications or another Web service—using standard protocols. Most importantly, a Web service can combine several applications that are of interest to the user; from the perspective of the end user, though, the service will appear to be a single seamless application.

Not surprisingly, Web services will embrace just about any application delivered via the Web and incorporating standard protocols, especially UDDI (Universal Description, Discovery, and Integration), XML, SOAP (Simple Object Access Protocol), and WSDL (Web Services Description Language), as shown in Figure 2.4. The goal of the Web services initiative is to have multiple applications interoperate seamlessly.

Readers should be aware that Web services will not be appearing on your desktop any time soon. The reason? Breaking up applications into components will take some time to accomplish. The real winners will be those organizations that are able to envision a future of Web services that go considerably beyond what any combination of applications is able to deliver today. Executable programs, another name for Web services, will give users tools to experience the Internet in more entertaining and engaging ways.

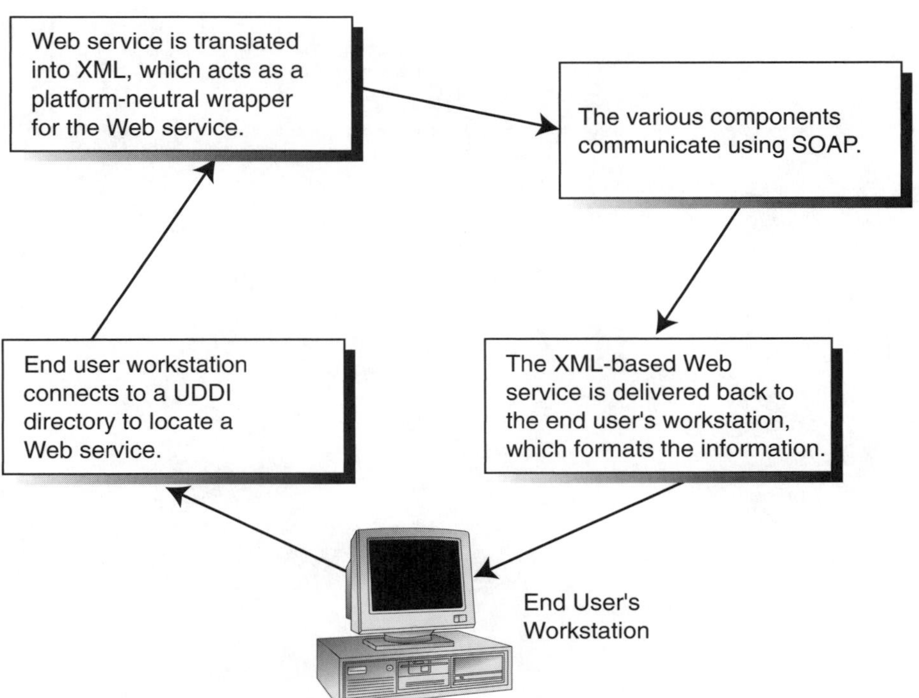

Figure 2.4 Shape of a Web service.

The Future

The Internet is still very much like a frontier. The U.S. federal government is very involved in extending the boundaries and capabilities of the Internet, funding a Next Generation Internet (NGI) initiative along with more than 180 American universities in a consortium called Internet2. The Internet2 initiative is focusing on three broad arenas: developing a faster backbone to the Net (very high-speed Backbone Network Service or vBNS), creating a more stable operating environment, and developing practical applications. Experiments are underway to provide a 3-D graphical user interface (ideal for medical applications, for example) and to create a kind of shared virtual office space (you can view a video of this prototype office by visiting www.advanced.org/tele-immersion/news.html).

In short, given the increasing bandwidth on both the backbone of the Internet and each individual desktop of mobile device, the possibilities for new and improved applications are almost endless.

CHAPTER 3

Internet Service Providers

Internet service providers (ISPs) give customers the infrastructure—software, equipment and services—to create an Internet connection with reliable, available, and scalable performance. In addition to the Internet, ISPs may provide access to the World Wide Web, USENET discussion groups, email, FTP (file transfer) and IRC (Internet relay chat), voice, domain name services, hosting, Web development and design, consulting, and e-commerce services. Today's technologies allow ISPs to connect customers to the Internet using a variety of communications media, including wireless and cable access, connecting to hardware that include telephones, laptops, and handheld devices.

Industry Outlook

The use of the Internet continues its rapid expansion, especially in commercial establishments where Web products and services have revolutionized the workplace as well as the marketplace. The number of Internet users worldwide will reach 1.17 billion in 2005, up from 400 million in 2000 (eTForecasts 2001). Large and midsize businesses are expected to more than double their spending on Internet technology, from $49 billion in 2000 to $110 billion in 2004, with the bulk being spent on streamlining supply chains and managing partners through corporate portals. According to a recent report from Cahners In-Stat Group, mid-market and enterprise U.S. businesses will also spend nearly $110 billion—or 26 percent of their total IT spending—on Internet infrastructure in 2004. This category accounted for just 15 percent of IT budgets in 2000.

Internet access is on the rise worldwide, with the most significant growth occurring outside the United States. The number of Internet connections in France soared 75.9 percent between December 1999 and December 2000. Meanwhile, U.K. Internet access increased 35.9 percent while in Germany Internet access rose 42.9 percent over the same period. See Table 3.1.

As the number of homes and businesses with Internet access increases worldwide, expect the number of Internet service providers (also called Internet access providers), some pure-play, others multiservice, to rise. ISPs are generally divided into three categories:

Local. Most ISPs are local, serving one municipality, county, or small geographic area. Eighty percent of the ISPs surveyed were labeled "local."

Regional. Regional ISPs are larger than local ISPs and serve more than one locality, but they are not national in scope. Their customer base can reach 10,000 or more.

National. National ISPs have multiple points of presence across the country, allowing unlimited Internet connectivity for customers. Some smaller ISPs expand their service range by contracting to use the large ISPs' point of presence (Lake 2001).

A recent survey of customer preferences found that the top five national ISPs were EarthLink, Excite@Home, Microsoft Network, Prodigy Communications, and America Online.

- EarthLink is the third largest U.S. Internet service provider in terms of the number of subscribers—4.7 million.
- Excite@Home, with its cable-modem service offering, is demonstrating that there is significant interest in alternatives to the traditional dial-up modem access using a telephone line.

Table 3.1 Internet Usage Worldwide

COUNTRY	HOUSEHOLDS CONNECTED	PERCENT OF POPULATION
United States	53,488,000	51.6
United Kingdom	8,487,000	35.9
Germany	9,976,000	29.2
France	4,178,000	19.6
Spain	2,031,000	15.6

Source: NetValue, 2001

- The Microsoft Network or MSN has nearly 5 million U.S. subscribers.
- Prodigy Communications is focusing on providing DSL connections to its customers.
- America Online, with 23.2 million subscribers, is the world's largest ISP. Its recent merger with Time Warner means that AOL will continue to focus on providing access to the Internet and proprietary content to its customers (Interactive Week A 2001).

Wireless Internet access is attracting far more interest in the ISP world with B2B markets expected to explode as companies realize an increasing rate of return on their investment. Wireless users, which numbered 40 million worldwide in 2000, will jump to 730 million in 2005, making up 62.1 percent of all Internet users (eTForcecasts 2001). Several other studies suggest that the number of U.S. wireless Web customers will increase from 4.1 million in 2000 to 96 million in 2005.

What does this mean for ISPs and their business customers alike? New markets, new products, new revenues. In addition, the dynamic intersection of market demand and supply could force a shake-out or consolidation in the ISP industry. Weaker service providers may falter if they are unable to meet the scale and scope of staggering network volumes.

Unless an ISP is able to provide more than simple Internet connection services and increase the reasons why a business should remain a customer, then the ISP will be able to compete only on price, a sure-fire recipe for disaster. ISPs that compete on price experience a higher-than-normal level of "churn"—customers who sign up and leave a short time later for a cheaper service. See Table 3.2 on page 44 for a list of the number of ISPs by region along with an indication of the range of services that they offer. Often the ISP must partner with other service providers—for example, an ASP—to provide these additional service offerings. Then an important issue arises: Who owns the customer? Who is communicating in writing, sending the bill, and providing support for the customer?

"This evolution of the Internet will stimulate the convergence of applications and services and allow them to reach well beyond their usual domains," says Neil Ward-Dutton, research director at Ovum. "The introduction of interactive digital TV services, media streaming, and the announcements of wireless strategies from IBM, Microsoft, Sun, Hewlett-Packard, and Oracle are just some examples of the early moves that are being made toward making Internet services available any time, anywhere."

For example, The MeT (Mobile electronic transactions) initiative, sponsored by Ericsson, Motorola, Nokia, Panasonic, Siemens AG, and Sony, released its first set of mobile e-commerce specifications in early 2001. These specs define how secure electronic transactions will be performed on a mobile phone, with privacy and security ensured by digital signatures and cryptography services. MeT estimates that there will be 1 billion mobile phone users worldwide by the end of 2002, many of whom will be equipped with mobile Internet-capable terminals, such as DoCoMo phones (Heim 2001).

TIP

For more information about The MeT, visit their Web site at http://www.mobiletransactin.org

The growth of Internet telephony—calling from a personal computer (PC) to an ordinary telephone or from PC to PC via the Internet—is growing and is putting great pressure on traditional telecommunications companies by offering a competing service at no cost. ITSPs (Internet telephony service providers) offer low-cost or even free long distance and international calls. Basic telephone handsets are beginning to appear on the market and are replacing the inconvenient/poor-quality headsets that are in use today. U.S. competitive local exchange carriers (CLECs) are starting to form relationships with these ITSPs in order to surpass traditional long distance carriers like Sprint and MCI. AT&T is so concerned about this that it has bought a 39 percent stake in the ITSP Net2Phone (Spring 2001).

How Does It Work?

For a monthly fee, the Internet service provider gives the business a software package (Web browser plus dial-up access software, if needed), user name, password, and access phone number. Equipped with a modem, you can then log on to the *Internet*, browse the *World Wide Web* and *USENET*, and send and receive *email*.

In addition to serving individuals, ISPs also serve large companies, providing a direct connection from the company's networks to the Internet. ISPs themselves are connected to one another through *network access points* (NAPs).

ISPs are also called Internet access providers (IAPs). IAPs generally provide dial-up access through a modem and *PPP* connection, though companies that offer Internet access with other devices, such as *cable modems* or wireless connections, could also be considered IAPs.

The terms IAP and ISP are often used interchangeably, though some people consider IAPs to be a subset of ISPs. Whereas IAPs offer only Internet access,

ISPs may provide additional services, such as access to leased lines (T-1 or T-3) and Web development.

ISP Offerings

What services does an ISP generally offer? The basics include a connection to the Internet (using a variety of communications technologies), Web browsing, USENET, email, Web hosting, Web design, information services, virtual private networks (VPNs), intranets, and Extranets

A summary of ISP characteristics as well as an indication of the range of services they offer can be found in Table 3.2 on the following page.

Internet Connection

For most business ISP customers, the days of a single 28.8 analog modem and a telephone dial-up are long gone. Those initial technologies have been replaced with enhanced digital networking tools that enable convenient, complete connectivity across the enterprise.

Connection types, detailed in the technology section, include dial-up, xDSL, cable modems, ISDN, T-1, T-3, and in some cases, optical fiber (OC 3) links.

Historically, ISPs have competed on cost and area of service coverage. The industry includes everything from "mom and pop" local setups with a couple of dial-in telephone lines to the national leaders with millions of customers.

One of the quickest and easiest places to begin searching for an ISP is www.thelist.com, a search engine and directory. You can search its database with more than 9,700 ISP listings by area code or country code or restrict searches to the United States or Canada. Searches can be limited to the type of services offered—for example, Web hosting and Web design.

Should you already have an ISP, you can rate your ISP and then compare your results with others by visiting the Web site http://www.cnet.com/internet. You will need to respond to 20 questions; then you can see how your ISP measures up.

Table 3.2 ISPs by Region

	NEW ENGLAND	MID-ATLANTIC	EAST NORTH CENTRAL	WEST NORTH CENTRAL	SOUTH ATLANTIC	EAST SOUTH CENTRAL	WEST SOUTH CENTRAL	MOUNTAIN	PACIFIC	CANADA
Subscribers	9,711	2,142	10,184	3,867	15,276	1,542	3,375	2,783	4,472	3,649
POPs	172	282	67	75	179	258	93	107	366	216
Employees	19	10	19	22	13	9	12	11	43	33
Start Year	1990	1994	1994	1992	1994	1994	1995	1994	1995	1994
Modems	487	2,078	1,991	508	345	276	458	4,098	1,599	325
Subs/Modem	20:1	1:1	5:1	8:1	44:1	6:1	7:1	1:1	3:1	11:1
SERVICES										
ISDN	70%	80%	70%	62%	85%	76%	86%	63%	66%	72%
DSL	74%	61%	40%	66%	56%	28%	64%	65%	71%	33%
T-1	83%	70%	77%	77%	78%	88%	88%	88%	72%	50%
Cable	4%	3%	7%	11%	9%	0%	2%	0%	4%	6%
Wireless	35%	30%	25%	30%	30%	36%	36%	37%	23%	44%
Web Hosting	100%	97%	93%	91%	93%	92%	93%	98%	91%	89%
PRICING										
Dial-Up	$20	$18	$18	$19	$18	$18	$18	$21	$19	$16
Dedicated										
Modem	$114	$85	$91	$103	$97	$109	$97	$118	$99	$95
128k	$193	$164	$225	$200	$216	$213	$195	$214	$222	$224
512k	$401	$468	$481	$400	$476	$609	$590	$406	$359	$481
1.544m	$1,169	$907	$1,003	$678	$903	$1,015	$1,111	$854	$929	$1,101

Canadian pricing has been adjusted to U.S. dollars based upon the conversion rate of .678104 to 1 (06/12/00)
BIA fn ISP Survey: Summary of Findings. BIA Financial Network, June 2000.

Case Study: The Business of Broadband

For companies especially, the case for getting broadband service—any way they can—is compelling.

An example is Glendora, California-based ChecKing Check Cashing Centers, which recently switched from dial-up Internet service to DSL for tracking customer records and rooting out scammers.

"Our reason was mostly cost," says Harry Clouse, ChecKing's CFO. Before DSL, each ChecKing location had several dial-up accounts, each with its own phone line. By consolidating these accounts in each of its branch offices into shared high-speed connections, ChecKing saved $200 per office per month—and got faster service to boot. "With 13 locations, that's $30,000 a year," says Clouse. "For a small business, that's significant."

But for ChecKing, switching to DSL also meant going from the familiar dial-up data and voice service delivery of a traditional telephone company to Mpower Communications, a relatively unknown DSL ISP. Start-up Mpower, a mere four years old, is based in Rochester, New York—a city almost as far away from Glendora as one can get without leaving the country.

"Needless to say, we had concerns about quality and reliability," says Clouse. "We had heard about the benefits of DSL, but we had also heard some of DSL's horror stories."

Indeed, horror stories abound. Because demand for broadband far outstripped the ability of providers to deliver it, long waits for installation were (and in many areas still are) the norm. Often, customer service personnel at the cable and telephone companies were ill informed about the new service, and many would-be customers couldn't find out whether broadband was even available to them. Worse, broadband service is often sold through third-party providers, which lease the lines from cable or phone companies. This has led to miscommunication about which organization is responsible for what—and plenty of finger pointing when things go wrong.

For ChecKing, the switch worked well—at least, for the most part. "The good news is that we got all of our offices on our DSL network," says Clouse. "The bad news is it took a few months to get it all done" (Medford 2001).

In addition to the basic service—providing Internet access—an ISP will typically provide a range of additional services for its customers. These additional services cover a broad range of activities, as noted in the following discussion.

USENET

Network news is the equivalent of a bulletin board system (BBS) or a discussion group found on private dial-up facilities like those on Microsoft Network and America Online, among others. Network news is organized under a set of broad headings called newsgroups. Typically, multiple discussions occur simultaneously within one newsgroup. The user can view the current discussion as well as review the prior discussions. In addition, the user can search for an article based on the author, subject, or summary.

Newsgroups are organized hierarchically. A newsgroup name consists of a few words separated by dots—for example, rec.music.a-cappella. The name becomes more specific as you move from left to right. Thus, rec.music.a-cappella is a recreational discussion, in the general category of music. And more specifically it is a discussion of singing without musical accompaniment (a-cappella).

Not all ISPs provide access to newsgroups. A set of free newsgroups considered to be of global interest come as a part of USENET. Access to USENET does not require the Internet (because USENET predates the Internet) although you can gain access to USENET using the Internet.

USENET consists of ten well-managed newsgroup categories. These categories include those shown in Table 3.3.

Table 3.3 USENET Discussion Groups

CATEGORY	DESCRIPTION
alt	Alternative viewpoints on any conceivable topic.
biz	Business products, services, and review.
comp	Computer science and related topics (computer hardware and software, sources of software, impact of computers on society).
humanities	Topics dealing with fine art, literature, philosophy.
misc	Groups dealing with employment, health, and a variety of other topics.
news	Groups interested in the news network. Important information for new users is to be found here.
rec	Groups that discuss recreational activities, hobbies, and the arts.
sci	Discussions focus on scientific research and the application of science. Includes both the hard sciences and the social sciences.
soc	Groups that address social issues including politics.
talk	Groups that debate controversial topics, including religion.

In addition to the official newsgroups there are a number of local or alternative newsgroups. For example, alternative newsgroups with groups discuss topics of interest to kindergarten through high school teachers and students, Institute of Electronic and Electrical Engineers, business people, biologists, and many others.

A complete list of the USENET newsgroups may be found by searching http://www.ibiblio.org/usenet-i/.

Also, if you visit http://groups.google.com/googlegroups/deja_announcement.html you can search the archives of USENET.

It should be noted that the servers supporting newsgroups are extensive and require sufficient processing power to handle thousands of inquires each day as well as to store a significant amount of information on the disk drives.

Email

Electronic mail (email for short) is probably the most popular and most widely known Internet application. The delivery of email consists of two parts: the time it takes to move the message across the network to your mail computer and the delays until you open and read the email. Checking your email regularly means that the utility of the service increases. In the year 2000, the number of email messages sent each day exceeded the volume of the regular paper mail delivered by the post office.

Email is a store-and-forward service in that the message is passed from machine to machine until it arrives at its final destination. This is similar to how regular paper mail is delivered. In the case of an email, the address is placed in a mail header rather than an envelope. The header has the **To:, cc:, From:, Subject:** information that is found at the top of all email messages.

The key to an email is obviously its address, which is sent to an individual and not just a computer. A computer acts as the mail agent—receiving and storing the individual's email until they log on to the network and "open" their email. The computer acting as the mail agent has a domain name. For example, the domain name might be **wiley.com**. The name of the specific individual appears prior to the domain name and the "@" or "at" symbol separates the name of the individual from the domain name. There are no standard naming conventions for identifying an individual within an organization. The rules followed by a specific organization are a combination of policy and the options that the email software allows. For example, the individual "John Smith" might be

john.smith@wiley.com or **j.smith@wiley.com** or **j_smith@wiley.com** or **jsmith@wiley.com** and so on in seemingly endless variations.

In addition to the fact that a great majority of all businesses and organizations assign email addresses to their employees, an individual can visit a host of Internet sites and sign up for free email service. Among the more popular are Microsoft's Hotmail.com and Yahoo's email service. The vast majority of ISPs provide a free email account for each business or individual that signs up.

Unfortunately, the popularity of email has led to the equivalent of paper junk mail. In cyberspace this junk email is called "spam." Deleting spam email messages can be a time-consuming task for most employees, especially if they have signed up to receive a "free" something at a Web site. Fortunately there are tools that will assist an individual in automatically deleting their spam.

Internet Relay Chat

Internet relay chat (IRC), or 'chat" for short, was developed in that late 1980s. It enables many people connected anywhere on the Internet to join live discussions. The IRC server is responsible for receiving and sending text messages to and from all of the participants in a discussion. The IRC server is able to handle multiple discussions simultaneously. Obviously, all of the discussions in the chat room are public (all messages are sent to everyone in the chat room). It is possible, though, for two or more individuals to move to a private chat room. A number of Web sites—Yahoo!, for one—provide directories of chat subject categories.

Some businesses have installed chat room software (the IRC server software) to facilitate discussions within their organization. This approach has been particularly effective for larger, geographically dispersed organizations.

Instant Messaging

A relatively new communications service called instant messaging enables you to create a private chat room with another individual. The instant messaging systems alerts you whenever someone on a list that you maintain is online. You then can initiate a private chat session with a specific individual, play games, and so forth.

America Online popularized instant messaging with its "Buddy List." Because there are no standards for moving messages from one network to another (yet), currently individuals using instant messaging can do so only with other individuals who use the same network. One popular instant messaging program is called ICQ (pronounced as separate letters, as in "I-Seek-You").

Voice

It is possible to use the Internet as a transmission medium for telephone calls. For businesses and organizations that have fixed-price Internet access, Internet telephony software provides essentially free telephone calls—anywhere in the world. The quality of these calls is not currently up to a normal telephone call, but it is improving day-by-day.

Some telephone applications—for example, NetMeeting and CoolTalk—come bundled with the popular Web browsers. There are also some stand-alone products that can be installed to facilitate telephone calling using the Internet. Although the most popular shorthand manner used to refer to Internet telephony as *voice over IP* (VoIP) the press will also sometimes refer to IP telephony or voice over the Internet (VOI).

Use of voice over IP obviously has the traditional telephone companies concerned about the long-term financial viability of providing telephone services.

A variation of VoIP is to use the Internet as a transmission medium for both audio and video signals, with the result that it is possible to conduct a videoconference using the Internet. Admittedly, some of the video pictures are a bit "jerky," but it can be an effective and cost-effective tool as opposed to using a more traditional videoconferencing provider.

Domain Name Services

It is not uncommon for an ISP to partner with one of the Internet domain name licensing companies to provide such services to its customers.

Consulting Services

Some ISPs will provide consulting services to their customers. These consulting services are typically fairly limited and usually involve designing Web pages, updating Web pages, and so forth. One reason for the limited services is that true consulting services require a larger and more experienced staff in order to add value to a consulting assignment.

As a result, some ISPs will partner with local or regional consulting organizations and introduce these firms to their customers who require more consulting services than the ISP itself can provide. The consulting company will typically pay the ISP a finder's fee that varies depending on the dollar amount of the consulting agreement.

Web Hosting

One obvious added-value service that almost all ISPs provide to their customers is to host the customers Web pages. The customer, in most cases, assumes responsibility for designing and updating the Web pages for the company's Web site; the ISP simply provides the computer(s), necessary disk space, and connection to the Internet.

Web Design

Designing a Web site is very much more an art than a science. Thus, while there are no hard-and-fast rules to follow, some general conventions have evolved over time. The problem with any Web design is that it must serve the purpose of the Web site—for example, is the Web site to provide e-commerce services, or is it a customer support site?

The observation that a Web site is good must be made from the perspective of the user rather than that of the designer. And even at Web sites with several years' worth of experience (for example, at Amazon.com), the number of users that start the purchasing process and fail to complete it is still quite high. Thus, it is not surprising that when a user becomes frustrated with the process to complete a task on a Web site they simply leave. After all, on the Internet a competitor is only one "click" away.

Thus, after a Web site has been made operational, make sure that someone responsible is constantly monitoring the various paths users actually take so that improvements can be made to the site and the frustrations experienced by the user are eliminated.

E-Commerce Services

An ISP can typically provide a business or organization with access to an e-commerce site. The ISP will assist in making the products provided by the company available for sale via the Internet. This is clearly one approach that has found favor by a large number of companies and organizations that have used this approach. An alternative approach is to become a partner with a portal that is organizing companies within one particular industry, for example, plastics, steel, automobile manufacturers, and so forth.

The financial rewards for companies that are using an ISP to operate an e-commerce Web site on their behalf have generally been disappointing. A customer or a prospect must have a compelling reason to visit a Web site in the first place and then even more reasons to return again and again. The key for a user to return is to have a very satisfactory experience the first time he or she visits a Web site. Thus, the expectations of a business's customer or prospect are usually quite high, and they must not be disappointed.

VPNs

A virtual private network (VPN) is a "private" network constructed using the public Internet to connect nodes. A VPN uses encryption and other security mechanisms to ensure that only authorized users can access the network.

Aside from the improved security afforded by a VPN, VPNs also provide directories, authentication, and, in some cases, content. Many companies are using the Internet as a wide area network, in conjunction with use of a VPN, as a means to promote remote access for teleworkers, after-hours workers, remote offices, and travelers. Using a VPN, an ISP can attract customers by providing efficient remote connectivity without the restrictions of point-to-point, dedicated access. By providing these services, the customer can avoid dealing with the day-to-day network firefighting.

VPNs can provide the IP approximation of Quality of Service control using specialized tunneling protocols, such as point-to-point tunneling protocol (PPTP) or Layer 2 tunneling protocol (L2TP), which establish restricted, secure channels within the Internet.

Intranets and Extranets

An *intranet* is a network belonging to a business or organization that is accessible only to its employees and others with appropriate authorization. An intranet is used primarily to share information about the company's products and services, manufacturing processes, its competitors, sales opportunities, product literature, and so forth. A number of organizations also use the intranet to compile and maintain the collective wisdom about the organization and what makes the organization distinctive and unique. This latter activity is often referred to as "knowledge management."

An *Extranet* is an intranet that has extended additional levels of accessibility to others outside the organization. For example, an Extranet will often provide access to and share proprietary information with business suppliers, wholesalers, distributors, and other resellers. The sharing of information will often result in a company's ability to reduce its levels of inventory, improve customer service, and so forth.

ISP Customer Benefits

The future of any organization in today's digital economy depends on how effectively it maximizes and leverages technology. In short, a company's ISP is its cornerstone for profitability, its technological platform as well as a battleground to recruit and retain clients. Thus network reliability, or the lack thereof, can have a deep and dark impact on revenues, customer satisfaction, and long-term competitive superiority.

ISPs promise business customers the ability to link strategic plans with client-focused processes that exceed individual as well as corporate performance metrics. Business customers, mindful of operational inefficiencies, outdated technology, and limited intellectual capital, seek support in delivering their core competencies to their stakeholders.

What Should an ISP Enable?

ISP business customers can and should expect the following:

- Guaranteed, instant high-speed access to the Internet whether from dial-up, DSL, ISDN, and T-1 networking.
- Improved employee productivity, provided they don't spend a lot of time surfing the Net for nonbusiness-related sites.
- Improved customer service, provided the company has a Web site that provides relevant information for its customers.
- Increase in speed –to market by improving communications within an organization and between a company and its customers.
- Safeguarding of the customer's data using state-of-the-art security protocols.
- Access to additional value-added services, for example, Web design and development and strategic e-consulting services.

Special Concerns for Business Customers

Speed doesn't matter if your employees, your customers, or your vendors can't access crucial data once they link to the Net. As we said earlier, live tech support is mandatory on a 24×7 basis for ISP business customers. Following are additional operational issues for businesses to consider before partnering with an ISP:

- Are there local telephone dial-up numbers or a toll-free number? Better yet, is there wireless access? Otherwise, telecom expenses could mount with business travel and telecommuting. Double-check with the phone company that the numbers offered by the ISP are indeed *local*.
- What's the network outage record? Redundancy, having multiple connections to the Internet backbone, is an essential ISP requirement. If an ISP

offers DSL or T-1 access, it should have multiple T-3 (43 Mbps) and even OC 3 optical links (155 Mbps) to the backbone.

- How many customers does the ISP have? What services do they receive? Ask for referrals.
- How much traffic can the bandwidth handle? Capacity counts. Does the ISP have sufficient lines, servers, and tech support staff to meet market demand? Can it ramp up as your business grows in scale?
- How long has the ISP been in business? Who are the investors? Senior managers? IT executives?
- How much of the application work is outsourced and to which vendors? Are the vendors domestic or overseas?
- Speaking of overseas, does the ISP have global capability? Can it support multiple languages for overseas subsidiaries and customers?

ISP Operating Responsibilities

The bottom line for ISP operating responsibilities is that all users are routed directly to a secure high-speed connection directly to a Tier 1 Internet backbone (Holden 2000). This will include the following:

- A secure, environmentally controlled computer facility.
- Full backup power.
- Direct fiber-optic links between the ISP and the Internet backbone.
- Dual circuits, with redundant routing to Tier 1 Internet backbones.
- Commercial grade equipment—for example, Cisco routers, Cisco catalyst switches, Sun Sparc Ultra 2 servers, Ascend Communication servers.
- Support for the latest modems like the Rockwell K56Flex and ITU v.90 standard for dial-up access and 64 Kbps and 128 Kbps for ISDN customers.
- 24 × 7 Help Desk support with well-trained employees who can quickly resolve problems for the ISPs customers.

ISP Service Checklist

The business ISP customer shouldn't just expect an affirmative response to the items listed in the checklist. Its ISP should be providing the latest commercial-grade systems and upgrades to perform at the highest end of Internet standards in each of these categories.

Disk space	Auto-responders
Data transfer speeds	Email forwards
Access logs	24-hour toll-free support
Statistics	Guarantees
Software	Telnet access
Email POP	Scripting
Accounts	Database access
Email	99.0 percent uptime
Virus monitoring and protection	Security monitoring

What Keeps an ISP Competitive?

Corporate customers choose ISPs based on the same benchmarks as households: outstanding service that's easy, fast, affordable, and reliable. Business users, however, have even greater requirements when it comes to ISPs: Server failures, bandwidth crunches, security breaches, and other service meltdowns can cripple, or even destroy, an organization regardless of size. It's imperative for business users to demand and expect 24 × 7 technical support for their digital assets. Successful ISPs provide not only the hardware and software to manage Internet communications but also the technical expertise and leadership to manage all levels of the customer relationship. Decreasing communication costs, increasing bandwidth capabilities, and explosive market opportunities create an ISP marketplace with robust choices of service and

Redundancy

Why is redundancy so important? On the Net, size does matter. The main lines of the Internet that carry the bulk of the traffic are collectively known as the Internet backbone. The Internet backbone is formed by the biggest networks in the system, owned by major ISPs such as MCI, Sprint, UUNet, and America Online's ANS. By connecting to each other, these networks create a super fast pipeline that crisscrosses the United States and extends to Europe, Japan, mainland Asia, and the rest of the world. But that doesn't mean that the network is equally well developed at every point along the route. The U.S. backbone has so many intersecting points that if one part fails or slows down, data can be quickly rerouted over another part, a feature called redundancy. Overseas, the network may have less redundancy and so be more vulnerable to slowdowns or breakdowns.

prices for ISP customers. ISPs must compete for limited revenue streams in an ever-evolving environment of efficiencies, partnerships, and data collection.

Some ISPs have found that by offering a solid, clearly written service level agreement (see Chapter 8 for further elaboration on SLAs) they are able to attract larger business customers, which translate into greater revenues.

Conclusion

It is only a matter of time before Internet products and services become the standard of all business transactions. Current and potential ISP customers must be prepared to develop and maintain integrated Web-enabled solutions across all business units, from human resources to data warehouse to customer support. Regardless of the type of application, it all begins with the Internet. In the next chapter, we examine application service providers, the next generation of Internet technology that allows companies to outsource software across their Internet connections.

CHAPTER 4

Application Service Providers

Application service providers (ASPs) rent access to application software over dedicated high-speed networks or the Internet. Representing a new competitive weapon in information technology, application service providers minimize time-to-market on new innovations through scalable information technology resources and infrastructure. An ASP takes the traditionally separate phases of a software implementation and bundles them together into a full-service offering. These phases include hardware and software license procurement, implementation, hosting operation, and maintenance of the application.

ASPs make world-class applications and information technology best practices accessible and affordable for businesses and organizations of all types and sizes. ASPs offer organizations digital freedom—the ability to leverage virtually everything in their computing environments to reach more users, with more applications, in more locations at record speeds. As a result, ASPs can minimize the risks, costs, and complexities of implementing new initiatives while increasing an organization's flexibility to capitalize on changing business conditions quickly. With an ASP service, even a small business can have access to the software tools that power the operations of larger organizations.

According to Dain Ehring, founder of Dorado.com, "The rapid pace of change created by the Internet completely antiquates the notion of annual software upgrades. E-commerce requires flexible software that can rapidly change with market conditions. Delivering applications as web-tone services is the only way to remain competitive" (TrendsReport 2000).

ASPs represent a convergence of IT and telecommunications in a way not seen before, as shown in Figure 4.1. While the availability of static data across the Internet was the engine that drove the popularity of the World Wide Web, the deployment of powerful applications and interactive services across wide area networks is a milestone development with far-reaching implications.

These are the very reasons application service providers have emerged—to give organizations of any size fast, predictable, affordable access to virtually any application. As a result, organizations are free to focus on the speed and competitiveness of their operations, unencumbered by hardware, software, database, network, and staffing constraints. Under the ASP computing model, even the smallest, most resource-constrained organization can access the best-of-breed technology solutions to level the competitive playing field in today's global, networked economy. As with other kinds of outsourcing, an ASP service can transform an organization by allowing staff to focus on the organization's core strengths and mission.

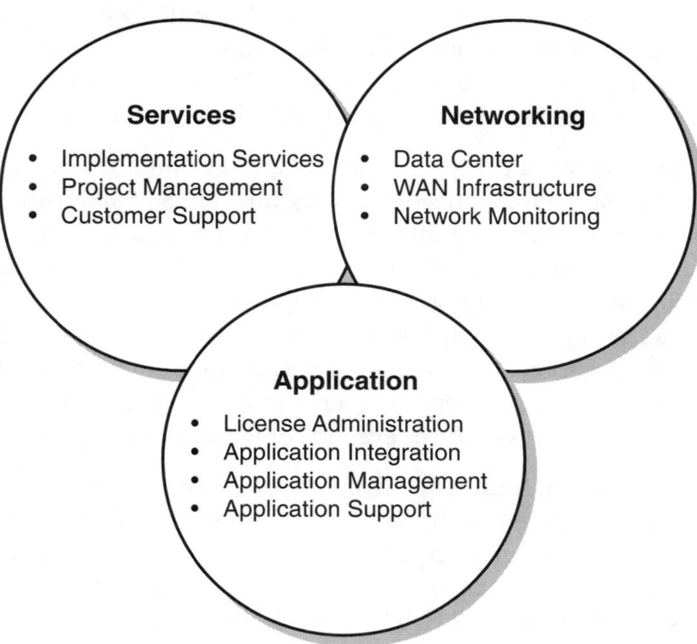

Figure 4.1 The ASP model.

What Is an ASP?

The ASP Industry Consortium, an international advocacy group focused on fostering greater understanding of and working to develop guidelines for the emerging ASP segment of the computer industry, suggests that an ASP can be defined as follows:

An application service provider manages and delivers application capabilities to multiple entities from a data center across a wide area network.

Several defining characteristics distinguish an ASP service (Cherry Tree 1999, 2000). Among these are:

The focus is on the application. The core value of an ASP service is providing access to and management of a software application that is commercially available. ASP services differ from hosting services, in which the focus of the service is on management of the network and servers, with minimal knowledge of the application(s). ASP services are also different from system integration consulting and business process outsourcing services. An outsourcing contract encompasses the management of entire business processes, such as human resources or accounting.

Under traditional applications management services (a type of service typically provided to large organizations by IBM or EDS), the customer already has acquired and deployed the application environment. Application management outsourcers take over management of that application environment, sometimes bringing it into their own data center. Under hosting service contracts, the customer owns the application and hands it over to the hosting company to operate, an approach different from that of an ASP.

It provides access to applications. Part of the value of ASP services is that businesses and organizations can gain access to a new applications environment (e.g., replace their old character-based system with a Web-based system), without making up-front investments for the software application's licenses, other third-party software licenses, servers, personnel, and other resources. The ASP, rather than the customer, either owns the application software or has a contractual agreement with the application software vendor to license and provide access to the application.

It is managed externally. Rather than being located within the organization, the application service is managed from a central location, or distributed locations, owned or under contract to the ASP. Staff and users access applications remotely—for instance, over the Internet or via leased lines, such as T-1 lines.

It offers one-to-many service. The ASP service is intended to be a one-to-many offering. An ASP typically partners with other application ASPs and other xSP vendors to package standardized offerings (providing for minimal or no customization) to which many organizations will subscribe over a specified contract period. For example, a company might gain access to an ASP service that provides accounting and human resources services.

IT outsourcing and application management services, conversely, are one-to-one, with each solution deployed to meet the unique needs of the customer organization.

A service contract is key. Many partners work together to provide an ASP solution. The ASP is the firm that is responsible, in the customer's eyes, for delivering on the contract—ensuring that the application service is provided as promised. If a problem arises (e.g., hardware problems with a server), the ASP is responsible for solving the problem, even if other companies provide the actual support. The ASP may warrant accessibility, reliability, and overall performance with a service level agreement (see Chapter 8).

Application service providers allow businesses of all sizes to outsource or rent software via the Internet, offering a simple alternative to expensive in-house technology. ASPs manage and deliver application capabilities to multiple users from a single data center across a wide area network. Within the industry, ASPs compete on their ability to provide excellent customer service and network reliability.

Industry Outlook

Over the course of the next three years, the ASP market is expected to grow dramatically. The growth curve is dependent on the wider availability of broadband and marketplace acceptance to the ASP concept. Initially, it was expected that small to medium-sized organizations would be interested in and using ASP services. Even the very largest organizations, though, are now beginning to utilize an ASP for one or more applications (Bianchi 2000).

Approximately $633 million was spent for ASP services during 2000. Industry analysts estimate that total ASP revenues will range from a low of $3.5 billion to a high of $12.3 billion in 2003 (see Figure 4.2). Market research group AMR Research predicts the ASP market will reach $4.7 billion by 2004, with an annual growth rate of 153 percent.

According to a recent survey, those organizations using an ASP service indicated that they currently are purchasing between two and six applications from an ASP. Some industry analysts expect that the total number of ASPs will decline over the next few years as companies merge, are acquired, or simply disappear.

A major reason for the emerging growth of the industry is the rising popularity of packaged software, which is richer in functionality and more config-

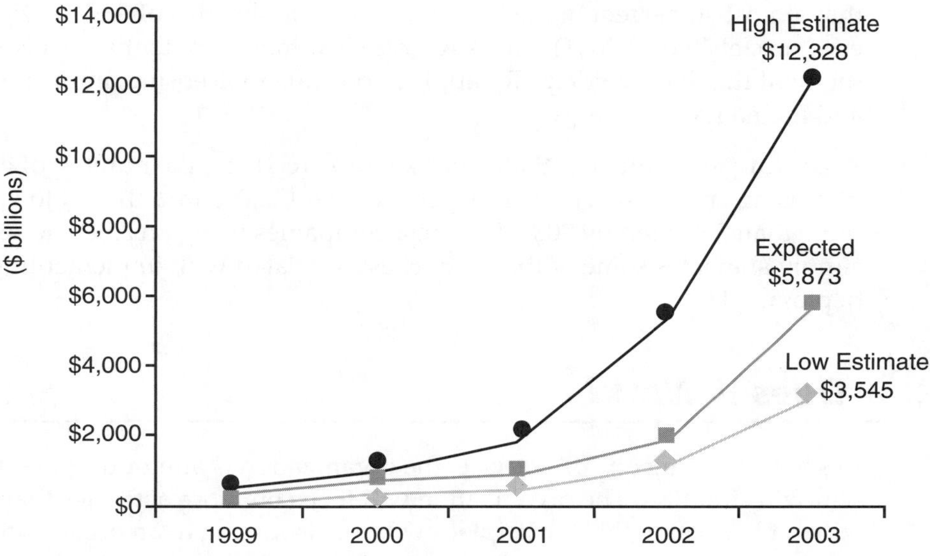

Figure 4.2 Expected ASP market growth.

urable than ever before. The chief drawback to higher flexibility, however, is the corresponding increase in time and cost to customize a system for an individual business. While some analysts say the ASP model has been slow to catch on, they believe a ubiquitous application such as instant messaging (the exchanging of email messages in near real time by two people using the Internet) could be the ticket to mainstream success.

A recent survey conducted by the Software & Information Industry Association indicated that 84 percent of the IT managers who responded are familiar with how the ASP model works and a full 75 percent are considering using an ASP service in conjunction with future software implementation projects. Only 25 percent indicated that their organizations were currently using an ASP service, and an additional 40 percent planned to do so within the next 12 months (SIIA 2000).

Mission-critical applications such as enterprise resource planning (ERP) and customer relationship management (CRM) were among the first to be offered by ASPs, but proved to be a tough sell to customers concerned about turning over control and security of their data to unproven service providers. Employees throughout the organization, on the other hand, use messaging and collaboration tools (Bhaskar and Jones, 2000). Several industry analysts suggest that software and service vendors still view the ASP approach as a key to reaching the small and medium-sized enterprise (SME) market and that almost 70 percent of businesses are open to the idea of ASP service delivery (Jaruzelski et al 2001). This suggests clear market potential in a customer segment that has avoided ERP applications due to licensing, implementation, and maintenance costs.

According to Cahners In-Stat, a market research firm, the number of companies using an ASP service was expected to be 136,000 in 2001 and to grow to more than 3 million by 2004. For most companies using an ASP, the service simply alleviates some of the headaches associated with implementing and deploying IT.

How Does It Work?

In short, by using an ASP service, the organization is attempting to set up a win-win situation: The organization will focus on those activities that will allow it to excel in the marketplace while outsourcing to an organization that excels at providing access to an application(s). The emphasis is placed on the *use* and not the *ownership* of the application software.

"The ASP model takes care of what I call the 'Tylenol factors' of applications—the maintenance, support, upgrades, and hardware. And we don't have to find and pay for staff to handle the applications," states Craig Kinyon, chief financial officer for Reid Hospital and Health Care Services, Inc., Richmond, Indiana (Gilbert and Mateyaschuk 2000).

Historically, most organizations have relied on a mixture of developing and maintaining systems in-house as well as purchasing packaged software products at an affordable price. Although it is sometimes overlooked in the buying process, most companies realize that it is necessary for them to recruit and retain an information technology (IT) manager and the associated support staff for the computer hardware, operating system, and network software, as well as the application software itself. Staff is needed to maintain the local area network as well as ensure that the computer workstations continue to operate in a normal manner. This support staff is typically responsible for maintaining and updating software with the newest releases of an office suite and other products, which allow the organization's other staff members to perform their jobs in a productive manner. Yet, IT managers are under tremendous strain—they can have a growing number of end users to support, an expanding network, an array of existing applications that must be supported, and new applications to install—all with a very limited number of qualified staff members.

Instead of maximizing the performance of the IT infrastructure and the end-user experience, an organization's IT department is consumed full-time with care and feeding tasks. Instead of developing new initiatives to leverage IT as a strategic weapon, the IT staff is flooded with a seemingly endless array of system problems, software upgrades, system patches, hackers flooding the email system, and more. When an IT manager does have time to scope out new applications that will improve the organization, the initiative is often killed because the application is too big, overly complex, or too expensive or it will take too long to implement. Thus, it is not unusual for any manager to find that he or she is at the end of the IT queue to resolve problems, install the latest release of a software application, and more.

An ASP can provide an organization with a high-quality application service that is run by trained professionals leveraging the best-of-breed systems and infrastructure. The ASP can assume responsibility for the day-to-day management of the application, freeing up scarce resources to focus on more strategic initiatives.

An ASP is more than just software—it is a comprehensive set of services that bundle the application software and system administrative services into one easy-to-use solution. In summary, an ASP vendor assumes responsibility for the following:

- Central site equipment: server(s), disk drives, tape back-up, etc.
- Application software
- Licenses for third-party software (e.g., Oracle or MS SQL Server, search engine software, operating system software, etc.)
- High-speed link from the application to a wide area network (e.g., the Internet)
- Backup of the library's data on a nightly basis
- Updating the application software with regular release of software enhancements and bug fixes
- Providing a help desk to quickly resolve problems
- Providing on-site training, if requested

Currently, more than 90 percent of companies using ASPs do so via the Windows environment. It is anticipated that the majority of ASP service delivery will migrate to the browser/Java environment in the coming three to four years (King 2001).

ASP Offerings

A growing trend in the packaged application space that is greatly benefiting the ASP industry is the move toward accelerated solutions for business.

Because an ASP generally uses designated technology to create its unique business solutions, it produces the required solutions in less time than an in-house IT group that deals with a broader range of projects and technologies. ASP customers pay a monthly or an annual fee to access applications instead of investing thousands, and perhaps millions, of dollars to create the software themselves. ASPs can also reduce the risk for companies, both large and small, that often occur when in-house technology teams attempt to launch and manage unfamiliar software. The ASP marketplace can be segmented into three groups:

Horizontal ASPs, sometimes called enterprise ASPs, volume business ASPs, managed application providers (MAPs), ASP application aggregators (AAAs), or aggregator ASPs, accumulate a range of applications and offer each customer the opportunity for signing up for the applications of their choice. These applications might include human resources, ERP, accounting, transportation, and more. The horizontal ASP will, in most cases, provide integration services so that one application can "talk" to another so that data need not be entered twice. For obvious reasons, a horizontal ASP will appeal to a broad audience, independent of any particular industry focus. Clearly, an important issue for the customer of such services is who is the single point of accountability when the customer is receiving several applications that are provided by multiple software development firms. Examples of companies that aggregate a broad range of applications include Jamcracker, USinternetworking, Corio, Breakaway, and Infinium.

The success of these companies will come if they are able to package and integrate the right set of applications for a target market. The integration allows data from one application to flow to another, as needed (e.g., employee data from a human resources application to become patron data for a library application). If they offer multiple ASP services as a part of the solution, an important issue to determine is who has primary responsible for providing customer support to each customer.

Vertical market ASPs that aggregate several applications will have appeal in one vertical niche of the marketplace (e.g., law firms, hospitals, retail, finance, hospitality, etc.). Examples of companies that aggregate applications for a vertical industry include CollegeNet, ExamBuilder, JurisDictionUSA, and LearningStation.

A specialist ASP, sometimes called a stand-alone ASP, will typically have developed or licensed a single application that it will then provide to its customers (e.g., library software, legal software, medical software and so forth). The strength of a specialist ASP is that the firm brings a depth of domain expertise to the development of the ASP service. Domain expertise refers to a thorough understanding of the business functions and the marketplace.

Typically, a specialist ASP will own the software or have extensive experience in integrating the application with other enterprise-wide applications. In some cases, the specialist ASP will be known as a Web Application Service Provider (WASP). Using a browser and HTML tags, a Web page can be built out of content originating from a company's site plus from WASPs. Partnering with a WASP for a search engine or stock price information and so forth can provide a seamless view because the look and feel can be made identical.

The ASP may have a local or regional focus or a national and/or international focus. In general, because the vast majority of applications are delivered via the Internet, the location of the ASP as well as where the application needs to be delivered (e.g., across a state or around the world) is no longer a major consideration.

The application software can come from three general sources:

- The independent software vendor (ISV) that has developed one or more applications to meet a specific customer need. The ISV may offer access to its software as an ASP service so that it is just one more in a series of ways to bring its products to the marketplace.
- A dot-com startup that would license another vendor's software and provide a set of bundled services to customers. A number of vendors have licensed ERP and CRM software, and these startup companies have had a mixed track record.
- A pure-play ASP company that develops its own software. This software works only as a service offering being delivered via the Internet.

ASP Customer Benefits

ASPs make it easier for organizations to gain fast and cost-effective access to best-in-class applications in order to do the following:

- Generate new revenue through increased sales vehicles such as e-commerce and customer resource management (CRM), to customer billing and sales force automation applications.
- Provide better customer service through online ordering/tracking and customer self-services, to call centers, order entry, and help desk applications.
- Enhance organizational knowledge through intranets, email, and groupware that enhances collaboration and streamlines communications, to data warehousing, data mining, and decision support solutions.

- Increase user productivity through personal productivity suites and contact management, to enterprise-class ERP and supply chain optimization applications.

Through application hosting, application service providers remove the burden of day-to-day IT management by assuming total responsibility for application rollout, updates, and ongoing maintenance and support. As a result, organizations are free to focus on core goals and objectives rather than difficult IT issues.

Increasing bandwidth and speed are giving software vendors the ability to host and manage applications for users, removing the software from the desktop or local server. The result is a shift in the business model of some software companies from traditional shrink-wrap products to software as a service.

> *The nature of software will be changing, software will be delivered in many cases as a service across the Internet instead of a packaged product.*
>
> Bill Gates, Microsoft

> *If you're a CIO with a head for business, you won't be buying computers anymore. You won't buy software either. You'll rent all your resources from a service provider.*
>
> Scott McNealy, Sun Microsystems

Larry Ellison, President of Oracle, believes that over the next few years, the company will stop being a traditional software company and deliver most of its technology to customers the way its Oracle Business Online operation does—as an online service for a monthly fee. Already, about 70 percent of the software in the new e-business suite is designed to be dished up this way (Hamm 2000).

Certainly, the outsourcing of information technology functions has been a familiar theme in both the profit and nonprofit sectors for the past 30 years. Outsourcing has enabled organizations to focus on what they do best and eliminate activities that were distractions. Factors that persuaded the decision makers in organizations to adopt the ASP model are shown in Table 4.1 (Zona Research 2000, 2001). And, according to another recent survey, the primary values that an ASP could offer to an organization are shown in Table 4.2 (Metzler 2000). It is significant to note that only 10 percent of the respondents indicated that reducing costs was the primary benefit that ASPs could offer their organization.

The convergence of application software and IT infrastructure toward an Internet-centric environment has enabled the ASP concept to emerge, as

Sales Force Automation

ASP applications provide tremendous opportunities and flexibility to sales reps, both in the office and in the field. Accessible by laptop, personal computer, or PDA, these SFA packages manage and host software for direct sales channels not only with basic contact files (names, phone numbers, emails) but with enterprise-wide processes like centralization that track goals and revenues.

Current ASP sales force automation packages provide even more than the basic contract information to sales reps. Some of these ASP packages can also track relationships (both official and unofficial), seniority, influencing factors, disposition, and other "soft" factors as well as change quotes into order forms dynamically. Some packages can even automatically "demote" an opportunity that has stagnated within a particular stage of the sales cycle (SPEX 2000).

How does using a sales force ASP benefit a business? It gives its sales team and their managers state-of-the-art information to make crucial, real-time decisions, create instant reports, and analyze and track key metrics. This is all available on a 24 x 7 basis, without first having to interact with an internal technology team because the information is being hosted and managed by the ASP. And this is all done in a reporting environment that packs a lot more power than weekly reports typed in Excel spreadsheets and then sent to regional or corporate headquarters.

shown in Figure 4.3. Software has evolved from custom, proprietary applications to off-the-shelf packages to the latest Net-centric software applications. Net-centric software allows Web-enabled communication and management of information content to e-commerce. In a similar vein, IT infrastructure has evolved from a proprietary mainframe environment to distributed computing, sometimes called client/server computing, toward a Net-centric milieu linking all stakeholders. As noted earlier, the ASP concept is revisiting the service bureau concept popular when mainframe computers dominated the scene.

Among the potential benefits that working with an ASP can offer a business or organization are these:

Improved ability to focus resources on core issues rather than IT concerns. In some organizations, information technology is more often perceived as a problem generator rather than a problem solver (Danziger 1977). Eliminating IT concerns by outsourcing responsibility for IT to an ASP allows the organization to focus on the quality and range of services that it provides to its customers.

Table 4.1 Importance of Factors Influencing the ASP Decision

RANK	FACTOR
1	Reduces total cost of ownership
2	Enables an organization to focus on achieving strategic business objectives
3	Frees IT resources to focus on mission-critical applications
4	Enables an organization to implement new applications more quickly
5	Reduces or eliminates application administration tasks
6	Better allocates costs by paying monthly fees versus large up-front purchase costs for applications
7	Enables seamless access to applications from remote offices and locations
8	Compensates for lack of internal IT resources
9	Provides the ability to have fixed, predictable application costs
10	Enables access to applications the organization would not otherwise be able to afford
11	Reduces time-to-market

Continuous access to the latest technology you need to run your business. Without the risks, costs, and administrative responsibilities associated with developing and maintaining the required IT infrastructure.

Faster access to the latest functionality. Clearly it is in the ASP's best interest to keep its computer environments as up-to-date as possible. The vendor can correct bugs and introduce new functionality much more quickly (weeks rather than cycles of four to six months). In addition, the enterprise department is not dependent on its organization's IT department to load the latest release of the software.

Table 4.2 Factors Influencing the ASP Value

FACTOR	PERCENT OF RESPONDENTS
Minimize the administrative burden of supporting applications	27%
Increased competitiveness	18%
Reduce applications deployment time	15%
Access to new applications	14%
Reduced cost	10%
Minimize technology risk	7%

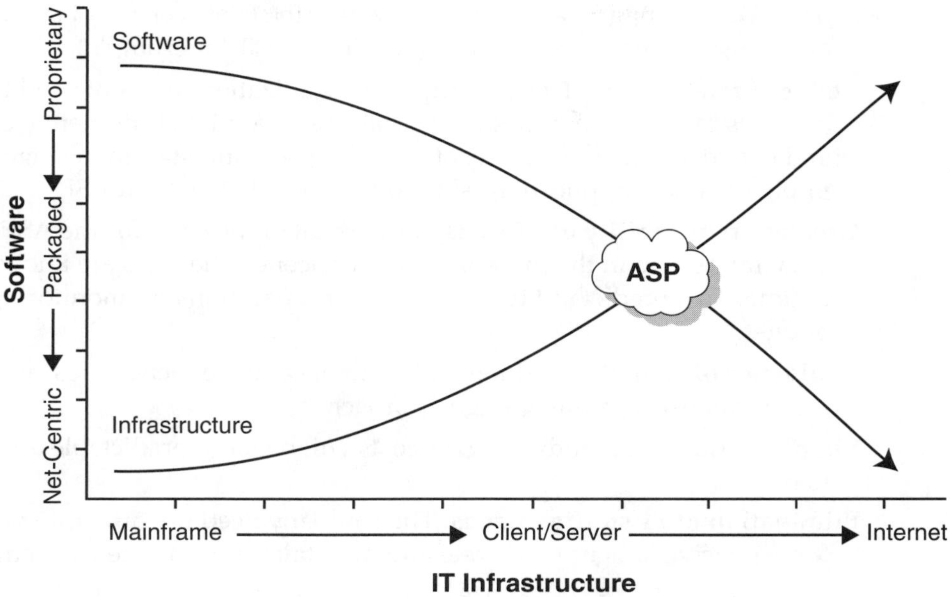

Figure 4.3 Emergence of the ASP.

Faster implementation of new applications and technologies. With reduced risk to the existing systems environment and lower impact on an organization's budget. Forty percent of customers expect that the return on investment (ROI) will occur within the first year of implementation, and another 25 percent believe that ROI will happen in less than two years (Wittmann 2000).

Access to a wider range of functionality and services. Through their own capabilities and with partnerships, ASPs can offer their customers a wider range of services, technologies, and application options than is possible for all but the largest organizations to handle on their own.

Easy application scalability. The ASP will allow the customer to add users or applications quickly as the needs in an organization change.

Access to comprehensive support services. Security, scheduled database and application back-ups, and a help desk to respond to problems and answer questions are provided. The ASP should provide training services as well as implementation consulting assistance.

Preservation of existing investments in legacy computers. Because the ASPs servers will handle the intensive processing required by today's sophisticated applications. Because the ASP will be delivering the application via a Web browser, older desktop workstations will, in most cases, be satisfactory and not need to be upgraded or replaced so that the latest version of the desktop operating system can be installed (Windows 2000, for example).

Reduced total cost of IT ownership. An organization does not need to spend precious capital on purchasing central site computer equipment (servers and disk drives), application software licenses, and staff to manage and implement new applications should they decide to use an ASP.

Greater predictability of IT costs. Because all of the costs for the ASP service are wrapped up in the monthly per-user license, the costs are known ahead of time. This predictability assists in the preparation and monitoring of a budget.

Avoidance of capital investments. In lieu of capital expenditures, an organization can use a pay-as-you-go approach.

Simplification of IT budgeting. IT costs will be more predictable and easier to budget.

Elimination of IT staffing needs. The company need not attempt to compete for expensive IT staff to operate and maintain its automated systems.

Surveys of organizations of all sizes have indicated that the total cost of ownership or TCO is significant and is significantly larger than the original purchase price of the application software licenses (Kapoor 1999). The TCO elements are shown in Figure 4.4. Support for hardware, the operating system, and the application software account for almost one-fourth of the costs. By far, the largest cost component is the staff necessary to provide the care and feeding of any automated system.

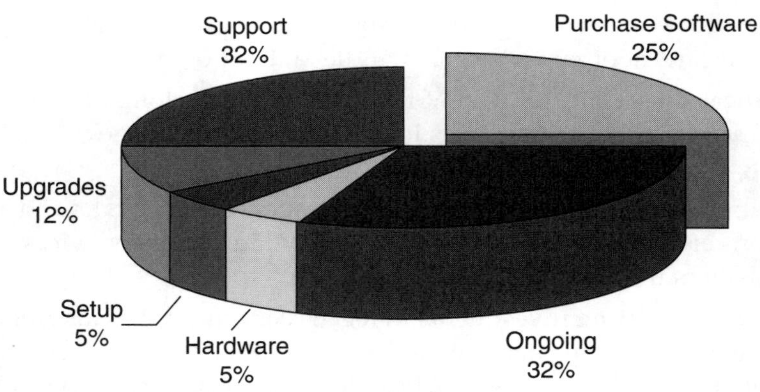

Figure 4.4 Traditional Five Year TCO Elements.

"What Can You Do for Me?"

In short, any organization will be asking the question, "Does the ASP service give me..."

... What I Want? Is the value high and the noise level low, or more specifically, does the organization gain access to the necessary application software and I don't have to think about it? Is the service timely and accurate?

... When I Need It? Just as the telephone company has worked hard to deliver a reliable dial tone, so too will prospective customers ask if the service "tone" is always on so that the application software is accessible by the organization's staff members when and where needed?

... Without Hassles? Does the ASP provide a service that is responsive, predictable, and reliable? Does the ASP vendor do whatever is necessary to resolve problems quickly?

Organizations of all sizes as well as individual consumers can benefit from this new ASP computing paradigm:

Large enterprises. ASPs can help large enterprises break free of the software upgrade and distribution monotony while helping these organizations to standardize on the same software applications and versions. In addition, ASPs can make it easier for global, distributed organizations to provide consistent application services to branch offices, mobile workers, and telecommuters. In this increasingly merger-prone environment, an ASP can help a company move online faster across diverse platforms and networks.

Small and medium-sized enterprises. Application service providers increase the competitiveness of risk-averse and resource-constrained small and medium-sized enterprises that could not otherwise afford the high-cost, technical staff training and support for rollout and ongoing maintenance of enterprise technologies, such as ERP and human resources. By renting world-class applications rather than purchasing low-cost alternatives, the ASP computing model gives these organizations an edge. ASPs enable these organizations to try new applications by reducing the level of investment risk.

Consumers. Application service providers promise to widen the reach of computing to a wide cross-section of people, especially those who have, thus far, not participated in the Internet age. Consumers who want software access without the associated cost and maintenance challenges of personal computing can contract with an ASP, just as they would sign up for Internet access or cable programming.

Clearly the Internet has shown that an organization does not need an application on a server or desktop. Yet, most organizations are still hesitant to give up too much too soon, especially mission-critical applications (Kearney 2000). Thus, a number of organizations that are using an ASP are using the service for niche applications (e.g., reporting travel-related expenses).

A recent survey conducted by the Information Technology Association of America (ITAA 2000) found the actual benefits for using an ASP service were the following:

- Gaining access to high-end applications
- Alleviating shortages of IT personnel
- Providing a guaranteed performance/uptime
- Increasing flexibility for the organization
- Reducing initial capital outlay
- Lowering IT costs over time
- Reducing time of implementation
- Improving security

Pricing

A recent research report from the Meta Group suggests that ASP prices jump 200 percent to 300 percent when even modest levels of customization (7 percent to 10 percent of function) are required. To be successful as an ASP, a company has to do much more than just license its software. Most ASP companies that Meta has talked with charge extra for integrating and customizing their software and see those services as a profit center and a way to differentiate themselves in the market. There are no flat standards for charging ASP customers. Many ASPs set basic pricing models according to the following metrics:

- The *flat monthly fee or fixed price* covers a service offering that provides a set level of functionality and services.
- *Variable pricing* involves using a fixed price at the low end of the service spectrum with additional variances at the higher ends. Exceeding set levels results in additional charges.
- A *subscription model* basically provides a specific number of users, sometimes called seats, with access to one or more applications and/or to specific modules within one application. For example, access to an application might cost $500 per seat per month. The customer pays a usage fee based on each registered user of the application, which can vary from a handful in a single department to thousands across a global enterprise.

- *Per employee.* The customer pays a usage fee based on the total employment headcount that governs a limited amount of time.
- *Per service.* Multiple products result in multiple fees.
- *Per CPU.* A usage fee is charged for every PC, laptop, or other hardware device that runs the ASP application.
- *Incentive-based (or performance-based) pricing.* The ASP is rewarded when certain performance levels are exceeded.
- An ASP might provide access to an application based on a *per-transaction approach*, for example, $5 per purchase order. Usually the per-transaction approach is employed only when an application is used infrequently or the value of each transaction is quite large. Transaction-based fees are used for e-commerce applications to match costs to revenues.
- *Risk/reward sharing.* In some cases, the supplier may be willing to take on some risk so that if the buyer is able to achieve some target goals that result from using the ASP's system, then the service provider will receive a portion of profits. For this pricing strategy to work, the metrics used to measure success must be carefully crafted and clearly understood by both parties.

The majority of ASPs will charge a system set-up fee, data conversion charge, implementation consulting service fees, and so forth, depending on the complexity of the application and the amount of customization that is required by the customer.

Some customers may, optionally, request a higher degree of system reliability. This increased system reliability will be reflected in higher annual charges. Just as there is no free lunch, in general any customer-requested "extra" will result in additional charges.

ASP Application Offerings

The available ASP offerings are quite widespread and include applications as a service from both Internet start-ups and the more established software vendors, as shown in Table 4.3.

A customer tracking survey by an ASP industry group released in February 2001 reported that communications, financial/accounting, and e-commerce offerings remain the most common types of ASP applications. The ASP Industry Consortium, an international advocacy group of ASP companies, commissioned the study listed in Figure 4.5 (Zona Research 2001). The survey asked respondents to list the types of applications their organizations are currently accessing from an ASP.

Table 4.3 Range of ASP Applications

CUSTOMER FOCUS	ENTERPRISE FOCUS	OPERATIONS FOCUS
Databases	Email	Expense accounts
Document management	Finance	Project management
E-commerce	Help desk (CRM)	Sales force automation
Engineering	Human resources	Training
Scientific	Marketing	Travel assistance
Office suites	Web sites	Library management

The higher adoption rate among communications, finance/accounting, education/training, and human resources applications probably have more to do with a tradition in those fields to outsource some portion of those activities. And, in most cases, while the application itself is important—for example, getting accurate payroll checks out in a timely manner is important—it is not central to what the company or organization does to provide value to its customers. This is in contrast to the important e-commerce and customer rela-

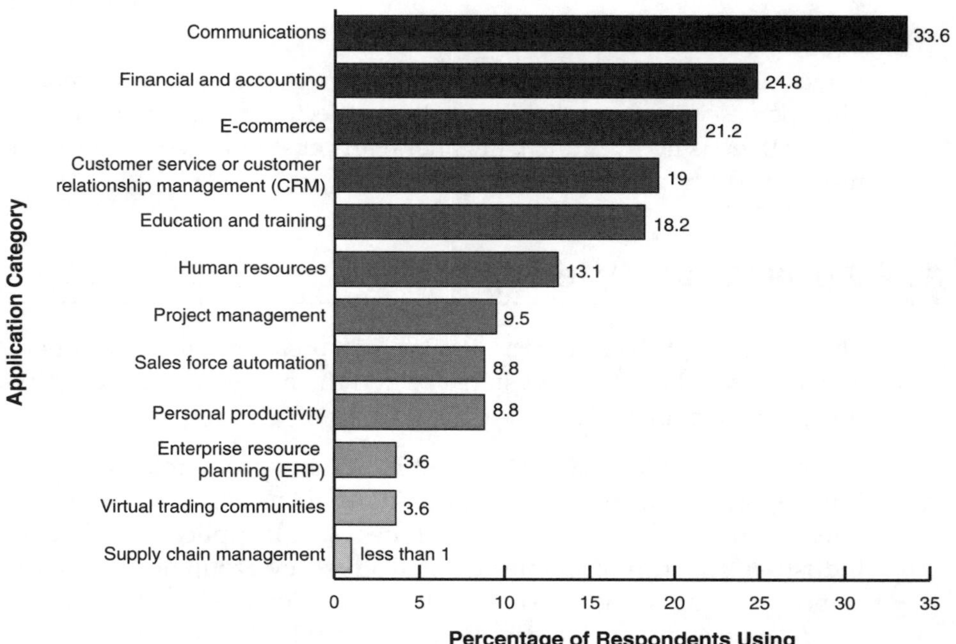

Figure 4.5 Survey of ASP application offerings.

tionship management or CRM applications that are more than likely outsourced to an ASP simply because the organization wants to roll out the application in a short period of time for a predictable cost. The applications that require a fair degree of integration both within the organization itself and between the applications from other companies are clearly achieving less traction in the marketplace.

The top-line benefits of using an ASP are also emerging from customers, according to the survey. For each of the first three-quarters, respondents cited a reduction in the total cost of ownership as the leading factor influencing the ASP purchase decision. While cost still ranked as very important, more respondents in the fourth-quarter ASPIC survey cited the fact that ASPs enable them to focus on achieving strategic business objectives, as well as enable them to implement new applications more quickly. Also cited more often than cost was the fact that ASPs free up IT resources so that they can focus on internal mission-critical applications.

What Should an ASP Enable?

An ASP business customer should expect the following:

- Guaranteed availability to application software for all employees of the organization, regardless of their location
- Increased employee productivity as the ASP will provide Internet-based training 24 × 7
- A higher level of service for the business's employees as a result of using the ASP service
- Increase in speed-to-market by improving the software installation process
- Safeguarding of the customer's data using state-of-the-art security protocols
- Access to additional value-added services, for example, strategic consulting services

Special Concerns for Business Customers

As with any new emerging technology that hits the marketplace, the ASP industry finds itself attempting to live up to the enormous amount of hype. And from this hype have come some popular myths. Here are some of the most prominent ones and the reality behind them.

It's All or Nothing

Wrong! This isn't dessert with Mom yelling, "You touch it, you own it," as she passes out the éclairs. There will be instances when customers will want to own software and maintain direct control. The total ownership model will be the best solution for some; other managers will continue to outsource certain areas like accounting and back-end office support. But for many managers, the costs of ramping up and running an application are going to outweigh the pleasures of ownership.

Nothing new here. Think about your paycheck for a minute. Thousands of companies for decades have outsourced payroll functions to service companies like ADP with nary an ounce of guilt or a second thought. Unless they are in the payroll business, managers didn't, and still don't, want to chuck time, money, and bodies down a big black hole building a state-of-the-art payroll system.

Now extend this train of thought to the new economy and do the math. Management teams that are building cutting-edge, in-house email systems are not building cutting-edge deliverables to bring to market.

Okay, Then It's an IT-Only Issue

Wrong! A recent study of ASP purchasing decisions by Zona Research showed that middle managers or higher made 89 percent of all ASP purchase decisions; IT teams were responsible for only 6 percent.

The no-brainer reason: Every IT department on this planet is tremendously overburdened right now; even those immune to the skilled labor shortage and operating fully staffed. They can't begin to support all the projects and programs driven by the competitive demand for technological innovation and initiatives from the legal, procurement, or marketing departments, never mind develop them.

"The ability to get IT involvement in a project is very, very difficult, yet the need is crucial. And getting more crucial as competitive trends increase," says Paul D. Mann, CEO of Informative Inc., a California-based ASP that provides online performance measurements by surveying customers and employees for Fortune 1000 companies like Cisco Networks, Nortel, and 3Com.

Hey, those companies certainly have the bucks and the brains to do their own market research. But they use Informative's real-time Web channels because, as Mann says, "it's not in their best interests with the rapid pace of change to support and upgrade" internal market research technologies.

"I like to tell our clients that we are virtually the department down the hall," Mann says.

So, Let's Outsource Everything

Don't be ridiculous. First, who will eat all the leftover food from the sales meetings? A recent research report notes that IT departments do not wish to be completely excluded from the ASP process, and frankly, they shouldn't be.

Obviously IT departments will feel more comfortable if any ASP sales efforts to departments within a business also involves them. IT departments want to be in charge of which applications are used and by whom. Without this control, they fear 'applications anarchy' could result, leaving a company's software standardization policy and systems compatibility crumbling (Zona Research 2000).

If It's on the Web, Everyone Can See It

Because security has been cited in some focus groups as ASP customers' number one concern, it is the number one deliverable for an ASP. As risks can never be eliminated entirely, it is up to service providers and their customers to decide how much risk is acceptable to address all potential points of failure. This includes physical threats such as fire or theft and technological risks like hackers.

Thus a top ASP is going to invest in cutting-edge, customized security with firewalls and redundant power supplies, ensuring a level of continual operations that most managers can't afford to replicate in-house. Paula M. Hunter, vice president of sales and marketing for c Me Run Corp. of Hudson, Massachusetts, says service providers create an IT collaborative model that melds the best of all internal and external resources into a highly secure environment. "You're not just getting cutting edge, you're getting experience that your own IT people won't be able to get," Hunter says, "From a technology aspect, ASPs are investing in a lot more security than most business professionals."

Outsourcing Will Save Money

With the industry so new, pricing models are still immature in the ASP marketplace. Forget comparison shopping. Hunter advises managers to do a cost-benefit analysis that measures labor and capital costs along with the actual costs of hardware and software.

"You're saving because you're not buying headcount," she says.

The savings also come from an accounting perspective. Leases or rentals are entered over time as business expenses whereas actual purchases of software are recorded at the point of sale as a one-time, and usually huge, capital expenditure.

For new and emerging businesses, that up-front hit can be hurtful or even deadly to cash-flow operations. Susan Hammond, a Massachusetts strategic planning consultant who works with start-ups and growing businesses, counsels senior executives to be extremely careful for that very reason.

For entrepreneurs, ASPs offer a way to retain equity dollars and reduce the amount of control given to outside financiers like venture capitalists or bankers. When entrepreneurs raise a round of money, they give up equity or ownership to the financiers. If entrepreneurs burn through that early round by buying thousands or millions of dollars of software, they will soon find themselves looking for fresh funding before the smoke can die down on the spreadsheets. And another round of financing means giving up more control of the business.

By paying deposits and fees on monthly or annual software rentals through ASPs, Hammond notes that entrepreneurs retain funds as well as control.

"An ASP may not be cheaper in the long run, but it is easier to manage on a cash-flow basis. It defers the cost of doing business over the life of the business instead of up front," says Hammond, a certified public accountant. "An ASP provides flexibility and improves the ability to compete because it shortens the time to market" by eliminating the need for internal staffing, training, and allocation of resources.

ASP Operating Responsibilities

Customers demand excellence. ASPs are like most other businesses when it comes to serving their customers: They compete on the basis of the quality, consistency, and efficiency of their products and services. Successful service providers will be those who contact their customers to notify them of service degradation or interruption before customers even know a problem exists.

In general, customers will expect higher standards of service from their ASPs than their own internal benchmarks. Soon, some may even be demanding that ASP service guarantees approach carrier-class reliability (that is, five nines, or 99.999% availability). A more realistic expectation would be for the ASP to be able to deliver a range of service levels that meet specific business needs of the customer.

Certain aspects of the ASP model can make pricing and billing potentially more complex than traditional data and voice communication services. Reasons include the ASP reliance on partnerships, customers' desires for a single bill, and the required integration of billing with other systems (particularly for usage-based models).

ASP Service Checklist

In general, an ASP can be expected to do the following:

- Create infrastructure, including connectivity, security, and applications, to deliver service to the customer.
- Provide customer application support.
- Manage customer expectations by accepting orders, implementing applications, and training end users.

Design of network connectivity is critical to the delivery of applications; in fact, some view network infrastructure as the heart of the ASP business model. The ASP data center should have processing and storage hardware and software that is continuously available, highly scalable, and flexible and that offers true disaster recovery capabilities. Both application access and data access should be continuously available.

In addition, ASP customer support is often the primary driver of an end user's decision, more so than the actual performance of the live environment. To ensure positive interactions, an ASP customer support system must include much more than a toll-free help desk, such as the following:

- Aggressive service level agreements (SLAs).
- Integrated and proactive processes for system, application, network, and SLA monitoring, management, and reporting.
- 24 × 7 call center support.
- Full data backup.
- Off-site storage of backup media and disaster recovery.
- Web-based, self-provisioning account management (adds, changes, and so on.) and support.
- Regular, professional maintenance and upgrades of all application software and server hardware.

Conclusion

There are three primary measures of success for an ASP service provider: revenue (sustained and growing), profitability, and customer satisfaction. A year or two ago the ASP industry barely existed. A year from now, who knows?

Case Study

A paper bag manufacturer was maintaining a system for order acceptance by means of application software made up of legacy applications, in-house-developed software, and the back-end database. Primarily, the samples were physically shipped to the distributors, and on selection the orders were placed. This involved time and money for the physical order booking.

The customer's objective for its application service provider was online display of the product catalog with daily updates to the distributors, providing restricted access, online booking of orders, maintenance of the original applications and databases, and implementation of a remote content management solution.

The ASP developed a three-part solution over 36 months. The back-end application was ported to MS SQL Database on NT Server running IIS, and the client applications were developed in a combination of Java, ASP pages, and Web client development.

Phase 1. Reverse engineering was adopted to analyze the current system's functioning. This was done to ensure the application performance, identify testing documentation, and eliminate redundant functionality. Phase 1 used primarily on-site staff with the client to understand the process of the organization.

Phase 2. System designing and development was done online with the Web enabler model. The designing consisted of high-level designing with the overall system requirements and application performance plans, and the detailed low-level designing for the detailed modularity of the functional modules. This phase consisted of a mix of on-site and off-shore staff, so as to ensure the smooth communication with the client and to enhance cost-effective solutions using part resources from off-shore teams.

Phase 3. Implementation and retrofitting was done. This consisted of system implementation and constructive feedback from the client for smooth functionality of the developed system. The entire implementation consisted of an on-site coordination team that was involved in system implementation and worked to understand the client requirements for fine-tuning the application, using off-shore resources (Octon Technologies 2001).

The research firm IDC forecast the end of the ASP acronym, despite the probability of rapid growth in the industry itself, and suggested that a newer term, "xSP," more accurately reflects the emergence and maturity of the ASP market. xSPs represent a broad range of service providers, offering all types of services including Internet access, applications functionality, and support for business processes. What separates xSPs from traditional service providers and unites them as a group is the underlying service delivery model. Successful ASPs will focus on providing services that add value to their basic application and provide integration services for their customers. It calls for service offerings to be delivered over a network, externally managed, based on a one-to-many business model, and priced on a service-fee basis (Flanagan (B) 2001).

Other technology research has urged companies to be very skeptical of the staying power of pure ASPs, noting that as of early 2001, even Corio and USinternetworking, the market leaders among pure ASP vendors, are yet to be profitable. Only the large outsourcers, which already have the necessary data center infrastructure and experience in integrating and customizing applications, are likely to have the staying power to survive in the ASP market, with the ASP segment probably as a small part of their total business (DeZoysa 2001).

Since the onset of the ASP industry, companies have been tinkering with the acronym to better explain their core competencies. xSPs differ from traditional service providers by delivering their service over a network and by managing that service externally. Among some of the newer terminology that sprouted as a result of the operant definition of the xSP acronym are systems infrastructure providers (SIPs) and process support providers (PSPs). This name issue simply reflects the fast transitioning of the service provider landscape, and especially the role that ASPs play in that environment.

Whatever they are called, and whatever the shakeout in the industry, the ASP marketplace is still in flux. Short-term challenges include building brand awareness and a customer base when network reliability and bandwidth issues still are an everyday factor for most organizations. The ASPs that survive and thrive will be the ones that go beyond the terms of their service level agreements with end users. They will act as strategic partners instead of outsourced vendors, embrace a passion for innovation and forward thinking, and volunteer to help create global best practices and industry standards.

Top 20 ASPs

For the month of October 2001

This is the list of companies that, in the view of ASPnews, are the world's 20 leading ASPs. For inclusion, companies must meet the following criteria:

- Have ASP and/or Web services as their core business
- Have a substantial and active customer base
- Be able to demonstrate proven revenue streams
- Be innovators within the ASP and/or Web services models
- Be recognized as a leader by others within the industry

COMPANY	DESCRIPTION	LOCATION
Agilera	Enterprise ASP	Engelwood, CO
BlueStar Solutions	Enterprise ASP	Cupertino, CA
Corio	Enterprise ASP	San Carlos, CA
Digital River	ASP, business ASP	Eden Prairie, MN
Intranets.com	Web service vendor	Woburn, MA
Jamcracker	ASP aggregator	Cupertino, CA
ManagedOps	ASP wholesaler	Bedford, NH
McAfee.com	Web service vendor, Web service aggregator	Sunnyvale, CA
NetLedger	Web service vendor	San Mateo, CA
OpenAir.com	Web service vendor	Boston, MA
Portera Systems	Vertical service provider	Campbell, CA
Qwest Cyber.Solutions	Enterprise ASP	Denver, CO
Salesforce.com	Web service vendor	San Francisco, CA
Surebridge	Enterprise ASP	Lexington, MA
Telecomputing	ASP and integrator	Oslo Norway/ Fort Lauderdale, FL
TriZetto Group	Vertical service provider, Web services ISV	Newport Beach, CA
Upshot.com	Web service vendor	Mountain View, CA
USinternetworking	Enterprise ASP, application infrastructure provider	Annapolis, MD
WebEx	Web service provider	San Jose, CA
WebSideStory	Web service provider	San Diego, CA

Top 20 ASP Infrastructure Providers

For the month of October 2001

These are the 20 companies that, in the view of ASPnews, are the most influential providers of software or infrastructure for the ASP and Web services industry. For inclusion, companies must meet the following criteria:

- Have a substantial and active customer base of ASPs and/or Web service providers
- Be active in their support and promotion of the ASP and/or Web services model
- Be innovators within the ASP and/or Web services models
- Be recognized as a leader by others within the industry

COMPANY	DESCRIPTION	LOCATION
Abridean	Infrastructure ISV	Halifax, Nova Scotia
BMC Software	Infrastructure ISV, infrastructure ASP	Houston, TX
Cisco Systems	Systems manufacturer	San Jose, CA
Citrix Systems	Infrastructure ISV	Fort Lauderdale, FL
Compaq	System manufacturer	Houston, TX
Computer Associates	Infrastructure ISV	Islandia, NY
Data Return	Application infrastructure provider, managed hosting provider	Irving, TX
Digex	Application infrastructure provider, managed hosting provider	Beltsville, MD
Hewlett-Packard	Systems manufacturer, infrastructure ISV	Palo Alto, CA
IBM	Infrastructure ISV, systems manufacturer, application infrastructure provider	Armonk, NY
IPlanet	Infrastructure ISV	Santa Clara, CA
JD Edwards	Enterprise ISV	Denver, CO
Lawson Software	Enterprise ISV, e-business platform vendor	Minneapolis, MN

Continues

Top 20 ASP Infrastructure Providers *(Continued)*

COMPANY	DESCRIPTION	LOCATION
Microsoft	Enterprise ISV, Web service vendor/aggregator	Seattle, WA
Onyx Software	Enterprise ISV	Bellevue, WA
Oracle	Enterprise ISV, enterprise ASP	Redwood Shores, CA
PeopleSoft	Enterprise ISV, enterprise ASP	Pleasanton, CA
Progress Software	Infrastructure ISV	Bedford, MA
Qwest	Hosting and access provider	Denver, CO
Sun Microsystems, iPlanet	Systems manufacturer, infrastructure ISV	Palo Alto, CA
Xevo	Infrastructure ISV	Marlboro, MA

The latest edition of the "Top 20" lists is available at: http://www.aspnews.com/

CHAPTER

Management Service Providers

Management service providers or managed service providers (MSPs) emerged in the last two to three years to fill the vacuum created by the shortage of IT personnel and by the explosion of dot-com companies without IT management of their own. Working on a contract basis, MSPs handle most aspects of Web site management or monitor the performance of servers located in a data center or even servers located at a company's site, from a remote site.

Companies and organizations have recognized their limitations when it comes to around-the-clock management and monitoring of their IT infrastructure. Offloading a non-strategic task such as server monitoring can make a lot of sense. When a business contracts with an MSP, it frees up IT resources to allow the company to focus on what it does best.

The hosting industry is undergoing a transformation, as customers' needs grow and their patience and ability to deal with increasingly complex infrastructure issues wear thin. MSPs are monitoring and managing servers, Web servers, particular applications (email), security, databases, and so forth. Some have referred to MSP offerings as the plumbing of the IT industry. Hiring an MSP may mean that a company does not need to worry as much about hiring network administrators, database administrators, security experts, network architects, and system administrators.

What Is an MSP?

The MSP Association, a nonprofit, international industry trade group that was launched in June 2000, provides a forum for discussing industry issues, sponsors industry research, develops open standards and guidelines, and establishes best practices, among other activities. As of July 2001, the MSP Association had over 100 members. Its definition of a MSP is as follows:

Management service provider companies deliver information technology (IT) infrastructure management services to multiple customers over a network on a subscription basis.

Like application service providers (ASPs), they deliver services via networks that are billed to their clients on a recurring-fee basis. Unlike ASPs, which deliver business applications to end users, MSPs deliver system and network management services to IT departments and other customers who manage their own technology assets. Thus, the MSP focuses on IT infrastructure to the exclusion of the applications running on the systems, as shown in Table 5.1.

Table 5.1 Possible MSP Selection Criteria

SERVICE CATEGORY	POTENTIAL SERVICES
Desktop	• Help desk • Asset/inventory • Remote control
Servers	• Monitoring • Alerting • Repair
Network	• Monitoring • Alerting • Repair
Database	• Monitoring • Alerting • Repair
Storage	• Storage hardware • Monitoring • Alerting • Repair
Security	• Monitoring • Alerting • Repair • Expert

The types of solutions that management service providers or managed service providers (MSPs) typically offer include products and services that enable companies or individuals to better manage computer systems, networks, databases, and applications, as well as the performance and availability of those critical IT resources.

Some MSPs are able to monitor a customer's network or Web server(s) remotely. Other MSPs perform this same service by installing an additional server on the customer's premises that enables it to monitor the customer's network, even if the link to the MSP is broken for some reason. Some MSPs are able to offer a full-service approach while others have staked out a claim that provides niche services, for example, security services (virus detection) for emails.

MSPs will be particularly attractive to larger companies and organizations due to the IT staffing shortage.

Industry Outlook

Industry analysts expect the demand for management service providers to grow almost exponentially with revenue estimates reaching as much as $11 billion by the year 2004 from an over all hosting market expected to reach $20 billion (Bannan 2000). Some companies will clearly benefit if they are able to outsource the operation of internal computer systems. The MSP provides management oversight for the operation of functioning systems and networks as well as providing the option for a company to avoid the capital costs associated with installing or expanding a computer network.

Total available data center space in the United States is growing from 33 million square feet to some 66 million square feet by the end of 2001. The investment to fuel this expansion is expensive and is costing an estimated $16.5 billion (Smetannikov 2001). Given this large investment, it is unclear how some firms will continue to operate given the competitive nature of the marketplace and the downturn in the economy.

Some MSPs don't own a data center but simply lease space and equipment from data center owners such as Exodus and WorldCom. Other MSPs have invested in their own data centers. Thus, it is not surprising that as the infrastructure service providers that build data centers have begun to move to provide MSP services. Thus, the infrastructure service providers will become a new source of competition in the marketplace. In some cases, these firms are known as managed infrastructure providers or MIPs.

Recently, a global MSP network was formed with the intention of helping MSPs improve their IT management outsourcing service by identifying and sharing best practices.

How Does It Work?

Management service providers make a significant investment in building the knowledge, expertise, and ability to use their own software monitoring tools, or they license third-party tools that have achieved prominence in the marketplace. These tools then allow them to provide niche services or a broad range of services, as shown in Figure 5.1.

To the extent that the MSP is able to provide a cookie-cutter service offering then it can begin to achieve economies of scale. To that end, some MSPs will work only with certain brands of hardware and software, which makes it easier for them to address problems and expand capacity. Loudcloud, a highly visible MSP, is following this approach.

The MSP will look after a site's servers, fix problems, configure and reboot computer systems when needed, and coordinate the many disparate elements that make up any site's technical underpinning. Other MSPs, such as SiteSmith and Nuclio, are willing to manage sites that run on diverse technologies.

Fees usually hinge on the size of the site. Some MSPs charge by the server while others look to the size of the database. The volume of traffic will also

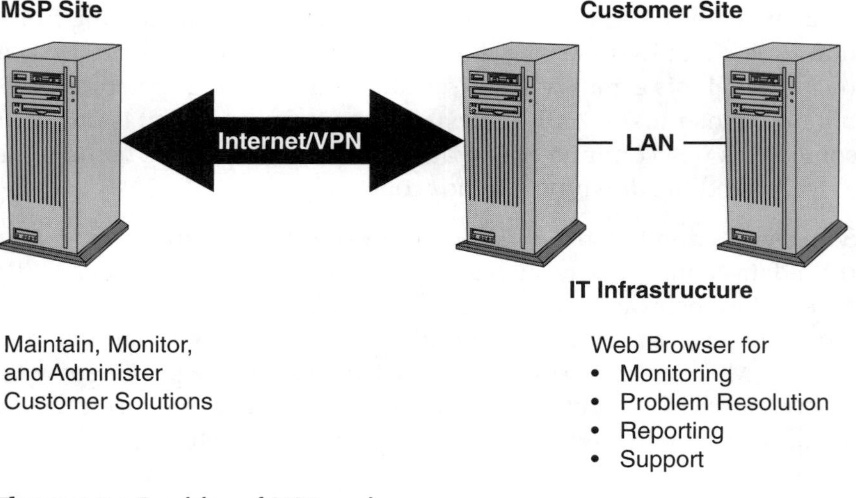

Figure 5.1 Provision of MSP services.

clearly have an impact on price—sites generating more traffic will require more computer resources in order to maintain adequate response times.

Clearly, the strength of an MSP is its ability to recruit and train knowledgeable staff. This capable staff is then complemented by processes and procedures which introduce discipline into the tools that are used and how those tools are utilized. Typically an MSP will utilize tools from fewer vendors than an IT shop would, but these tools are much better understood and employed to maximize the value of their use. This brings simplicity and replication to the work environment within the MSP.

Aside from providing significant physical security safeguards, significant environmental systems must be in place to overcome the electrical, heat, and humidity requirements of computer systems. This is especially true given the increasing density of servers located in racks and thus the increased demands for air conditioning. Backup electrical systems are mandatory, especially in California with its challenges surrounding the constant and reliable delivery of electrical power. Issues associated with data centers are discussed in greater detail in Chapter 9.

MSP Offerings

Management service providers typically offer products and services that enable companies or organizations to better manage computer systems, networks, databases, and applications, as well as the performance and availability of those critical IT resources. A convenient way to subdivide the MSP offerings is by the type of business:

Enterprise MSP services. These solutions support a company's internal IT-managed infrastructure, including desktops, servers, networks, databases, storage, and security.

e-business MSP services. These solutions focus on a company's transaction-intensive, Internet-based business capabilities including Web servers, storage, networks, databases, security, and performance management.

A visit to the MSP Association Web site (www.mspassociation.org) will allow you to conduct a search, using a variety of selection criteria to limit your search results. The selection criteria, as noted in Figure 5.2, will enable you to find a number of MSPs that could potentially meet the needs of your company or organization.

Some MSPs adopt an all-or-nothing approach to providing a service while others are more flexible. For example, some MSPs provide off-hours system management oversight support for email servers, Web sites, and so forth.

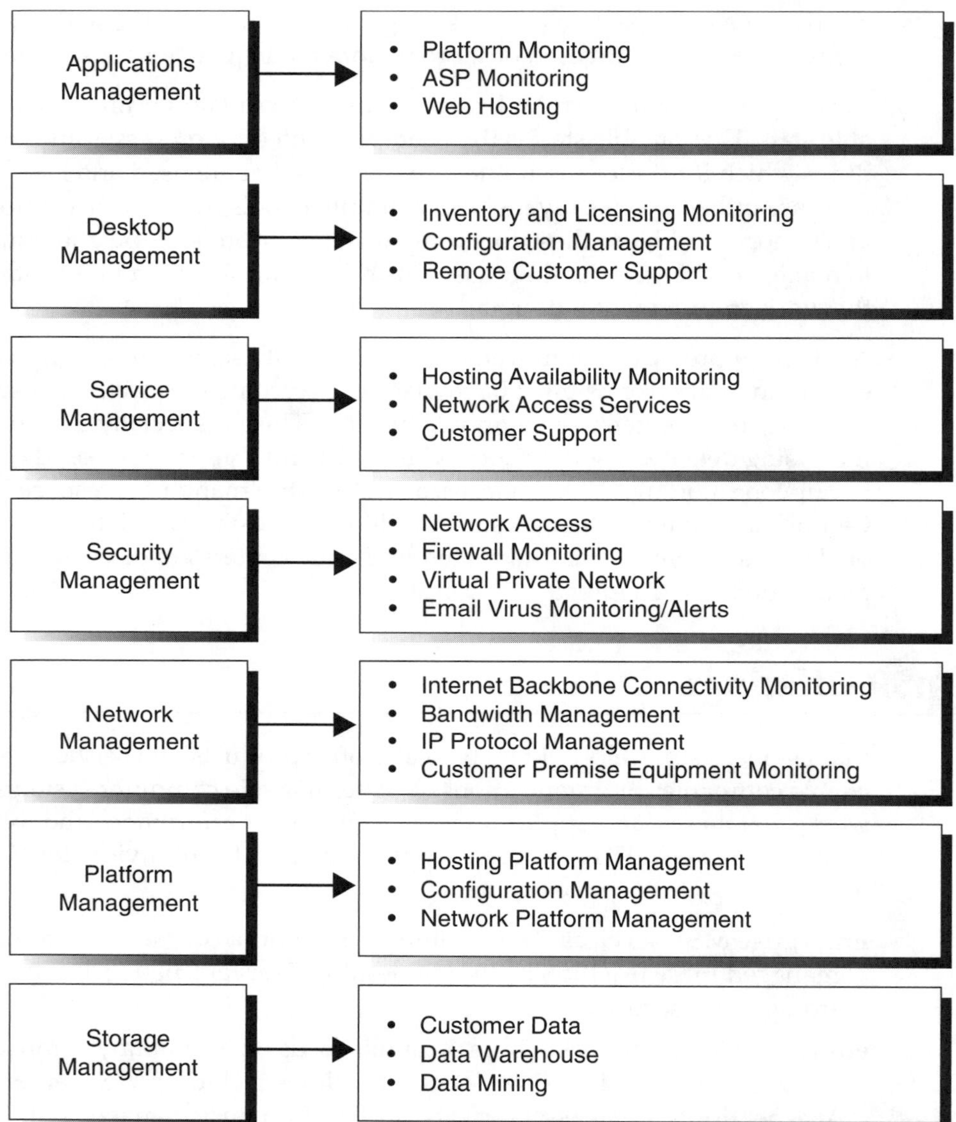

Figure 5.2 Possible MSP services.

It is the management of the IT infrastructure that sets apart MSPs from their cousins, infrastructure Service Providers or Internet Data Centers that provide the physical space, and in some cases the equipment and software itself. If the customer owns the computer system equipment and provides staff for

Build versus Outsource?

David Wither, manager of network infrastructure at Cleveland-based Marconi Medical Systems, faces IT challenges. With 5,000 people at 60 sites—22 of them overseas—the company depends on its network being available around-the-clock.

Wither saw two alternatives to keep the network up and running 24 hours. One was to build its own network operations center. But covering more than 8,700 hours per year requires 8 people, a supervisor, and $1 million in hardware and software, Wither says. The other option was to outsource the job.

Wither decided to hire Silverback Technologies, an MSP based in Billerica, Massachusetts. Marconi Medical pays $4,000 per month for the Silverback management server, which monitors routers and a variety of critical servers at Marconi's main office and remote locations. Marconi has also contracted a network integration firm to deliver response-and-fix services for another $3,500 per month. Wither says he figures that for $90,000 per year—or the cost of an experienced network manager—he gets $1 million worth of network management.

"Plus, if it doesn't work out, I can always terminate the deal," he says.

Wither also likes that Silverback's service doesn't require any overhaul of the IT staff's existing management tool kits. Both Marconi and Silverback use the Simple Network Management Protocol instrumentation built into most servers and switches.

The non-intrusiveness, combined with a relatively low cost, makes it much easier for network executives like Wither to opt for an MSP, especially when compared to the high cost of deploying traditional frameworks.

Wither has one note of caution for those moving ahead with MSP plans: Any problems in the company's infrastructure will quickly become apparent as the MSP learns more about the devices managed across the network. In his case, inconsistencies in Marconi's IP addressing scheme caused Silverback to raise some flags. Once those issues were brought up, Silverback was able to identify the devices in question (Liebmann 2001).

the operation and maintenance of the system, then the space in the data center is usually referred to as collocation.

MSPs have origins from three main sources: start-ups, hosting companies, and software companies. Regardless of its origin, the MSP needs to have sufficient size and experience to convince potential customers that it provides value for the money and that it will be around for the long-term.

In some cases, MSPs will team up with an infrastructure service provider to provide services with a single service level agreement and a single bill to customers. For example, Totality has teamed up with Conxion. Conxion focuses on the data center while Totality concentrates on the managed services being deployed.

Among the MSPs with more name recognition than some of their competitors are Altaworks, AssetMetrix, Brix Networks, Chapter 2, Coradiant, Data Return, Envive, Exodus, FrontLine, FusionStorm, Genuity, HiFive, InteQ, InterOPS, Intira, Loudcloud, Luminate, NaviSite, NetIQ, NetSolve, Nuclio, Peakstone, QuantumShift, Rackspace.com, Silverback Technologies, SiteROCK, SiteSmith, SpeeDEV, StrataSource, Telenisus, Totality, Triactive, and UUNET.

And in the face of an economy with continuing financial uncertainties, it will not be unexpected to see MSPs and infrastructure service providers agreeing to work on joint ventures and partnering in other creative ways in order to be more responsive to the needs of their potential customers. Partnering provides a way to fill in the holes of a service offering so that the customer is concerned only with dealing with a single vendor with guarantees provided in a single service level agreement.

MSP Customer Benefits

The appeal of the MSP model is that it eliminates the need for companies and organizations to buy, maintain, or upgrade IT infrastructure, which typically requires a major investment of capital, highly technical expertise, and a considerable expenditure of time. In addition to appealing to ASPs, the services of an MSP are also attractive to small and midsized firms that prefer not to invest in a large IT staff.

Outsourcing the IT infrastructure allows a company or organization to concentrate on its core competencies that add value for their customers when they purchase the goods or services offered by the company. MSPs help companies and organizations prevent work outages, and lost revenues, by ensuring that their systems stay up and are running efficiently around the clock.

The MSP approach furnishes a practical solution to the continuing shortage of qualified IT professionals and the increasing complexity of systems, networks, databases, and applications.

One significant benefit that an MSP can bring to the table is to provide clarity about the response times end users actually experience. An MSP can do the following:

- Determine application functions that give the worst response time.
- Determine application functions that are the most popular.
- Provide capacity planning metrics—for example, machine availability,

CPU usage, memory usage, disk usage, and network bandwidth.

- Help eliminate emotional issues associated with end users complaining about response times.

With this information the company can tune its system with the assistance of the MSP. Tuning is important because it does the following:

- Lowers equipment costs
- Increases user productivity
- Improves user attitude
- Allows greater system reliability due to lower equipment stress
- Reduces applications errors
- Reduces administration troubleshooting time

What Should an MSP Enable?

An MSP partner should provide the following to a customer company:

- Leasing of any necessary computer equipment and software.
- Proactive monitoring and management of the contracted components and/or service.
- Access to a 24 × 7 help desk for assistance, if needed.
- Immediate cost savings.
- Relief from the costs and pressures of attempting to recruit and retain skilled IT talent.
- Help for the customer organization to focus on its core competencies.
- Standardized processes and procedures to facilitate change management.
- Knowledgeable and trained staff to provide oversight management to a computer system or network.

Special Concerns for Business Customers

Two primary concerns when selecting an MSP are technical competence and financial health. Does the MSP have experience with the combination of equipment and software that you need for your operation? Does the MSP have a set of procedures in place to deal with site problems and system crashes? What is the process for escalating problems to the attention of management of the MSP as well as to the customer? If the MSP wants to complete an initial inventory or analysis of the customer's infrastructure, that's a good sign.

Creating and operating an MSP, especially an MSP with multiple data center locations, requires a significant investment. Are the prospects for the MSP to be operating profitably likely to occur in the short term or long term? If long term, how long until the MSP runs out of cash?

Is the MSP willing to sign a service level agreement that is balanced in identifying the responsibilities and consequences of various activities for both parties? Is the MSP willing to be flexible enough to meet the unique needs of the customer? And exactly what does a managed service mean? For example, if the service is to manage a company's firewall, are some or all of the following activities covered—ensuring proper configuration, applying the latest patches, ensuring stability and availability, and monitoring the traffic that comes to the firewall?

In some cases, the existing IT staff will be reluctant to turn over responsibility for monitoring and managing of their infrastructure. Yet, this is not new because the rise of the MSPs is yet another in the evolution of outsourcing services that started with data centers in the late 1980s and early 1990s.

Businesses are encouraged to be cautious about selecting the "low-priced spread" because you often get what you pay for. This is particularly true when an organization is selecting an MSP that will provide security services.

MSP Operating Responsibilities

Service is the *raison d'être* for a managed service provider. And the service will, of necessity, be orders of magnitude better than its customers could provide in-house. The cost of the service may or may not be less than the cost for what could be done in-house. While the software used to provide the management service is crucial (after all, it is this software and how it is used that differentiates the MSP), the MSP will need some quality network connections so that it can provide the service. These network connections will include the following:

- Direct links between the MSP and the Internet backbone (Ewens et al 2001).
- Dual circuits, with redundant routing, to Tier 1 Internet backbones.
- Quality commercial-grade equipment—for example, routers, switches, and servers.
- 24 × 7 help desk support with well-trained employees who can quickly resolve problems for the MSPs customers or alert them of a potential problem (Liebmann 2001).

MSP Service Checklist

Generally, a MSP can be expected to do the following:

- Create the necessary infrastructure, including connectivity, security, and applications, to deliver service to the customer.
- Provide customer support with a 24/7 help desk.
- Offer reasonable yet responsive service level agreements (SLAs).
- Provide proactive processes for system, network, and Web site monitoring and management.
- Provide full data backup for those MSPs providing access to a data center.
- Provide off-site storage of backup media and disaster recovery if a data center is used.
- Offer Web-based, self-provisioning account management (adds, changes, and so on.) and support.
- Provide regular, professional maintenance and upgrades of all application software and server hardware.

Conclusion

The growing dependence on businesses and organizations of all sizes on technology, coupled with the increasing difficulty of hiring and retaining qualified technical staff, has created an environment where outsourcing some IT management services can be very appealing. Clearly, the needs of any one organization will be different from those of another, yet there is sufficient commonality of these needs that MSP companies have developed the processes and procedures for dealing with a variety of IT services.

CHAPTER 6

Wireless Service Providers

Today there are some 45 million mobile workers (based on a definition of an employee who spends more than 20 percent of his or her time away from the office). He or she may carry a cell phone (85 million in use in the United States), a pager (54 million), or a palmtop, handheld, or laptop computer (30 million). Yet a majority of these individuals find it difficult to connect using wireless technology to obtain the information when and where they want it (Seybold 2000).

Wireless service providers allow immediate access to the Internet without physically plugging a portable device like a laptop or cell phone into a telecom or power outlet. This instant wireless access would allow business customers to monitor sales accounts, access employee records, and monitor supply-chain relationships without tethering a hardware device to a work area. The keyword here is mobile: Wireless service moves when and where you do. Business customers already have a wide variety of broadband options like T-1 lines for high-speed, dedicated Internet connections. But those looking for portable end-to-end solutions to access data, applications, and services with increased reliability need to look at wireless as a potential strategic choice.

There are at least four reasons why the wireless service provider market is expected to grow significantly in the next few years.

First, a variety of wireless standards has been adopted and is being implemented both in hardware products and in software applications.

Second, product prices continue to decline as standards-based products are being produced in increasing quantities.

Third, new wireless applications are almost continually being introduced and adopted by companies and organizations. Not only do these applications improve the productivity of the organization, but they allow individuals to move about within their work environment and still be able to send and receive information.

Fourth, organizations and individuals are becoming increasingly reliant on mobile communications. The combination of handheld and laptop devices means that an employee can respond immediately to a request for up-to-the-minute information by a customer or prospect.

What Is a WSP?

Wireless service provider (WSP), sometimes called a wireless application service provider (WASP), is a company that offers transmission services to users of wireless devices (handheld computers and telephones) through radio frequency signals rather than through end-to-end wire communication. A WSP offers cellular telephone service, personal communication service, or both.

Wireless carriers are eager to recoup the investment they have made in building and enhancing their wireless networks. Some research analysts suggest that mobile phone subscribers will represent about 60 percent of the total U.S. population by 2004. Wireless carriers are anxious to add more uses and subscribers to their wireless networks by embracing access to the Internet, mobile entertainment, and m-commerce.

Technology executives who already have wireless projects in place or about ready to be rolled out into the marketplace, are concerned about integrating the technology with existing wired systems and providing security for wireless applications, according to a recent survey by *CIO Magazine*. *CIO* administered the survey from December 8 to December 18, 2000 by email and received 170 responses from executives from companies ranging in size from less than $50 million in revenues to more than $10 billion in revenues (Pender and Ware 2001).

Providing access to information that would be of immediate value to employees tops the list of current wireless applications rather than B2B or B2C portal tie-ins, as shown in Figure 6.1. These active wireless applications utilize a variety of technology protocols with U.S. cellular phone leader code division multiple access (CDMA) and the wireless application protocol (WAP) leading the list; see Figure 6.2. And wireless-enabled PDAs—for example, the Palm and BlackBerry—are the preferred device ahead of pagers and digital and analog cellular telephones; see Figure 6.3.

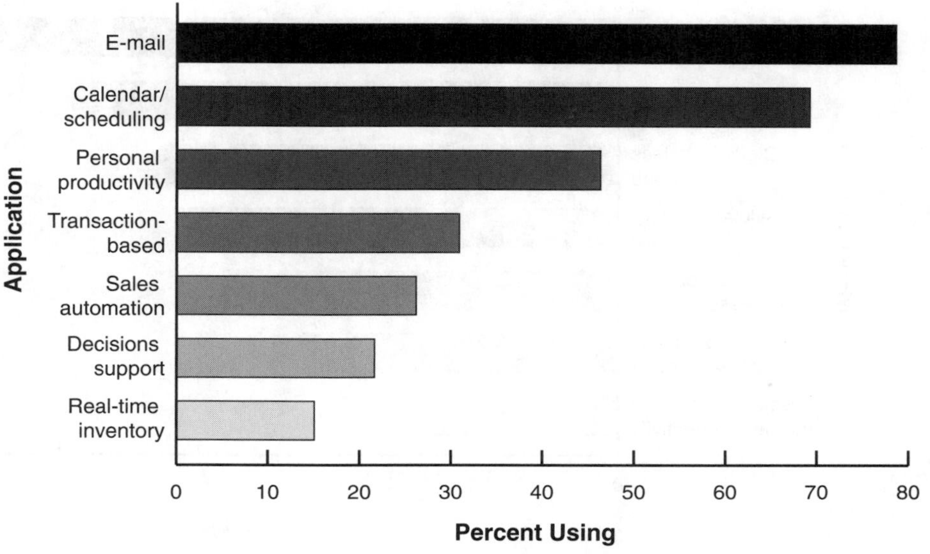

Figure 6.1 Types of wireless applications currently supported.

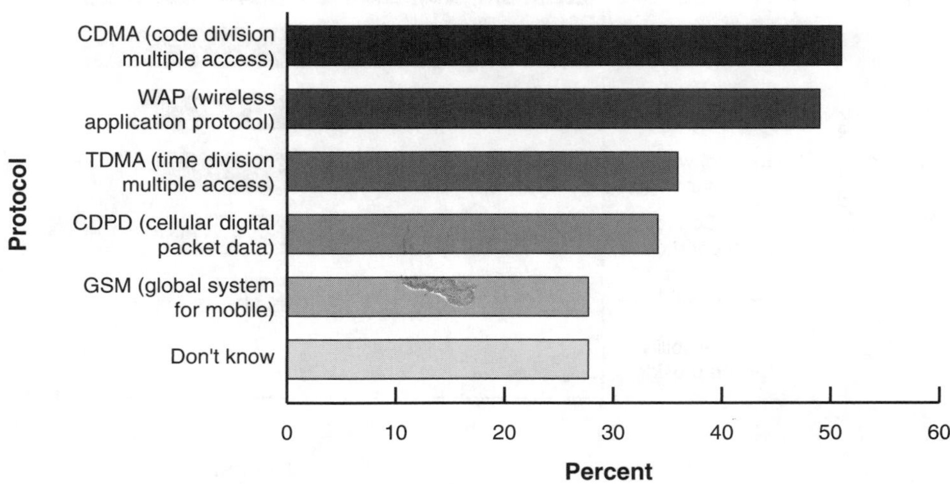

Figure 6.2 Popular wireless protocols.

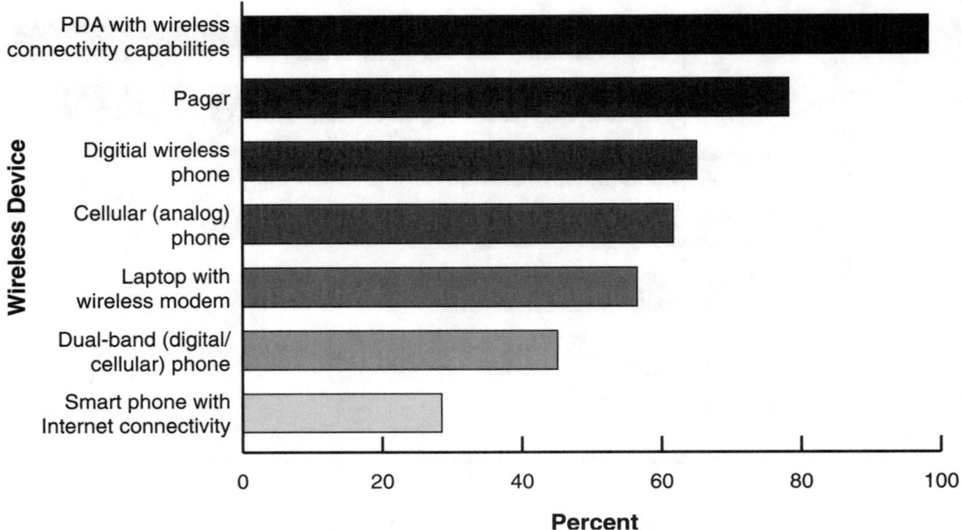

Figure 6.3 Wireless devices currently supported.

The top challenges facing the implementation of wireless technology are familiar themes: system integration, security, end-user support, and reliability; see Figure 6.4. For those businesses that allow customers wireless access to their systems, the dominant challenge is security; see Figure 6.5.

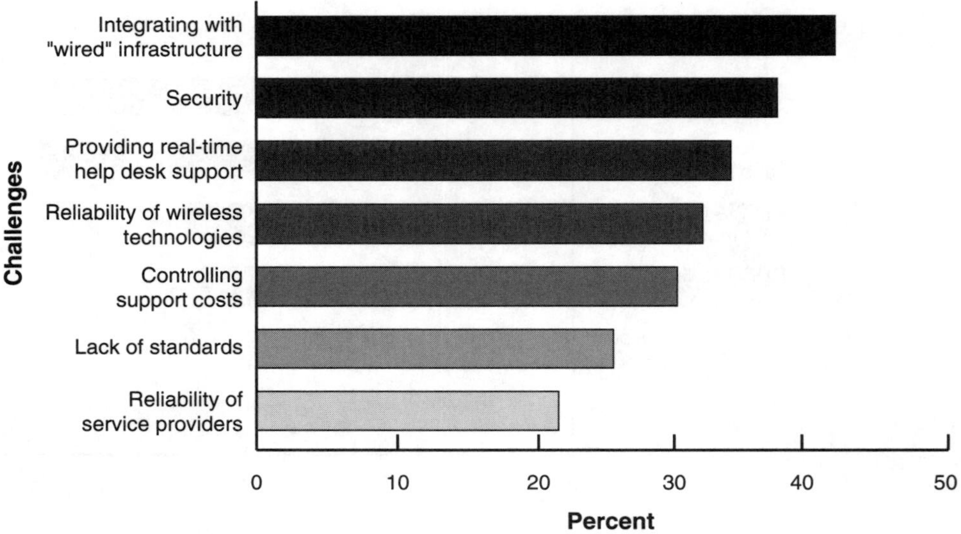

Figure 6.4 Top three wireless challenges.

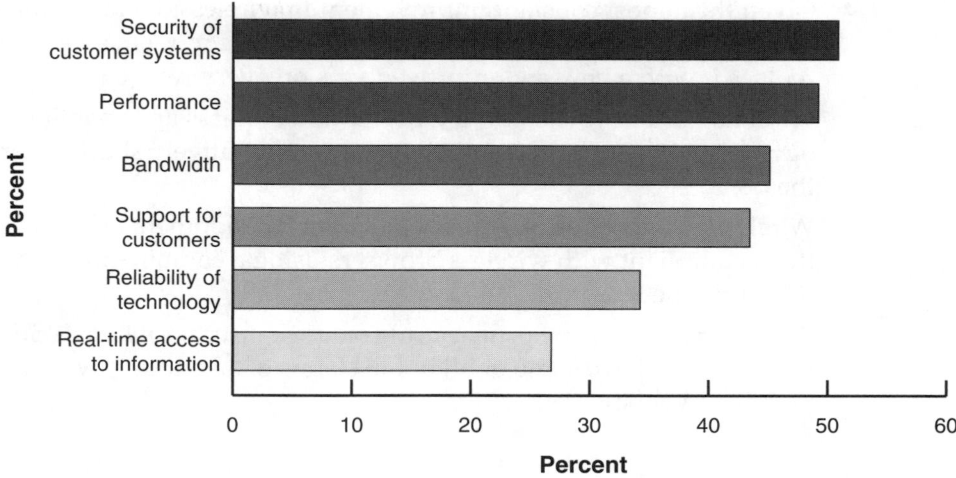

Figure 6.5 Biggest challenges to access wireless.

It is important to recognize some basic truths about wireless:

- Data moved by wireless is slower than that moved by wires and is likely to remain so for the next several years.
- Given the slow data transmission speeds, users do not spend time surfing the Internet. Rather, wireless access to the Net is more about retrieving very specific information to meet a particular information need.
- Users can use wireless to receive emails and other alerts, sometimes called "push" technology, as well as "pulling" information from the network. Alerts lets mobile workers monitor critical business events, and they thus can act immediately once notified.
- Most wireless applications do not employ graphics given the slow data transfer rates. The focus is on easy-to-read information.
- The true value proposition for any enterprise is where information and transaction bottlenecks frequently occur. Thus, wireless has great appeal where a business process is improved and the employee's productivity is therefore enhanced.
- No single U.S. wireless network provides total "anywhere" coverage. Rather, various networks provide regional coverage.

- Given the almost constant improvement in wireless data transmission speeds, most users will throw their existing data modem away and replace it with a new and improved version every two to three years.
- Wireless has not yet achieved a perception that it is an "enabling technology" due to the primitive user interface and relatively short battery life of the devices.
- Wireless applications require a significant development effort to make them compliant with wireless browsers using a combination of XML and XSL style sheets.
- Always remember the primary rule of any consumer when deciding whether to believe some or all of the claims of a vendor: caveat emptor (let the buyer beware!).

Industry Outlook

Industry experts forecast that wireless applications and mobile commerce, currently raging in Europe, will be the next big Internet explosion in North America. By 2003, 40 million mobile devices will be used for Internet access in the United States alone. The worldwide market for smart handheld devices will grow to more than $26 billion by 2004 as shipments rise from 12.9 million units to 63.4 million units. Smart phones will represent the fastest growing segment of these devices, increasing from 480,000 shipments in 2000 to more than 23 million in 2004 (Hogan 2001).

Another research firm suggests that sales of wireless Internet applications will reach $37 billion by 2002. Despite the tremendous interest in wireless Internet-based applications, currently wireless data accounts for only 2 percent of all wireless traffic according to Warren Wilson, senior analyst for Summit Strategies (Goldman 2001). Yet, the demand is sure to grow as companies move to extend existing applications rather than searching for a wireless "killer app." All of this suggests that the separate worlds of wireless and the Internet are converging so that users will be able to have access to the Internet whether they are in the office or traveling, as shown in Figure 6.6.

A recent survey of small and medium-sized business, conducted by Sage Research, found that about half the firms would be using wireless applications by August 2001 (Walker 2001). Some two-thirds of the companies were satisfied with their wireless experience although only 44 percent were happy with the security of the wireless networks. By 2004, the wireless LAN market could reach $1.7 billion, starting from $300 million in 1999. Other industry analysts suggest that the overall wireless market is expected to grow to $12 billion by 2003.

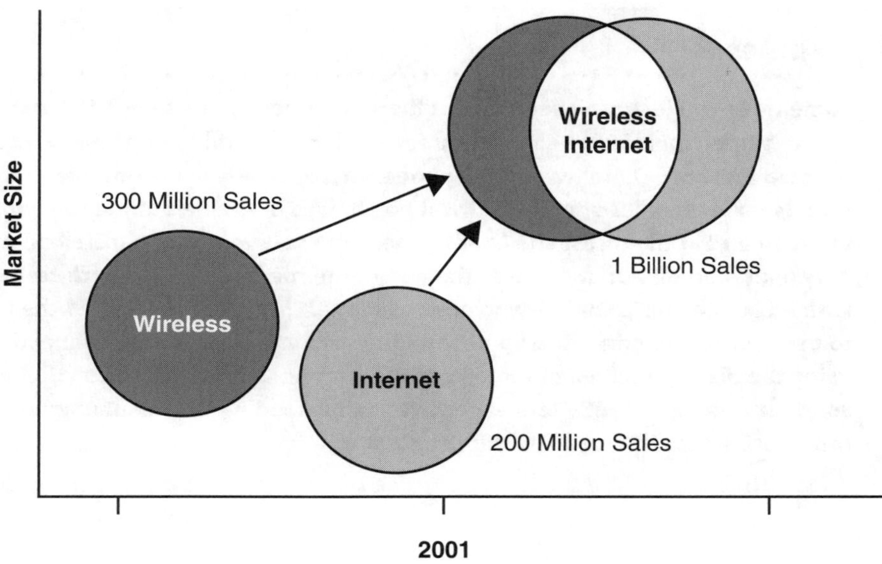

Figure 6.6 The converging worlds of wireless and the Internet.

According to a recent survey of customer preferences, the top five fixed wireless providers are these:

- Sprint's Broadband Direct
- Taligent, which filed for Chapter 11 bankruptcy and offers its SmartWave fixed wireless service in 43 U.S. markets
- Winstar Communications, whose goal is to provide wireless T-1 (1.5 Mbps) service to every desktop
- XO Communications, which operates both a backbone and a local service using Local Multipoint Distribution Service (limited to a 2.5 mile reach from each antenna)
- Nucentricx Broadband Networks, which operates in 93 U.S. markets (Interactive Week B 2001)

The same survey also identified the top five mobile wireless providers:

- AT&T Wireless, which has significant revenues and more than 16 million subscribers

Why Wireless?

Sometimes you just can't seem to get there from here ... A site in a U.S. national forest wanted an Internet connection for a solar-powered laptop computer at an isolated location. There was no telephone service available beyond the end of the road (some five miles short). Electrical power was available both at the end of the road and at the forest site (solar panel). The solution was to install an ordinary (external) dial-up modem at the end of the road, connected back-to-back with a LongRanger 2020 in asynchronous mode. This solution allowed the laptop to use normal Windows dial-up networking software to make the connection, using the dial-up modem at the end of the telephone line. This fixed wireless solution was significantly less expensive than extending the telephone line along the forest across the road (UC Wireless 2000).

- Sprint PCS, which now has more than 10 million subscribers and a popular Wireless Web service
- Nextel Communications, with nearly 6.7 million subscribers, which offers three services—two-way radio, digital cellular, and short messaging
- Verizon Wireless, which has more than 750,000 DSL subscribers and offers three services—mobile messaging service, mobile office using a cell phone, and SmartPhone, which is a PDA wireless phone combination
- Cingular, the merged operations of BellSouth and SBC Communications, which has more than 20 million subscribers (Interactive Week C, 2001)

Wireless service providers, many of which are now active in the ISP or ASP space, are rallying to bring customer-centric technologies to the business marketplace that go beyond the basics of email and a Web browser. Take, for example, Anoto's wireless technology that allows anything written, drawn, or scribbled with pen and on paper to be digitized, stored, and wirelessly transmitted to any electronic device: personal computer, mobile phone, or laptop. This Anoto suite of technologies includes a pen with built-in technology and enhanced paper that, when used together, enable direct storage or transfer—via Bluetooth (a radio frequency technology for cordless computer links)—of handwritten information to optional digital storage media, an email receiver, mobile telephone, or fax machine.

Other emerging wireless technologies include the following:

Speech recognition. Speech recognition is a combination of computer hardware and software that recognizes spoken words. Systems that require an extended training session are said to be speaker dependent. Some systems require that the speaker speaks slowly and distinctly; these are called discrete speech systems. Recently, major improvements have been made in continuous speech systems—voice recognition systems that allow the individual to speak naturally. Such systems are useful in instances when the user is unable to use a keyboard to enter data because his or her hands are occupied. One potential use of a continuous speech system would allow delivery and other transportation personnel to ask for directions on a portable phone and then view a map delivered on a wireless-enabled screen.

Intranet usage. Off-site employees can download specific information from internal applications and other information content such as account or order status while traveling or telecommuting.

Digital-cellular positioning systems. This person-to-person locator could track mobile personnel—say, physicians and paramedics in a hospital setting.

Advertising management. Instant coupons, special sales, and online discounts can be beamed to targeted retail customers just as they drive by the store, outlet, or the product itself within a store.

We'll talk more about customer benefits later in this chapter. Right now, this is the bottom line for business customers of wireless technologies: whether cost-benefit analysis favors being first to market now using nascent wireless technology or waiting to upgrade with improved third-generation technology and risk competitive defeat in a Web-enabled global marketplace.

How Does It Work?

Not surprisingly, wireless technology has developed its own rich vocabulary of acronyms as the technology has matured through three generations. In the first generation, Advance Mobile Phone Service (AMPS) was used only for providing voice via cellular analog signals. With an analog transmission, the message is sent as a continuous electrical signal. According to the Cellular Telecommunications and Internet Association (CTIA), as of mid-2001 there are about 113 million wireless subscribers; of these, some 40 million are still analog customers.

The move from first-generation to second-generation digital technology occurred in the early 1990s. In digital transmissions, conversations are converted to ones and zeros or a combination of on and off pulses of electricity. Using digital circuits, the networks could accommodate more simultaneous calls, and the calls are clearer because there is less noise due to interference.

Case Study: Wireless in the Workplace

Meet Advantage Sales & Marketing, a grocery sales and marketing firm based in Irvine, California. A leading player in an industry formerly known as "grocery brokers," Advantage acts as a middleman, supplying large and small groceries alike with products to fill their shelves. The company represents some of the biggest names in retailing, including Mars, Uncle Ben's, Quaker, Del Monte, Bumblebee, and Johnson & Johnson. Advantage never takes possession of the actual goods. Instead, it does the legwork of setting up orders and deliveries.

According to Kat Lemons, the National Web Department Manager for Advantage, the grocery marketing industry made a giant shift 3 years back. For the 30 years prior to that, grocery brokers worked locally, supplying only the businesses in their area. The shift to national coverage happened at the suppliers' request. They preferred to work with large companies that could service stores on a national level, rather than maintain relationships with small companies in each market. Advantage grew to national prominence by buying out some existing companies and merging with many others, says Lemons. When she joined, Advantage had 1 office with 300 associates. It now has 80 offices, with 10,000 associates, not including offices in Canada. Getting those offices to work with the same information was a major challenge. Because these weren't new offices, but established ones with set ways of doing things, Advantage faced the added burden of snapping people out of their old ways.

The first hurdle then, in what would become a two-part solution, was to create a portal, one accessible to anyone in-office or out, client or associate. This would provide a central repository of current information.

"We needed something that would function like a network within an office, but that could be accessed by all of our different offices," says Lemons. "That was the main reason we decided to put a portal into place."

To build its portal, Advantage chose to work with DataChannel Inc., a Web development company based in Bellevue, Washington. Lemons says her company was impressed by DataChannel's attention to security concerns. Client data needed to be protected. "We couldn't have Mars logging in and seeing Motts information, and Johnson & Johnson logging in and seeing Unilever information," she says.

Advantage was also swayed by DataChannel's security concerns and knowledge of XML, Lemons says. Putting all its data in XML was crucial to the second part of their solution, making the intranet available for wireless workers.

The carriers providing digital networks had to choose from three competing technologies to transport calls. These technologies include the following:

Not that all field worker information comes through the intranet. Advantage relies on PenRite, a "hugely complex" program, says Lemons that holds millions of pieces of product data. Sales representatives enter orders and make changes through PenRite, syncing their data with the main office at the end of the day via modem. PenRite runs on Windows CE HPCs, so representatives are issued clamshell-style handheld devices. The company currently has 3,000 handheld devices in use.

At the moment, says Lemons, load balancing for the intranet is done by two Compaq Windows NT servers, running Microsoft Sequel database software. Each server has two 800 MHz processors and 35 GBs of hard drive space. When the intranet finally goes wireless, Advantage will switch to four servers, with two application servers on the front end and two database servers on the back end.

"The end goal is to have interactive connectivity in a wireless mode with the database itself," says Kevin Paugh, CIO of Advantage, "so that when a rep is out in a store, he or she make a change that's immediately replicated in the database itself."

Unfortunately, the coverage for any wireless system is spotty at best on a national level. For Paugh, that's a major problem. If he can't give all his reps wireless access no matter where they roam, he doesn't think it's worth doing.

"It's hard to say at this point where it's all going," says Paugh. "Since we're a national enterprise, we can't have brownouts in certain areas. We have to have total coverage in the U.S. for this to work."

Then there's the issue of the wireless standards themselves. WAP might be leading the pack, but it's not without its detractors. Indeed, the race for dominance is far from over. "We don't feel the wireless standards are firm enough yet to pick a platform or an interface," says Paugh.

Finally, there's the problem of getting the right handheld for PenRite, the customer-tracking application Advantage uses.

With all that up in the air, it will be some time before Advantage reps give up their wired connections.

"Wireless right now is too in the future to say. I'd love to have it first quarter, but I can't say that's going to be done," says Paugh. "To our mind and what we've understood, the standards are not complete enough at this point to go ahead and just do it. So until that time, we'll still use modems." (Drier 2001)

- Code Division Multiple Access or CDMA (the choice of Sprint PCS and Verizon Wireless)

- Time Division Multiple Access or TDMA (the choice of AT&T and Cingular Wireless)
- Global System for Mobile Communications (GSM), a form of TDMA, widely used in Europe and Asia, and the choice of VoiceStream

CDMA, popularized by Qualcomm, transmits voice and data along a spread of radio frequencies. Each conversation is digitized and then tagged or identified with a code. The mobile phone or device deciphers only those portions of the data with that particular unique identifying code. There are about 80 million CDMA subscribers worldwide with almost 30 million of these in the United States. CDMA networks carry data at 14.4 Kbps.

TDMA divides the radio frequency into time slots and then assigns slots to multiple calls. According to the Universal Wireless Communications Consortium there are 61 million TDMA subscribers worldwide and about 31 million in the United States. TDMA carries data at 9.6 Kbps.

GSM, a variation on the TDMA technology, has more than 475 million subscribers worldwide but only about 10 million customers in the United States and Canada. Users of one GSM service are able to use their phones in many different countries—a big advantage when traveling internationally.

Providers of wireless networks are now moving to embrace the third-generation technology, called 3G. New 3G networks will mean speed for data communications—up to 2 Mbps. The 3G networks will double the voice capacity of networks and allow "always-on" Internet connections so that users can receive emails and other services.

CDMA carriers plan to move to a 3G technology called CDMA2000 in a phased implementation process. TDMA carriers will incrementally increase the capacity of their networks by implementing a number of different technologies. These include General Packet Radio Service (GPRS), which will move data up to 115 Kbps. This will be followed by Enhanced Data GSM Environment (EDGE), which will be implemented to provide data speeds of 384 Kbps. And finally, there will be a transition to Universal Mobile Telecommunications System or UMTS (sometimes referred to as Wideband CDMA or WCDMA). The higher bandwidth that will be a part of 3G networks won't happen until 2003 or 2004 in the United States. By the end of 2002 it is anticipated that 90 percent of the world's 1 billion mobile telephone subscribers will be on systems evolving toward WCDMA.

All of these seemingly confusing technologies are shown in a graphical form (see Figure 6.7, which shows the evolution of these first-generation to third-generations technologies).

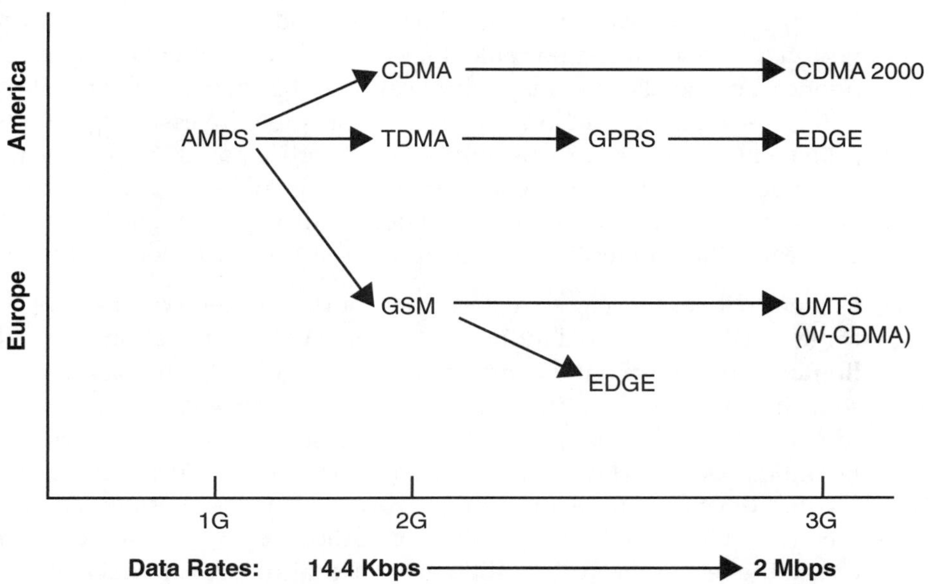

Figure 6.7 Evolution of wireless technologies.

Bluetooth, an interesting new technology named after the tenth century Viking king Harald Bluetooth, is a short-range radio frequency-hopping technology that allows wireless devices to connect to other devices within 30–100 feet operating on an unlicensed worldwide frequency of 2.4–2.4835 gigahertz. Bluetooth allows phones, PDAs, and laptops to connect with one another. When two or more Bluetooth-enabled devices are within range of one another, they automatically start communicating. Currently one of the impediments to a broader acceptance of Bluetooth technology is the high cost of a transceiver. And because Bluetooth uses the unregulated 2.4 GHz band, carriers are hard pressed to collect fees from users. A second impediment is that of interference (802.11B and HomeRF both use the same radio frequencies). And a third problem arises from the incompatibility of Bluetooth with other wireless standards.

Analysts expect that Bluetooth-enabled products will reach 11 million units in 2001 and exceed 1 billion units by 2005. The market value of these units is expected to exceed $5 billion in 2005.

Its original utility was to replace the wiring and cables between PCs and peripherals or between portable devices such as handheld computers, cells phones, and headsets. A major application of Bluetooth in the wireless arena will be its ability to link local access networks to wireless access points in public places like airports, restaurants, and office parks. A business traveler could be stranded in the Frequent-Flier Lounge of his or her favorite airline and still be able to access files at the home office via the Internet once he or she beams the Bluetooth-enabled laptop to the airport's local access network.

Current wireless services are here now courtesy of the Wireless Application Protocol (WAP), a global industry standard. WAP applications, though, are limited, curbed by content and channel boundaries. Brownout areas can squash service: no roaming, no phoning. Users must also contend with teeny-tiny screens that can display only special Web pages designed to support Handheld Device Markup Language (HDML), Wireless Markup Language (WML), or other micro-languages, instead of HTML. These wireless-ready Web sites, usually without graphics or audio, are few and far between relative to the rest of the Web's millions of sites, and they can make Net surfing on a mobile device as frustrating as riding a goldfish in the rain.

The confusing array of acronyms and services can be better understood by examining Table 6.1, which focuses on the radio frequencies used by these services.

Table 6.1 Wireless Services and Their Associated Radio Frequencies

FREQUENCY	LOCATION	INTENDED USE	TIME FRAME
700 MHz	United States	3G	By 2004
824–849/ 869–894 MHz	North America	AMPS cellular	Now
1850–1910/ 1930–1990 MHz	North America	PCS	Now
890–915/ 930–960 MHz	Outside North America	GSM	Now
2 GHz	Outside North America	3G (UMTS/W-CDMA)	Soon
2.4 GHz	World	IEEE 802.11	Rolling out
2.4 GHz	World	Bluetooth	Rolling out
2.4 GHz	World	HQ Cordless Phones	Rolling out

WAP's Up?

WAP is a secure specification that allows users to access information instantly via handheld wireless devices such as mobile phones, pagers, two-way radios, smart phones, and communicators. WAP supports most wireless networks and is supported by all operating systems. Operating systems specifically engineered for handheld devices include PalmOS, EPOC, Windows CE, FLEXOS, OS/9, and JavaOS.

WAP is not a single entity but a set of protocols and specifications. The point of this standard is to serve Internet contents and Internet services to wireless clients and WAP devices, such as mobile phones and terminals. According to a recent study by International Data Corp., the number of people using wireless devices to connect to the Internet will increase some 728 percent by 2003. That's an increase from 7.4 million U.S. users in 1999 to 61.5 million users in 2003.

WAP-enabled devices often run *microbrowsers*—Web browsers with small file sizes that can accommodate the memory constraints of handheld devices and the bandwidth constraints of wireless-content distribution. Although WAP supports HTML and XML, the WML language (an XML-derived language) is specifically devised for small screens and one-hand navigation without a keyboard.

WML is scalable from two-line text displays up through graphic screens found on items such as smart phones and communicators. WAP also supports WMLScript. The scripting language is similar to JavaScript but makes minimal demands on memory and CPU power by stripping features down to basic functionality. A consortium started by Unwired Planet, Motorola, Nokia, and Ericsson created WML.

Networks

Wireless networks are not one-size-fits-all. Rather, various wireless networks have evolved that provide a range of services and are priced accordingly. What follows is a brief review of networks designed for one-way paging, 1.5 paging, two-way paging, wireless packet data, dial-up data access, and in-building wireless LANs.

One-Way Paging

One-way paging networks are designed to provide building penetration. Paging systems typically simulcast a message to multiple base stations in order to improve the coverage area. One-way paging systems use higher-power transmitters when compared to cellular and PCS systems today.

Paging systems typically limit messages to type and length of message, for example, numeric-only (telephone numbers, for example) or alphanumeric messages. The latter are usually limited to either 80 or 256 characters per message. Worldwide, short message service (SMS) subscribers are sending some 16 billion text messages a month. Yet, lack of a universal, open standard for wired and wireless instant messaging is limiting the growth of the industry. In some cases, wireless SMS service providers are providing translation software to allow their subscribers to send messages across disparate networks.

Four types of paging systems exist:

- *Private paging systems* are limited to a small geographic area or building. They are purchased, installed, and operated by a company using a radio frequency assigned by the FCC for private use.
- *Local paging systems* cover a specific geographic area or city.
- *Regional paging systems* are designed to provide coverage for a larger geographic area. In some cases, a nationwide paging service will break its service into regional paging systems.
- *Nationwide paging systems* obviously provide a broad geographic coverage. They must broadcast each message across the entire country because the system has no way of knowing where you are located at any point in time.

1.5 Paging

A 1.5 paging network broadcasts the message and allows the user to acknowledge receipt of the message. Providers of this service include MCI, PageNet, and WebLink wireless. The 1.5-way pager has a built-in transmitter that lets the network know where the pager is. It also acknowledges receipt of a message. Because the 1.5 paging network knows where each subscriber is, the network can accommodate a greater number of subscribers. If the paging system does not know where a subscriber currently is (the pager is turned off), the system can store the message until such time as it can delivery it—store-and-forward capabilities.

Two-Way Paging

Two-way paging service allows the subscriber to receive and send paging messages. A subscriber can respond to a page or send a message to another two-way pager. Messages can also be sent to a fax machine. Motorola and Glenayre make two-way paging devices.

Wireless Packet Data

Packet data networks are important, and their importance will increase over time. Using packet data allows the user to connect to the organization's LAN or his or her own desktop computer (Geier 2001). If this connection is made using the Internet, then it is likely that middleware software and a secure connection through the firewall software will be required. Currently there are five packet data networks available for use by a company:

- *Motient* provides coverage for about 90 percent of the United States. Data transmission speeds on the network are usually 19.2 Kbps in most major cities and 4.8 Kbps for the rest of the coverage area. Most customers are corporations with fleets of users that use the service to extend their own services wirelessly. Good coverage for users in buildings was an initial design requirement. Typically major customers have a dedicated telephone line connecting to the closest Motient office. Pricing is such that Motient is not concerned with the volume of data transmitted by a customer.
- *Metricom's Ricochet networks* are available in three metropolitan areas: San Jose/San Francisco, Seattle, and Washington, D.C. The network has also been installed in some airports and on some university campuses. The network is designed primarily for devices that are at rest within the area covered by the network. Ricochet looks like a dial-up connection to a user with data speeds of 33 Kbps possible.
- *Cellular Digital Packet Data* (CDPD) has coverage for about 50 percent of the United States. Rather than a single nationwide network, CDPD is a collection of systems implemented by several analog cellular providers. This option has attracted the majority of wireless modem vendors. In-building coverage is spotty, and it is possible to surf the Net with a portable device using this service.
- *BellSouth Wireless Data* is a data-only network with solid in-building performance. This service covers about 90 percent of the United States. Data in-bound and out-bound speeds of 8 Kbps can be achieved. This network is designed primarily for text transmission.
- *ARDIS*, owned by Motorola, provides service coverage for about 90 percent of the United States, but is limited to a data rate of only 19.2 Kbps. The network focuses primarily on service dispatch applications.

Dial-up Data Access

Dial-up data access typically requires a wireless modem (internal or external) that is connected to the portable device, that is, a PDA, cell phone, or

Case Study: Wireless CRM

Many companies with customer relationship management systems are finding that they can't get leads to their sales forces fast enough. As a result, some are giving their field sales forces personal digital assistants with wireless access to the Internet and to their corporate networks, hoping that the technology is now at the point where it can solve that problem.

Aprisma Management Technologies, which sells infrastructure management software to help e-businesses control their networks, is in the process of making data from its lead management system available on sales associates' handheld devices, using new wireless capability from MarketSoft Corp. A new release of MarketSoft's eLeads management software is designed to transmit sales leads to any device that can receive email via wireless networks.

Aprisma hopes wireless notification will help salespeople turn more prospects into buyers. "The quicker we can get those leads into the hands of our sales team or our channel partners, the better opportunity we have to turn it around into real revenue," said Aprisma vice president of marketing Darren Orzechowski.

The typical flurry of leads comes when Aprisma demos its products at trade shows, advertises in print publications, collects names through its Web site, and makes outbound telemarketing calls. The company stores that personal, business, and contact information in a database.

The lead management software resides on Aprisma's server. The company's IT staff wrote a short script that customized the lead management software's rules engine. This "engine" prioritizes prospects and routes different lead types to separate sales reps. Those reps can use a secure browser interface to determine how they are to be notified of new leads—for example, whether they want them via fax or email.

The eLeads system will deliver prospect data to Internet-ready wireless devices in the form of email, letting Aprisma avoid dealing with the Wireless Application Protocol (WAP), which translates Web content to different handheld form factors (Kemp 2000).

laptop. Wireless dial-up access can move larger files, handle faxes, and accommodate other situations not suited for packet systems. Currently, each mobile device requires a different connector and interface because there are no connectivity standards. Bluetooth, which is a "wireless cable," has the potential for resolving this problem. Bluetooth-enabled devices are seemingly being announced weekly.

In-Building Wireless LAN

The IEEE 802.11 standard provides for interoperability between devices that have wireless modems manufactured by various vendors and the organization's LAN. Thus, users have immediate access to file servers, printers, and databases, regardless of their location within the building. 802.11A-enabled devices provide data speeds of up to 11 Mbps (and with 802.11B, 54 Mbps is coming) over distances of 400 feet although data speeds will decline when encountering walls or metal obstructions. An in-building wireless LAN consists of two components: a base station that is connected to a wired LAN and the network card (internal or external) that is a part of each device. The break-even point for an in-building wireless LAN is from 8 to 12 devices. The Wireless Ethernet Compatibility Alliance or Wi-Fi provides a testing and certification service for vendors of 802.11 devices.

One of the advantages with this technology is that you always have connectivity, even as you move your notebook computer from meeting to meeting or from building to building. Thus, there is no need to rush back to your office to check your email messages, learn of a schedule change, and so forth. And as 802.11 networks get installed in airports, the busy traveler will be able to remain connected without plugging into network plugs. Wireless 802.11 networks have even connected two Ethernet-based LANs found in two separate buildings. 802.11 cards provide an alternative to Bluetooth, and it should be noted that 802.11 and Bluetooth do not work well in the vicinity of each other.

It is likely that midsized and large companies and government agencies as a part of their network infrastructure will use the 802.11A standard. 802.11B networks will be used in areas that the pubic can access—for example, airports, hotels, and other similar facilities.

A study by the Wireless LAN Association found that almost 90 percent of respondents indicated that their wireless implementation had been successful and that typically the payback period was less than one year. Using wireless applications was economically beneficial in that the average per-user savings were almost $16,000 per year. The payback periods were fairly consistent across all industries: retail, manufacturing, health care, office automation, and education.

Some of the advantages of using a wireless LAN include the following:

- Improved productivity using service mobility
- Quick and easy installation
- Flexible installation
- Scalable equipment
- Reduced cost of ownership

Some of the practical considerations when moving to a wireless system are these:

- There are lots of wires supporting the endpoint transmitters located in the building walls and ceilings. The wires include data cables as well as electrical power connections.
- The signal range is between 150 and 200 feet, and a wireless transmitter can support about 15 to 20 simultaneous users.
- Some building construction materials may block the radio signal and thus create a "dead zone."
- A wireless network requires end-user authentication as well as end-user support when a problem arises. For example, a user making a financial transaction using a wireless device needs to know that the connection is secure and not subject to a security breach during the transfer (this type of security breach is usually referred to as a man-in-the-middle attack).

WSP Offerings

Wireless service providers provide a wide range of service offerings from basic data transmission to the ability to access Web-based wireless applications.

There are a number of wireless applications, as noted in Table 6.2.

Table 6.2 Types of Wireless Applications

MAINSTREAM	BLOSSOMING	ANTICIPATED
Data collection	Medical (bedside) monitoring	Project team collaboration
Inventory	Emergency room check-in	Virtual offices
Point of sale	Financial trading	Consulting teams
Hard-to-wire buildings	Cargo tracking Outdoor events Hospitality check-in Student networking Home networking	On-site training Mobile intranet Notification when customer needed good/service is ready

Mobile Phone Service

One of the more popular services is to provide access to data and other information via the ubiquitous digital cell phone. In addition to providing the traditional telephone service, the small telephone device is also enabled so that it can send requests for information and display the results of the query.

Unified Messaging

A unified messaging service will combine messages from a variety of sources. For example, voice mail, email, fax, and pager messages are combined into a single service so that the customer is able to view and act on all of the messages he or she has received, regardless of the manner in which the message has arrived.

Calendars

The calendaring function is very possible. It allows individuals who are mobile to make new appointments for themselves and for others because they are able to view a collaborative calendar for a number of individuals that are members of a team, department employees, and so forth. This allows the person away from his or her office to see if appointments have been made on his or her behalf while he or she has been in a meeting or traveling in an automobile or airplane.

Contacts

A Rolodex function gives the mobile employee access to name, address, telephone number, email address, and other pertinent information for his or her fellow employees, customers, prospects, and suppliers.

Instant Messaging

Mobile instant messaging, similar to PC-style instant messaging, may soon be an optional service. A planned service would allow the user to maintain a list of messaging "buddies" as well as detect when a person is available for messaging.

MP3

Some new phones are being produced that provide a built-in MP3 player.

Service Provider Case Study: Enterprise

This large enterprise manufactures precision metal parts and assemblies. Its products are used in aerospace, communications, and computers. Recently the company instituted just-in-time inventory management to be more competitive. With its facilities in more than one building, it faced the question of how to implement this new inventory method cost-effectively. With critical data residing in buildings spread across its campus, the first step was to network the offices together. One option was to get permits, trench, lay cable, and go from there. The other was to do it wirelessly. After comparing the costs, the wireless option seemed to be the only feasible answer. Not only was laying cable costly; it was also time-consuming, and the company wanted to get things going immediately. Information from the manufacturing production plants needed to be sent to the main office. A wireless service provider offering wireless Ethernet bridge services appeared to be the simplest to install and provided a significant cost savings over competitive products. The company was impressed to see how simple it was to install the necessary hardware. With such a quick, solid implementation, the enterprise was able to focus its attention on manufacturing and its new inventory management system.

Internet Connection

A wireless connection to the Internet allows the mobile individual to gain access to a variety of Web sites that provide a wireless interface to facilitate access to information. The individual so empowered can accomplish much in a short period of time.

Information Services

Internet-based information services allow an individual with a wireless connection to learn of late-breaking news and make a reservation for a restaurant, car rental, airline flight, and hotel, among a wide variety of other services. One of the more popular information services is to obtain a map providing very specific routing information so that the individual can move from point A to point B.

Data Access on the Corporate Network

For mobile employees and, in some cases, for customers, providing access to the corporate network can have some very positive benefits. When wireless access is provided the user can view information about current inventory levels, receive or send email messages, and locate contact information for an employee or supplier; these are just a few examples of the potential usefulness that can occur.

Location Services

A location service allows an individual to be tracked automatically by the system. Typically the individual would wear an ID badge or device that either periodically sends a radio signal to a receiver or responds when queried by a radio frequency device. The system then tracks the location of the individual and presents this information using a map of the building.

Automated Payment and Billing

A wireless automated payment and billing system would enable an individual to order a meal at a restaurant, pay for a rental car, stay at a hotel, pay for groceries—well, you get the idea. And the payment or billing would be handled automatically at the time of completing the transaction without need to stand in one more line in order to complete the paper work.

Customer Benefits

Flexibility is probably the key benefit to customers using wireless technologies. Literally, the workplace world becomes a global office without walls or stairs.

In addition to the freedom of portability, other benefits of wireless technology include the following:

- Improved efficiency of operations
- Increased productivity levels among mobile employees
- Improved customer service and responsiveness to customer inquiries
- Simplified network management
- Increased revenues
- Lower maintenance costs

What Should a WSP Enable?

A wireless service provider should provide to its customers the ability to extend access to existing applications as well as access to new Internet-based applications. With wireless the organization should be able to do the following:

- Provide Internet access to mobile employees including Web browsing and email using a variety of devices
- Achieve full integration with the existing wired network
- Allow wireless LAN installations if wired LANs are either prohibitively expensive or physically impossible
- Achieve instant deployment and/or LAN extension, with no need for rewiring or adding HUB ports

The best place to locate a WSP in your area is to visit the Web site www.wirelessadvisor.com and choose the U.S. Wireless Carriers–Alphabetical Guide under the Resources section. This Web site will allow you to input your Zip code or select a major city by name to determine the list of potential WSP partners in that area.

Special Concerns for Business Customers

How can you make electronic systems, computers, and communications networks—including wireless applications—work within your company or organization?

- Determine how mobile your customers or employees want or need to be and the potential benefits of wireless solutions. How frequently do they need to access data? What is the environment in which mobile users operate—urban/rural, indoor/outdoor?
- Ensure that you understand how wireless fits in with your organization's goals and objectives.
- Determine how to make wireless access possible—will it be necessary to rewrite business applications to support mobile users? What devices will need to be supported—laptops, PDAs, pagers, cell phones?
- Select the appropriate wireless standards for maximum compatibility for both customers and employees.
- Select an appropriate systems architecture and prepare a phased implementation plan.
- Prepare a written report that justifies the use of wireless that includes a cost/benefit and qualitative analysis (see Chapter 10 for more on the preparation of this report). What incremental revenue opportunities exist by performing services/sales at the point of customer contact?
- Make sure that you select the right technology and system integration partners—xSPs (Broadbeam 2000).

Key Questions to Ask about Wireless

Ask Yourself:

What tools are you using now? Do you need to integrate a wireless solution with your existing infrastructure and databases?
What benefits do you expect short term? Long term?
Does your potential "partner" understand your business?

Ask Your Potential WASP:

What and where do you connect? What devices? What partners and what is their coverage?
How long have you been in business?
Who are your customers? Talk to actual paying customers about their experiences.
What's your vision of the future? What technologies are going to win?
What will the service cost?
What is your business model (how do you generate revenues)?
How much customization is required to meet your needs?

WSP Operating Responsibilities

There are six important issues surrounding the development and deployment of a wireless service or application. These include devices, coverage, security, user experience, scalability, and availability.

Devices

The greater the array of devices to be supported, the longer the development cycle. The wireless service provider should be very clear about what devices are and are not supported. Also, the greater the variety of devices, the more the service provider's help desk personnel will need to become trained about the characteristics and problems associated with each device. An application that works well on one device may have nothing but problems when implemented on another device.

Coverage

The area in which the wireless application is available or, in other words, the coverage of the wireless service, is an important factor in the success of a wireless application. In the United States, coverage is often spotty and unreliable, even in the largest cities.

Security

Ensuring the security of the device involves using the device ID or the user ID to verify that they are authorized to use the wireless network. Due to the frequency with which theft of wireless devices occurs, relying on the device ID is not recommended. The integrity of the data being passed from the device over the wireless network is ensured using encryption.

User Experience

Users become frustrated with wireless applications either because of the loss of coverage (they are disconnected from the network) or because the user is required to make frequent visits to the wireless network to complete a task or transaction. Too often, designers of wireless applications seem to ignore the requirement that frequently accessed information should be the most easily accessible. Giving control to the user so that he or she can modify menu options and create shortcuts will empower users and ensure that they will remain as customers.

Scalability

The ability to scale an application smoothly is especially important given that wireless airtime is expensive. It is particularly important to avoid degradation of performance at the server level as loads increase. Distributing the processing will, in large measure, help improve the scalability of an application.

Availability

Using redundancy will improve the system reliability on the server side of an application. The reality is that the user is likely to experience being disconnected from an application due to a lost signal or a wireless network problem. It is not unusual for a user to be disconnected after sending requests to the application server via the wireless network six or seven times. After being reconnected, the user should be able to pick up in the same place that he or she was before being disconnected.

WSP Service Checklist

Generally, a wireless service provider can be expected to do the following:

- Provide the infrastructure, including connectivity, and security to deliver service to the customer. In some cases the WASP will also provide access to an application. For the wireless service provider, the location and density of its communication towers will determine its coverage within a geographical area.

- Provide customer application support.
- Manage customer expectations by articulating in clear language what the service provider is and is not responsible for.

Design of the network connectivity is critical to the delivery of applications; in fact, some view network infrastructure as the heart of the wireless service provider business model. The WSP should have sufficient computer processing and storage capacity so that the network is continuously available and highly scalable and offers true disaster recovery capabilities. In addition, the customer support provided by the WSP is critical to ensuring a great experience from the customer's perspective when problems will inevitably arise.

To ensure positive interactions, any customer-support system must include much more than a toll-free help desk, such as the following:

- Assertive service level agreements (SLAs).
- Proactive processes for system, network, and SLA monitoring management and reporting.
- 24 × 7 help desk assistance.
- Off-site storage of backup media and disaster recovery.
- Web-based, self-provisioning account management (adds, changes, and so on.) and support.
- Regular, professional maintenance and upgrades of all application software and server hardware.

Conclusion

Clearly there is strong demand for the wide range of services provided by a wireless service provider (WSP), and this demand will only grow quickly. And companies that have successfully implemented wireless applications have done so by thoroughly researching the capabilities and limitations of the technology and then embarking on projects that can be realistically achieved.

The prime audience for wireless services is not the B2B market. Wireless services can help an enterprise to integrate processes that lower IT costs and increase returns on investment. Linking back-end databases to screen displays that can display only four lines of text at a time does have its challenges, however. The first and foremost is cost. Wireless enterprise services are not going to be available at bargain-basement prices until the technologies reach maturity and competition between wireless service providers heats up.

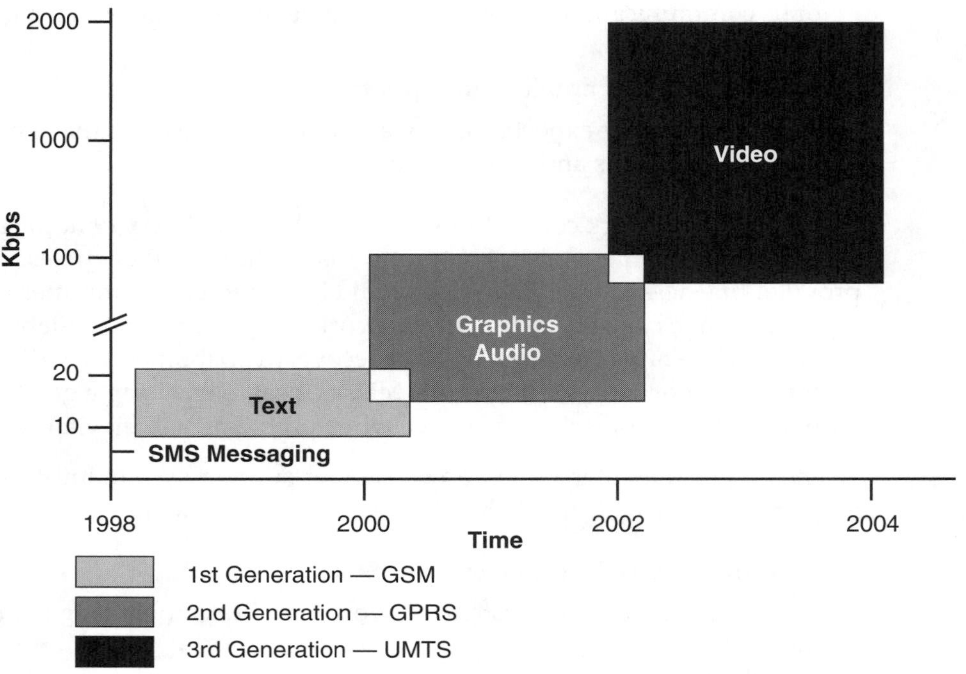

Figure 6.8 Three wireless generations.

Unlike traditional ISP usage, with flat monthly or annual pricing models, wireless phone applications are priced much like current cellular phone pricing models. Wireless users are charged per Web call or per minute. And bandwidth is very crunched. Speeds can be as slow as 7.2 Kbps (yawn). But then there's also Metricom's Ricochet wireless service, slated to be in 21 urban areas by the end of 2001, whose speeds of 128 Kbps rival the delivery rate of DSL. And as is shown in Figure 6.8, the coming generations of wireless will provide even more bandwidth for the mobile worker.

So what are we waiting for? Super-cellular phones, smart phones with or without embedded Web browsers, two-way pagers, handheld devices, and, as we saw with Anoto, digital pens are in the pipeline. So is a wireless network that lets intelligent vending machines accept cash-less payments for beverages and snack food while at the same time allowing the network to ship marketing, management, and maintenance reports back to the home office.

Wireless service providers and wireless application developers are racing to create a marketplace using key drivers like affordable price points, scalable design, sustainable security, and the future compatibility of wireless technologies.

CHAPTER 7

Other Service Providers

Since Gutenberg, technology has always been driven by newer, faster, better bits and pieces. The service provider industry is no exception. As service provider vendors vie for limited resources in an exceptionally competitive landscape, the service provider model is being expanded to provide an increasing array of flexible and efficient models for customers, many of which are service providers themselves with others ranging from enterprises of all sizes.

This isn't just about leasing some data center space somewhere in the middle of the night. Improvements in integration protocols discussed in earlier chapters allow for easier management of niche services like hosting service providers, Internet telephony service providers, infrastructure service providers, and content service providers.

As these and other service provider models emerge, it should be noted that all are under extreme pressure to provide demonstrated results in relatively short time frames. Areas in which a service provider must demonstrate excellence include customer satisfaction measures, service level management, the ability to scale at the process level including provisioning and deploying of systems for customers, and the quality of the team with resource and staff readiness. As emerging service provider operational and pricing models mature, vendor fallout will occur when service providers fail to pass along cost savings as well as sophisticated upgrades to their customers.

Whether the services are basic or ballistic in size, strategic IT managers demand support that brings value to their entire organization, not just the techie teams. And, with apologies to Gertrude Stein, a firewall is a firewall is a firewall, but the technical support surrounding that firewall is going to be the value proposition for the end users and the SP vendors.

This chapter offers a brief overview of emerging service providers, top applications, key market players, user demands, and future trends.

Hosting Service Providers

It's not just about ISPs any more. The HSP focus includes Web, collocation, and dedicated hosting options as well as outsourced Internet data center solutions. Leading HSPs are tripling the capacity of their Internet data centers to support improved network management that can accommodate end-to-end service level agreements.

A hosted service provider or HSP is sometimes called a network service provider (NSP), a computer service provider (CSP), a capacity service provider (CSP), a wholesale service provider (WSP), a collocation data center (CDC), a data center service provider (DCSP), a storage service provider (SSP), an application hosting provider (AHP), a hosting service provider (HSP), an internet infrastructure service provider (IISP), or an application infrastructure provider (AIP). These firms provide the physical space and network access for a customer's servers but do not furnish staff to manage the operation of the servers. Firms that provide this type of service include Exodus, Interliant, Loudcloud, Digex, Genuity, Qwest, and Concentric.

In recent months, HSPs have expanded their offerings, especially in the shared server segments, to meet additional user needs like testing labs, performance optimization tools, customized facilities, and application integration. Price points, based on fairly elastic demand, offer a wide range of offerings including dynamic upselling and upgrades.

Industry experts segment the HSP market into two categories: hosting types, which essentially focus on servers and rack space in the data center (called collocation centers), and business-size types, which essentially focus on penetration rates. Collocation centers provide basic infrastructure including floor space for servers, electricity, physical security, and network connections.

Several market research firms reported strong demand for Web hosting, revenues reached more than $1.5 billion in 1999, with the market divided into shared, complex, custom, and collocation segments. The Web hosting services market will likely grow steadily in the face of the downturn in the economy.

You can easily determine the kind of performance visitors to your Web site experience if your Web site is hosted by an HSP or your ISP or xSP. Simply visit http://webservices.cnet.com/ping/ and enter your site address and the name of your hosting provider. CNET's SiteSpeed Meter will test your Web site's performance and compare it to that of other hosting providers.

Web Hosting Solutions

Shared hosting solutions, which have the lowest barriers to entry, provide high-volume, bundle-access service across many shared servers. Note that the trend is away from the shared solution option and toward dedicated hosting solutions, which place an HSP user's site on a single or several specified servers. Look for shared hosting SP vendors to follow their end users into the dedicated hosting upgrades.

Custom hosting solutions are upgrades from the dedicated hosting solutions, giving end users complex hosting services and a customized solution, and a higher price point as well. Collocation HSP solutions allow the end user to use the vendor's rack space and bandwidth, again at higher price points.

A typical HSP vendor offering may include the following:

- Network services like transport, access, hosting, security, and content distribution and performance services.
- Network services platform, an integrated platform for building, deploying, and managing e-business solutions. Genuity's famed Black Rocket is its network services platform.
- Network solutions and integration services provided by the HSP and, in some cases, its service provider partners.

HSP Market Leaders

AT&T, Concentric, EarthLink, and Verio lead the shared hosting market while Digix, Exodus Communications, Genuity, IBM Global Services, GlobalCenter, and UUNET are seen as the movers on the dedicated hosting side. HSPs offer end users products from market-leading vendors like Sun Microsystems, Cisco, and Microsoft. The stakes remain high, and as such, market leaders continue to upgrade and improve their user offerings to go beyond basic offerings

For example, Exodus launched late in Q1 2001 a new Web portal, myExodus.com, which provided Exodus customers with access to a variety of operational management tools and applications provided by Exodus and its third-party application service provider (ASP) and managed service provider (MSP) partners, including: monitoring and reporting; network and systems administration; customer support, and account management. Exodus, at the same time, launched its Enterprise System Monitoring (ESM), accessible via the portal, to give its enterprise users real-time, improved updates on system performance key events and historical trends. Yet, despite these initiatives, Exodus has experienced revenue shortfalls as the economy has turned down.

Key industry drivers on the demand side on which HSP vendors must focus are increasing outsourcing among large businesses and rapid Web site adoption among small businesses. The proliferation of hosting service providers, data center buildouts and capacity expansion, and product and service development are most frequently listed as the key supply-side drivers.

HSP User Demands

HSP users, especially B2B dot-coms and other service providers, want their vendors to grow when they grow. Greater availability of bandwidth plus tighter management of architecture growth, security, backup, and monitoring aspects of their hosted environment also top the list of HSP user demands. As with all SP relationships, HSP users want to reduce internal time and costs associated with management and hosting administration without sacrificing reliability or scalability. HSP users want their vendors to grow when they grow.

To measure the benefits of Web hosting services, IDC developed an ROI model based on the following:

- The total costs of building, operating, and managing an Internet data center compared with the total costs for Web hosting services.
- The sum of projected savings over a forward-looking three-year period.
- Increased revenue and reduction in costs generated by increasing Website uptime over a forward-looking three-year period.
- An acceptable rate of return on capital (the actual rate will vary by type of organization and policy of the business).

Thus if the ROI numbers work, hosted service provider customers should expect to do the following:

- Generate new revenue streams faster, uniting content delivery and sales.
- Get to market ahead of competitors as well as reduce time-to-deploy margins, both at significantly reduced costs.
- Extend market reach to new customers.

HSP Case Study: TWA

TWA, hoping to harness the potential that the Web-enabled technologies offered airline companies, first hooked up with Digex in 1998 for basic Web hosting, network, and e-commerce services. That level of support has multiplied as TWA's business strategy expanded its use of e-business channels. When Digex configured TWA's initial Web site solution, it consisted of one Web server and one database server—an Ultra 1/170 and an Ultra 2/2100 both running Solaris 2.5.1. A 13GB RAID Level 5 drive handled data storage needs while a Compaq ProLiant NT running CheckPoint served as the site's firewall. The system also employed an e-commerce service to ensure that the online storefront would always be dynamic and interesting as well as a secure place to shop.

Since the initial site was launched, Digex has recommended and implemented a series of upgrades, including beefing up site security with a Nokia 440 running CheckPoint. That moves along significantly increased site traffic, leading to a need to upgrade the existing Web server with two Web servers operating behind a dedicated Cisco Local Director to provide fault tolerance while running Solaris 2.6. The database server remained the same while the MTI RAID 5 drive is now used to process the massive log files the site generates from the approximately 15 million hits it gets each week.

Today, TWA remains a Digex customer with 24/7 x 365 support and monitoring services as well as its own dedicated account manager. The daily reports TWA receives through WebTrends and SiteScope help the marketing staff at TWA spot trends and develop programs to take advantage of the changing marketplace.

Early in 2001, TWA expected to generate $100 million in Internet revenue, far exceeding its total Internet investment. The revenue generated by the site certainly underscores the growing importance of the Web and e-commerce to their business.

It will be interesting to see how big of an impact the September 11, 2001 terrorist attacks in New York and Washington DC will have on the airline industry's use of the Internet to provide services and generate revenues.

HSP Future Trends

Of course, greater higher-performance expectations at higher cost savings are expected. But how? Data center controls are expected to be a key competitive advantage as hosted apps, content distribution, and streaming media integrate into more managed and professional services for optimal enterprise results.

IDC forecasts continued growth in the custom segment but significant decline in share of total market as HSPs transition to standard, scalable products. And the collocation segment will experience significant growth based on three factors:

- Collocation has the lowest barriers to entry for the new HSPs.
- Collocation best serves ASPs and content distribution network services, which will experience rapid growth.
- Current collocation providers will incorporate elements of complex dedicated hosting to move upstream.

Hosted service provider insiders expect users to eventually be able to add any type of service to their basic HSP offering as increases in bandwidth allow for more and more components of customized packaged services.

Infrastructure Providers

In addition to hosted service providers, it is possible to contract for a variety of infrastructure components—for example, servers, data storage, databases, database administration services, network monitoring, and security services. A veritable potpourri of xSPs provides this wide range of services.

An Internet infrastructure service provider (IISP) or an infrastructure service provider (ISP) delivers turnkey solutions ready to operate Internet network and supporting services for business customers. This includes the provisioning of infrastructure, technical issues, network design, installation and operations, and business functions such as billing and provision of help desk services.

Solutions

According to research conducted by the University of California at Berkeley, the amount of digital information produced in the world is doubling as often as every two years. The rise of the Internet Protocol as a storage protocol is occurring at the same time that the storage industry is experiencing significant growth. According to the Gartner Group, storage revenues will grow from $37 billion in 2001 to more than $66 billion in 2004. And demand for storage capacity is expected to grow 80 percent on a compound annual basis during that same period of time. Storage service providers (SSPs)allow businesses to take advantage of leading-edge storage technology without the significant up-front capital investments required for purchasing and managing the storage.

Once IP protocols are used, stored data becomes indistinguishable from other data on the network. This reduces the necessary investment in people and equipment, which results in IP-based storage being cheaper than most other alternatives. Currently data can be moved at 1.5 Gbps, but within the next year, this should increase to 10 Gbps. IP standards-based equipment is still being introduced to the marketplace.

There are two approaches to providing additional disk space: network-attached storage (NAS) or a storage area network (SAN). A network-attached storage device has its own network address and is a server that is dedicated to file sharing. An NAS device delivers the data to the user, and the device need not be located within the server but can be located anywhere on the local area network (see Figure 7.1). NAS systems communicate at the file level. By separating storage area traffic from LAN traffic, efficiencies are increased for both.

The SAN, which is a high-speed sub-network of shared storage devices, is usually the choice for large-scale, high-performance networks where fast access is crucial (see Figure 7.1). SANs are highly dependable and expensive to purchase and install. SANs communicate at the data block level—their secret to hyper-fast transfer speeds.

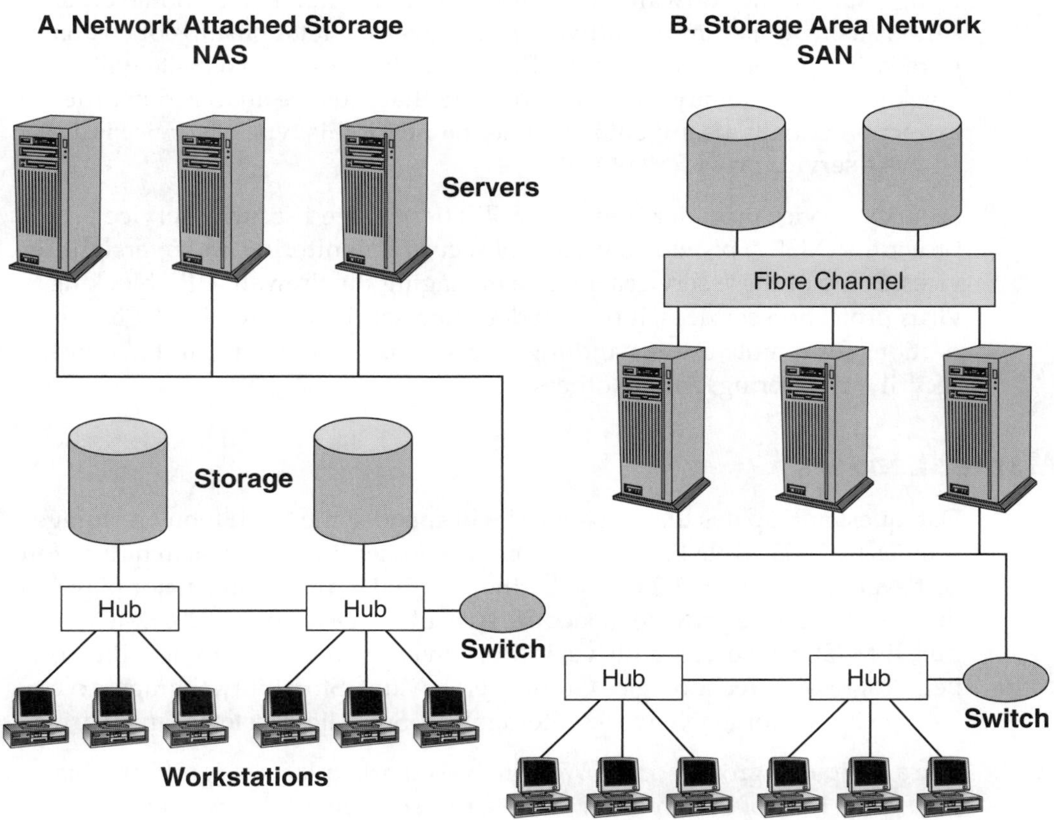

Figure 7.1 Storage architecture.

Some have suggested that accessing storage via the Internet will be as commonplace as the dialtone is to the telephone network (Erlanger 2001).

Other xSPs will provide both data storage capabilities and licenses to a specific relational database management system (RDBMS) such as Oracle, MS SQL Server, DB2, and so forth. The database service provider (DSP) is able to obtain better pricing through volume discounts than a typical small to medium-sized organization is able to achieve (Kane 2000).

Other xSPs will design, maintain, and monitor the performance of both internal and external networks for its customers. These service providers usually install an additional server at the customer's site to facilitate the monitoring of the network. The network service provider (NSP) is often able to offer specific suggestions about improving the performance of a network by eliminating bottlenecks before a problem becomes significant.

Data mining service providers (DMSP) will take a chunk of data from a customer, on a one-time basis or on an ongoing basis, and examine the data using data mining software that looks for patterns in the data. Some organizations using data mining software to discover the relationships of customer purchasing patterns, for example. Even a moderate-sized Web site will quickly generate terabytes of Web log data that must be analyzed in order to extract potentially useful data. Another name for this type of service is a Web analysis service provider (WASP).

Security service providers (another SSP!) or managed security service providers (MSSP) provide a variety of security monitoring and oversight services. Some of these services include managing the firewall, URL blocking, virus protection services, intrusion detection services, providing VPN connections for remote users, handling Web site risk assessment, and network security monitoring, among others.

Market Leaders

Dataquest anticipates that businesses will spend some $46 billion on storage utilities by 2003 while Enterprise Storage, another industry research firm, forecast expenditures of $11.2 billion by the year 2004. Among the major players in the storage service provider space are Articulent, Driveway, EDS, EMC, Exodus, IBM Global Services, Idrive, Intira, NaviStor, ManagedStorage, Pro Softnet, Progressive Technologies Group, ServerVault, Storability, Storage Access, Storage Link, StorageNetworks, StorageWay, Sun Microsystems, and Xdrive.

The anticipated growth of the Web analysis marketplace is significant. Starting from a base of $100 million in 1999, this segment of the market is expected to grow to $1.25 billion by 2004. Key WASP vendors include WebSideStory, Keylime Software, and Visual Insights.

The security service providers market is anticipated to grow to almost $1.7 billion by 2005 from $140 million in 2000. Vendors in this market include Affiliated Computer Services, Counterpane Internet Security, Jerboa, Riptech, Telenisus, TruSecure, and Veritect, among others.

User Demands

Businesses and organizations are faced with the need to significantly add disk storage capacity on a year-after-year basis. While a majority of organizations are able to plan for and manage the installation of additional disk storage space, the option of outsourcing data storage can be an attractive one. In particular, using remote data storage as an automatic backup option can be attractive in that the backup data is stored remotely. Normally, the backup data (removal disk drives or tape) needs to be physically transported to an off-site location to ensure the utility of the data itself.

SSPs allow a customer to buy only as much capacity as he or she needs (and to add more capacity easily when needed). Customers don't have to invest in their own storage infrastructure and personnel. Storage typically costs about $20,000 per month per terabyte for basic storage on demand. Additional services—for example, scheduled backup and restore, real-time data replication, and high availability SLAs—not surprisingly, will cost more. Obviously, putting such a valuable commodity as data about a company's customers in the hands of another is a serious decision. Such an approach calls for a clear plan of how to move the data quickly and easily from one SSP to another SSP or to move it back in-house should the need arise.

Unfortunately, once data is stored, it doesn't take care of itself—companies seeking storage must contend with management and operational costs. It costs anywhere from $25 to $35 a year to manage and maintain a single megabyte of storage according to the Enterprise Storage Group. Ultimately, storage can wind up costing more than 50 percent of an overall IT infrastructure costs.

Dealing with the mountains of Web log data that are routinely generated by a Web site can be a daunting task. Web analytic software tools such as Accrue, NetGenesis, and WebTrends provide this kind of data analysis, but they can be very expensive to purchase (in some cases, more than $250,000 for the software alone) and install locally. A WASP company can provide this as a monthly service starting at $2,500. The monthly service cost is based on a combination of the amount of data that needs to be analyzed (the direct result of the number of hits to a Web site) plus the level of detail that needs to be provided.

One of the strengths of employing a WASP service is that it can track a customer's true path through multiple domains. Customers access real-time Web traffic reports, and the formatting of the reports can be customized.

Managed security service providers save companies money by reducing staff and cutting installation and maintenance costs associated with deploying security hardware and software. In addition, because the MSSP staff become very knowledgeable about security issues, they can take a proactive approach about making recommendations to their customers to improve the overall security of the IT department.

One of the biggest reasons why companies are willing to hire a security service provider is that the company does not have enough staff members with adequate anti-hacking skills to know what to do when an intrusion detection system generates an alarm. And while the IT staff shortage is generally well known there is an even greater shortage of skilled security people. The annual *InformationWeek* salary survey indicates that the median income for system security staff is about $70,000 (Schactman 2001).

Future Trends

As the Internet Protocol becomes more and more persuasive (incorporated directly into more hardware and software products) the use of the Internet to gain access to infrastructure resources grows. For the infrastructure service providers, they must be able to deliver a clear and compelling set of reasons why customers will want to act on their value propositions. Their value propositions can be any of the following:

- Lower costs
- Faster time to benefit
- Greater availability
- Higher security
- No need to recruit IT personnel

Internet Telephony Service Providers

Internet telephony service providers (ITSPs), which include telecoms, ISPs, and even cable TV companies, create and manage Internet protocol-based data connections of voice and fax data, once solely carried over the public switched telephone network (PSTN). These ITSPs are known for their low, some might even say cheap, prices, which have made them the darling of Web-savvy consumers with offers like "Call anywhere in the U.S. for FREE up to 5 minutes" and "international calls as low as 3.9 cents per minute." Price points aside, enterprises and B2B service providers have remained cool to the concept, instead waiting for improvements in infrastructure like voice quality, latency, compression algorithms, and quality of service.

ITSP first debuted as software applications that let two people talk via their personal computers. Static-like echos and other sounds marked those early conversations. Now ITSP allows users to make direct calls on a telephone over an IP network. IP networks also allow users to transfer large bundles of information such as videoconferencing, multicasting, and faxing, all business-critical processes. To date, pure-play ITSP firms remain relatively unregulated, unlike traditional phone service providers, which are subject to federal and state utility laws, some of which date back to the 1930s.

Some industry experts say that the time has now come as converged networks create new opportunities using applications like wireless and speech recognition protocols as part of basic outsourced managed and monitoring services. The quality of the sound has become indistinguishable from that of the PSTN.

Business users will find multivendor and multiple protocol options to voice and fax traffic over current data networks based on packet telephony standards based on networking, multimedia, and digital signal processing fundamentals. Today, most Web-to-phone services are sold to communications portals and e-communications companies.

Solutions

ITSP applications range from prepaid and postpaid calling cards for services on voice-over-data networks to enterprise call/contact centers with the ability to handle both voice and data contacts. Other applications allow carriers to enter new markets quickly and generate additional revenues by establishing their own calling card business or by reselling calling card services to other service providers.

Enabling technologies include basic telephone handsets, which plug into the personal computers. New handsets, including cordless units, will soon be widely available and will allow the user to dial on a conventional keypad rather than a keyboard and mouse. When combined with the growing availability of broadband always-on Internet access, this removes most of the inconvenience of calling from a PC.

A communication service provider (CSP) is a generic term used to encompass all forms of communication (phone, mobile, wireless, and fax). CSPs can provide end-to-end connectivity for organizations at a single location, multiple locations in the same city, and multiple locations in multiple states or countries.

Market Leaders

Calling Card Services for PacketIN Solutions is part of Lucent's recently announced SurePay suite, and it is available for deployment on converged networks. And ITXC webtalkNOW! Service gives portals, ITSPs, ISPs, and other Internet-based companies a turnkey solution for offering self-branded, retail, Web-to-phone service to their customers. Dialpad, one of the largest ITSPs, uses advertising to support free service to any fixed or mobile phone in the United States, from any PC connected to the Internet, anywhere in the world.

In addition, the traditional telephone companies are beginning to recognize the value of providing an integrated solution for all forms of messaging to their customers. Thus, customers would be able to see, on a single screen, all of the voice mail, email, and faxes that have been received. A set of tools allows the recipient to respond in the best possible manner, taking into consideration the urgency and the form for the message that is preferred by the sender.

User Demands

In this arena, the customer is looking for convenience. Regardless of where he or she is located, in the office or traveling with a mobile device of some kind, the individual would like to have immediate access to all messages—regardless of their form.

Future Trends

Internet telephony service provider offerings are likely to become integrated with other xSP service offerings. In addition to providing integrated message services (voice mail, email, and fax), customers will also see product offerings that allow them to hear text messages (for example, emails) using their cellular phones. And the flip side of voice recognition software is that users will be able to speak commands and messages and have the system respond appropriately. For example, a user with a cell phone would be able to send a fax or email message using voice recognition software.

Content Service Providers

The Internet has evolved from a mechanism for transporting text and simple images to a vehicle for use of multimedia and other bandwidth-intensive content that demand higher service levels.

A content service provider (CSP) is a company that provides data, information, images, audio files, and video streaming capabilities for inclusion on the Web. A customer signs up to receive specific data or information within a stated time period, for example, every 10 minutes in the case of stock price ticker tape information. The "content" or "syndicated content" is then incorporated into a Web site. Thus, when an end user clicks on some portion of a

Web site to view the weather, obtain a stock price quote, or look at a map of a city, he or she has actually left the original Web site and is now at the content service provider's Web site.

A content management service provider (CMSP) is a company that aggregates data and information from a number of sources and then provides this information to its customers as if it were a content service provider. A data service provider or DSP is another name sometimes used for a CSP. With a content service provider, a customer specifies what content, services, catalog information, and streaming media he or she wants, and the CSP takes care of the rest. In some cases, the content can be dynamic so that the result for the end user is a customized experience.

There are a number of roles that a content management service provider can provide. Among these are the following:

Content Generation

- Generation means the creation of original or licensed content into distributable form.
- Content is digital information with which an end user interacts. The digital information may consist of items as disparate as streaming media, games, software applications, Web pages, emails, or text.
- A news service provider that maintains a network of up to the minute news that others license would be in the content generation space.

Content Aggregation

- Aggregation involves the collection or absorption of various content components into a menu of offerings. Content is not always aggregated.
- Aggregated content is usually bundled or sold in various pricing structures designed to maximize the return on investment.

Content Formatting

- Formatting means modifying or repurposing of content from one form to another, for the purpose of conforming to a predetermined or templated look.
- Formatted content provides uniform display capabilities.

Content Verification

- Verification tests the consistency and integrity of the content for invalid links, inappropriate messages, and version control.
- Content verification is critical for all content providers.
- A content provider can perform the content verification service or outsource it.

Content Transcoding

- Transcoding occurs when pages are dynamically converted—for example, HTML or .jpg images—to automatically format correctly for the end user's device.
- Transcoding ensures that various devices can view things the same way a PC does. It provides an assurance to content providers that their content will display correctly across devices.
- An MSP that did data synchronization on a hosted basis would be an example in the verification space.

Content Distribution

- Distribution means delivering content to a third party.
- Technologies, which make distribution more efficient and effective, can give a content provider a source of competitive advantage.
- A service provider who distributes data on behalf of a content provider is often called a content distributor.

Content Reporting

- Reporting provides results of content consumption patterns, content delivery, distribution, updating efficacy, and other associated data. Typically, the reports can be printed or viewed online.
- Reporting services allow content providers to evaluate the efficiency of their delivery channels, improve their customer service, and personalize/customize their content for individual and groups of users.
- Content service providers that receive, parse, store, mine, or make data available in defined or enable ad hoc reports to be created are sometimes referred to as reporting providers.

Solutions

Online service provider (OSP) companies include AOL (America Online), CompuServe, MSN (Microsoft Network), and MSNBC (Microsoft/NBC), among others. They usually provide Internet connectivity similar to an ISP's, but unlike an ISP, they also provide their own content. Some of this content is proprietary and is accessible only if you are a member (subscriber) of that network.

There are a host of other content service providers that will provide a business or organization with access to a wide variety of information resources that can be integrated into a public Web site, an intranet, or an Extranet.

Examples of these information resources include stock price quotations, information about companies, the weather, sports, the latest news from Associated Press or United Press International, and so forth. The information can be quite broad or narrowly focused to better meet the needs of the end users.

Market Leaders

Content service providers usually provide a Web interface that allows customers to manage what content is distributed to whom. Examples of service providers in the content or content management space are Ellacoya Networks, Isyndicate, Streetmail, and Trapezo. Content is also directly available from primary publishers, for example, the *Wall Street Journal*, Forbes, Inc., Nexus/Lexus, and others. In addition, similar content can also be obtained from information aggregators.

Some of the content service providers can be classified as being expensive solutions that provide an abundance of content that is geared toward use by specialists. Examples of companies in this group of "one-stop-shopping" providers include Dialog, Factiva, MarkIntel, and Lexus/Nexus. These companies have very large databases that go back a number of years and carry high price tags in order to gain access to the data.

A second solution uses the free Internet search engines, such as Yahoo!, Excite, and Alta Vista as well as other less expensive content service providers like Company Sleuth, Individual.com, and Northern Light. These companies tend to use information from press releases, public filings at government agencies, and other similar news from a limited number of sources. Prices for these services range from free to moderate.

One of the important factors that will differentiate an expensive from a free-to-moderate content service provider is the currency of the information being viewed. Real-time information typically commands a price premium. One of the other important features for considering a content service provider is whether an individual user can personalize the Web page and receive an email alert about fast-breaking news.

User Demands

Content management systems will support many contributors and editors and the many different ways that they work together. Workflow and collaboration are important areas that can differentiate systems. Due to the almost constant pressure to provide personalization, the content will appear on different platforms—for example, Netscape and Internet Explorer, mobile devices and kiosks.

Is the content available as a preformatted page or portion of a page in a cache, or is it retrieved from a database on demand? The latter approach can be slower from the perspective of the end user. Are there any technical or other restrictions on the use of the content? Is it possible to incorporate images, audio files, and video files?

Regardless of the form of the content and how and where it is stored, the end user is really interested only in the end result—delivery of the required content with acceptable response times. Some content management service providers team up with Akami to push content out to and deliver it from a point closest to the end user. With its 22 high-capacity data centers (called content access points or CAPs), Akami is able to improve performance by reducing the number of hops that content must make across routers. The Akami approach is particularly effective when streaming media is being utilized. The use of Akami, epicRealm, or Digital Island is often referred to as a content delivery network or CDN.

Future Trends

As the Internet continues its evolution with the introduction of new technologies and new user interfaces, the one constant will be that users will want to have access to relevant content. As the underlying bandwidth technologies continue to evolve so that the end user has a fatter and fatter pipe to his or her desktop or mobile device, users will expect quality content.

The goal of the content service provider as well as the content management service provider is to be poised so that they can deliver what the customer wants when they want it. In short, the service provider needs to be a customer-focused organization.

Conclusion

Clearly there is strong demand for the wide range of services provided by the other service providers—hosting service providers, infrastructure service providers, Internet telephony service providers, and the content service providers. Depending upon the particular service provider segment, growth will vary from quite strong to struggling. The tremendous diversity of service offerings means that any business or organization is likely to find more than one service provider that will meet their needs.

CHAPTER 8

Service Level Agreements

A service level agreement (SLA) is a type of contract between a service provider and a business customer that clearly outlines the rights and obligations of both parties. Service level agreements define the responsibilities of a service provider and its customers by outlining the service offering as well as the supported products, measurement criteria, reporting criteria, and quality standards for that service. In some cases, the service level agreement is called a performance level agreement (PLA).

The rise of the service provider models, the evolution of e-commerce, and the maturity of network infrastructure have raised the service expectations of customers. As a result, SLAs define the responsibilities of an IT service provider and the users of that service. The SLA also identifies and defines the services provided as well as the supported products, measurement criteria, reporting criteria, and quality standards for the service.

Due to the newness of the xSP industry, there are few documented or benchmarked trends to serve as industry standards. As awareness of service provider benefits increases, industry experts expect that SLAs will become the leading purchase factor.

Industry analysts expect that worldwide outsourced spending will increase from a mere $10 billion in 1998 to as much as $151 billion by 2003.

As a part of defining and delivering on SLAs, the xSP must determine what level of service to guarantee to its customers. These decisions should take into consideration the business risk assumed by the xSP for guaranteeing a particular level of service to the customer at a specific cost.

A good SLA is a tool that works to benefit the service provider in three ways:

- It encourages customer loyalty. If the customer is happy with the service levels he or she is receiving, then the SLA is a reminder of what the customer might lose by changing service providers.
- It provides a very specific target for the provider, thus helping to ensure that higher levels of service are not routinely provided (when they are not needed or charged for). The written SLA provides a clear roadmap of the service level expectations that the customer has and is expecting to receive.
- The preparation of a mutually agreeable SLA assists the service provider in setting the customer expectations appropriately, especially in the area of implementation.

An SLA should be written from the customer's perspective in clear, simple language. All legalese and technology jargon should be minimized, and for what remains, it should be clearly defined at the beginning of the agreement. The SLA spells out the service levels to be provided and the penalties to be imposed for shortfalls. Yet, not surprisingly, buyers have discovered that not all SLAs have been created equal. Some employ too much undefined jargon (that is open to interpretation) as well as statistical sleight –of hand. Is a network availability standard based on the network being available to all customers or only for one specific customer?

Despite the relative newness of the xSP industry we are seeing the evolution of service level agreements that take on more of a customer focus, as shown in Table 8.1.

Some progressive information technology (IT) departments use an SLA to define the level of services that they can provide to their customers within an organization. An SLA can be used internally to define expectations for everything from help desk services to network performance and availability, appli-

Table 8.1 Evolution of the Service Level Agreement

FROM	TO
Technical perspective	Customer perspective
System availability is important	Exceptional availability is better
System components measured	Actual customer experiences measured
Reporting after the fact	Real-time reporting

cation performance and availability, and other internal processes that are important to their customers (Andress 2001).

Managing SLAs effectively is fast becoming a key operational strategy for xSPs and their customers, who both must determine accountability for service problems, prioritize resolution, and leverage their respective IT investment planning. The SLA defines the choices of service levels that are being made. The SLA must make very clear how service levels are measured. Such clarity will eradicate hours of unnecessary discussions and miscommunications on all sides.

Increasingly, business executives who hire service providers require active SLA verification to show that the service provider will indeed deliver the outsourced IT solutions that are promised. These validation tools, while expensive, are crucial to ensure that the SLA is being managed correctly across all channels.

A well-negotiated SLA significantly reduces the scope for disagreement that may arise in the course of the business relationship. The source of the largest number of disputes is likely to be the gap between the actual performance by a service provider and that which is expected by customer based on the terms of the underlying SLA. Even the most carefully drafted SLA will not prevent disputes between the parties from arising. There are always unforeseen circumstances or matters where the parties genuinely cannot agree. In such a case, the parties will need to resort to a dispute resolution mechanism.

The SLA should also provide the customer with specific notification by the service provider should a number of financial standards fall below minimum levels. This will allow the customer the opportunity to assess the risk of continuing the service or looking for a replacement service provider in order to provide an orderly migration from one service to another. Receiving notice that your DSL ISP provider is going out of business in a few days is not good news for any business or organization that relies on access to the Internet to conduct business.

Types of SLAs

It is recommended to have certain types of SLAs, each covering a certain IT aspect or area, or to make a clear distinction in service catalogs between the services that are candidates to be split into separate SLAs. A few examples of these different types of services or SLAs are the following:

- Access to the Internet
- Desktop services

- ➢ Application services
- ➢ Project services
- ➢ Network services
- ➢ Hosting services
- ➢ Customer care services

Each will have its own set of service levels, processes to support them, and skill set and systems and service management tool requirements. This distinction will make the service provider's business model, its organization, and the provided services manageable in a more efficient and effective way. (Pappalardo 2001).

SLA Case Study: LTU

Today's college students have far greater access to information resources and academic tools than ever before with the availability of the Internet. College and university campuses not only have the challenge of assuring students and faculty that they will have access to the Internet, but they must also make sure that their limited bandwidth is being used mainly for academic purposes.

A perfect example is LT University, which has a typical campus of a few thousand students, many living on campus, and 2 x T-1s connecting the campus to the Internet. The LTU network administrator and technical experts from its ISP ran tests to see how much bandwidth was being used by the students on a typical weekday afternoon. Around 60 percent to 70 percent of the traffic going to the T-1 links was FTP (the Internet file transfer protocol). Additionally, the ISP's real-time traffic monitoring graph immediately revealed that the great majority of the FTP traffic was using TCP port numbers associated with Napster and other popular applications used for MP3 file download. It also found that at times, users from outside the campus accessing servers within the dormitory subnet were, in fact, taking up a noticeable amount of bandwidth! This is often viewed as a use of the networking resource clearly outside the organization's objective.

LT University has taken advantage of the ISP's service level agreement management solutions to manage its on-campus bandwidth usage proactively by writing and enforcing policies, which prioritize and actually guarantee specific bandwidth to academic applications. The students living on campus can still use "entertainment" and file sharing software, but at an appropriately scaled level. The result is network usage that meets academic goals while maintaining open access for both students and faculty.

In order to guarantee a particular level of service, the service provider must determine the potential risk factors that are within its control and those that are not. The service provider should decide the contents of an SLA only after careful evaluation of all of its performance risk factors and their respective causes. Ultimately, the price of a retail product should reflect the SLA conditions as well as the service provider performance risk. The SLA should include metrics and, whenever available and practical, industry ranges. Some xSPs offer only a standard SLA designed to fit all customers. A popular option, however, is the tiering of service levels—such as gold, silver, or bronze—that allows customers to choose the level of support that best suits their business needs.

Key Components of an SLA

A service level agreement governs the scope, quality, and availability of services. This document becomes a tool for both parties to identify the responsibilities, problem resolution and escalation procedures, and the performance and cost monitoring process. It should be understood that the best agreement in the world would not work if both parties were not able to meet their respective responsibilities. Customers who insist on maximum service provider responsibility at rock-bottom prices will rarely find that the project will be successful. The demand is irrational because a basic business principle is that risk is rewarded with money. Customers who insist on irrational terms are simply issuing demands.

One of the ironies of the service provider industry is that customers have learned that they need to have contracts "with teeth" to get the high levels of service that they need. xSPs that realize that even though they need to provide a good SLA to their customers, in reality the SLA is a piece of paper and that what customers really want is high-quality, reliable service.

Among the broad issues that should be addressed in a service level agreement are the following:

Definitions. All industry jargon and abbreviations must be clearly defined to prevent possible misinterpretations.

Description of service. What the service deliverables are, when they are delivered, and where must be defined. Where the service is delivered is known as the point of service delivery (POSD). There may be multiple POSDs.

Responsibilities of the customer. Possible topics in this area might include appointing a single point of contact, specifying what version or release number of Web browser will be supported, ensuring that the customer's

LAN and ISP connections meet minimum standards, and so forth. Failure caused by a customer's infrastructure will, in most cases, invalidate an SLA.

Responsibilities of the service provider. Issues that should be addressed in this section include what specific services are being delivered, provision of Internet-based support or help desk services, and alerts when the service will be unavailable.

Level of integration. The customer may wish to have the service provider integrate one or more applications with existing customer-developed applications or with another service provider application. The specific data elements and transactions that need to be integrated should be identified in great detail.

Duration of the service. The time the agreement is in effect may range from one to five years. What is the start date of the service?

Installation schedule. When will the service start? Will the service be rolled out in phases?

Confidential information. Both the customer and the service provider will have information that will need to remain confidential. This section should define what information will be considered to be confidential and what shall be done to protect that confidentiality. This section should clearly address the need to keep the customer's data confidential and the consequences should data be accidentally or explicitly compromised. Failure to protect the confidentiality of a customer's data is a clear breech of a warranty to keep data confidential.

Ownership of customer data. This defines what data belongs to the customer and in what format it can be exported. The customer should have periodic copies of his or her data sent to him or her or stored in a specified location. Should the customer decide to move to another service provider or bring the application in-house, the agreement must allow the customer to retrieve his or her data without asking permission from the existing service provider.

Ownership of trademarks, copyrights. The ownership or interest in the service provider's trademarks, copyrights, trade names, know how, and trade secrets should be addressed.

Security. The measures being taken by the service provider to ensure the security of its data center and of its customer's data should be clearly articulated. How are security intrusions reported? Is a security audit performed by an outside, qualified third party? Are the results of these regular audits shared with all customers? Are the service provider's employees bonded?

- Physical security. What precautions does the service provider take to ensure the absolute security of its data center?

- Applications, network, and platform security. How are issues such as user authentication, firewalls, virus scanning, and intrusion detection to be addressed?
- Data backup. How frequently are a partial and a total system backup performed? Is the backup data stored off-site? Are service provider employees bonded (McWhirter 2001)?

Environmental concerns. The ready availability of electrical power is an assumption that can no longer be made (if indeed, it was ever a safe assumption). What safeguard measures are in place in the event that power brownouts or blackouts are experienced? How long would a system be down? Backup power systems are complex, and an uninterrupted power supply (UPS) will have a limited time period in which it can provide power. And if electrical power is limited, what effect will it have on the air conditioning system? As the computer density per square foot increases due to thinner systems located in racks, increased heat output must be countered.

Performance metrics. What business and technical metrics will be used to evaluate the service being provided? It is critical to specify what calculation criteria will be used to measure each metric. Most importantly, data for all metrics must be easy to collect, and it must be automated. The agreement should identify what are the target metrics, minimum acceptable metrics, and unacceptable metrics. A majority, if not all, of the metrics should be automated so that both the customer and service provider will have ready access to the same set of data.

Problem resolution. Topics might include ways in which a customer can contact the service provider's help desk, hours of help desk operation, timeframe to respond to inquiries, time needed to fix different levels of software problems, and so forth. Among the specific issues that need to be addressed are problems associated with local hardware and Internet connectivity, problems connecting to an application, and problems associated with usage of the application itself.

Payment. Typically, payment is normally made in advance on a yearly, quarterly, or monthly basis.

Performance bond. The customer should consider asking the service provider for a performance bond, depending on the value and importance of the service being provided.

Service enhancements. Ways in which the customer can make suggestions for enhancing the service, ownership of the enhancements, and so forth are addressed in this section. The procedures to be followed by the service provider when installing new software updates and bug fixes should be spelled out. For example, the amount of testing that must be performed before the new software is installed in an operational system should be addressed.

Service levels. Several warranties might be included in a SLA. Among these are the following:

- *Service availability*. System reliability for the service will meet a minimum of *x* percent during any given one-month period. Optionally, the warranty might focus on the hours from early in the morning until the time when the business closes. Thus, there may be different standards, depending on the needs of the customer.
- *Service reliability*. System reliability, or the reciprocal measure downtime, is usually expressed as a percent, for example, 98 percent system reliability and 2 percent downtime. Consider a typical month with 30 days and 24 hours a day. That is a total of 720 hours or 43,200 minutes of service availability if there is no downtime. As shown in Table 8.2, the amount of system downtime can be considerable, depending on the level of system availability.

  The cost of moving from one level to a higher level of service reliability will be significant because the service provider must add more equipment and software—for example, adding redundant equipment and more sophisticated software to improve the reliability of the service. One approach to improve reliability is to employ duplicate disk drives (this is often called RAID or Redundant Array of Inexpensive Disks).

  In addition, the amount of downtime that will be experienced in any given month will not occur in one single downtime incident; rather,

Table 8.2 System Availability and Downtime

AVAILABILITY LEVEL	AMOUNT OF DOWNTIME PER MONTH
95%	36 hours
97%	21.6 hours
98%	14.4 hours
99%	7.2 hours
99.3%	5.0 hours
99.5%	3.6 hours
99.7%	2.2 hours
99.9%	43.2 minutes
99.99%	4.3 minutes
99.999%	24 seconds

the end user is likely to experience multiple incidents of service unavailability, lasting a few seconds, minutes, or hours. In addition, some of the available hours will be scheduled for downtime due to system upgrades. Typically, the majority of customers are not concerned about what happens to the system from midnight till 6 a.m. but are concerned only with having the system be available when the customer's staff members are working.

Is availability measured end-to-end or just within a service provider's proprietary network? Is all downtime counted, or must downtime exceed a minimum threshold? Is availability measured over a calendar month or over a daily, rolling 30-day average?

- *System response times*. Response times will vary by type of transaction—for example, searching, editing a record, saving a record, and so forth. The variability of response times is a given for an Internet-based service. In addition to average response times, peak response times might also be identified. The anticipated volume of transactions should also be identified. Response times need to be measured for the server, the database, the application, and customer support.
- *Scalability*. As the number of users grows over time and as use of the service provider occurs over time, data volumes will also grow. What are the plans of the service provider to cope with hundreds, thousands or tens of thousands of users (Bhattacharjee 2001)?
- *Other service levels*. The customer may be interested in having the service provider agree to additional warranties. These will need to be negotiated with the service provider.
- *Exclusions to service levels*. Possible exclusions to system availability might be events such as routine maintenance, customer-caused outages, *force majeure*, and other events beyond the reasonable control of the xSP.

Remedies. Should the service provider fail to achieve the agreed-on warranty(s), then a remedy should be clearly stated—for example, prorating a portion of the fee paid by the customer as a credit for future service. The goal of any remedy is to ensure that the customer has the attention of the service provider. Rarely do penalties reimburse the customer for the total amount of the loss. Given a multiplicity of service metrics, there should be a corresponding number of remedies and consequences (Gerwig 2001).

Account management. This agreement sets up a single point of accountability between the service provider and the customer. The type of SLA reports that will be provided along with the time between data capture intervals should be identified. How the reports will be accessed—for example, via the Internet, sent via email, and so forth—should be agreed on.

Change management. In high technology, change is relentless and constant. Both the customer and the service provider must be able to make changes to the SLA quickly and easily—for example, add seats, change a warranty, and so forth. SLAs support live environments; hence SLAs should be considered as live documents. The SLA must continue to evolve over time. Scalability issues should be addressed so that the customer can quickly add or subtract levels of service. Iron-clad contracts put relationships into a bind (Rosa 2001).

Software escrow. A software source code escrow agreement may be necessary if the service provider is providing access to an application or is providing an e-commerce-enabled Web site. Should the service provider go out of business then the customer would have access to the software. The software in an escrow account should be administered by an experienced third party.

Force majeure. How are acts of God and other disasters going to affect the service? Can the physical and technical security elements of the service provider be audited independently and certified?

Termination. The amount of notice that either party must give to terminate the Service Level Agreement should be defined. What kinds of assistance and services the service provider will extend to the customer to migrate their data to a new system (Raths 2001)?

Limitation of liability. What liabilities does the service provider assume, and what are the limits of liability?

General terms. Issues such as notices, governing law, independent contractors, and so forth should be addressed.

There are several caveats about what to avoid in a service level agreement. These include the following:

- An SLA that is unachievable—for example, a guarantee of 100 percent system availability.
- Vague and unmeasurable goals and objectives for the SLA.
- An agreement that does not include both technical and business metrics.
- An SLA with penalties that do not kick in when a service outage or other problem occurs.

Negotiating an SLA can range from a few days to a number of weeks of intensive conversations to agree on all the details of a service level agreement, assuming that both parties have a solid understanding of what is involved. Increasingly, attorneys with experience in drafting SLAs are being used to help customers receive the assurances they are seeking.

SLAs and the Federal Government

The Information Technology Association of America has developed some guidelines for an application service provider (ASP) service level agreement (SLA) for the federal marketplace (for a copy visit http://www.itas.org/asp/itaaslafed.pdf). Because most ASP agreements by a federal agency are likely to be with a commercially available service, the contracts are likely to be formed under Part 12 of the Federal Acquisition Regulation. Most importantly, FAR 12.01 states that the government should, where possible, purchase commercial items, including commercial ASP services.

In addition to some standard terms and conditions for IT agreements, SLA guidelines for the federal marketplace cover 13 broad areas:

- Service level
- Security
- Tracking and reporting
- System performance
- Remedies
- Upgrades
- Contingency, backup, and disaster recovery
- Support and help desk services
- Termination
- Ownership
- Intellectual property indemnification
- Indemnification by customer
- General

These guidelines, developed by the ITAA, will be of value both to potential customers of xSPs, especially customers looking to contract for an ASP service, and to service providers. The ITAA also has a companion document that readers are likely to find of value—ITAA's "Application Service Provider (ASP) Service Level Agreement (SLA) Guidelines" (for a copy visit http://www.itaa.org/asp/itaasla.pdf).

SLA Implementation Plan

A simplified SLA implementation plan requires the following:

- Assess the SLA
- Secure management commitment
- Designate service level managers
- Educate the involved parties
- Assess the current services and service levels
- Gather customer feedback
- Solicit feedback
- Complete the implementation of measuring and monitoring activities
- Implement and manage the final SLA
- Conduct service level reporting

Managing successful SLAs has a lot to do with communicating and managing expectations. Service level reports, frequent meetings, and periodic audits are the perfect vehicles to establish this goal. The language that is being used during those meetings and audits and in those reports should be easy to understand and leave no doubts about the provided levels of the services. The goal is to establish a working relationship in which both parties are partners who are seeking a win-win situation.

And remember the rule of the four "Ss": Short, simple documents get signed sooner.

The Information Technology Association of America has developed a set of guidelines to assist federal, state and local governments develop and understand the terms and conditions of service level agreements (the text of ITAA's ASP SLA Guidelines for the Federal Marketplace can be downloaded from their Web site—http://www.itaa.org).

Performance Metrics

A majority of SLAs use performance metrics that are technical in nature and are often hard to understand. A recommended approach uses both business-oriented metrics and technical metrics. Metrics are used to better understand how the service affects a business or organization. In addition, metrics are often employed that address the quality of service only after a significant period of time has elapsed. Metrics that are utilized in a much shorter time

SLA Case Study: Genuity

Genuity is upping the service level agreement ante in a high-stakes guarantee game that experts say is as much about market bragging rights as customer dollars and cents. The ISP announced recently that new and existing dedicated Internet access customers are covered by enhanced SLAs. Genuity now guarantees that traffic traveling between its points of presence (POP) will not exceed 55 millisecond (msec) of round-trip latency.

Previously, the company guaranteed that round-trip latency would not exceed 65 msec. The improved SLA also guarantees that users will not sustain more than 0.5 percent packet loss. The ISP's previous SLA ensured no more than 1 percent packet loss. Both guarantees are based on monthly averages. Genuity is now offering the strongest packet-loss guarantee in the market.

AT&T was first to offer a packet loss guarantee below 1 percent, with an SLA that states users will not sustain more than 0.7 percent packet loss. Genuity now stands only with Cable & Wireless, which was the first ISP to offer a minimum round-trip latency guarantee at 55 msec. But analysts note that these changes are not noticeable to the average customer. Genuity's SLA for network availability remains unchanged, guaranteeing 99.97 percent network availability. That guarantee includes the customer's local-loop connection if ordered through Genuity. UUNET and AT&T also include their customer's local-loop connections in their network availability guarantee if ordered through the service provider.

Genuity customers are still missing performance monitoring tools. If they want to know monthly latency and packet-loss statistics on Genuity's network, they must request that information from the ISP. If Genuity missed any of its SLAs, the user has to contact the ISP and request the credit due. Without a site that lets users easily check to see if their ISP is living up to its guarantees, ISPs should offer customers automatic credits, experts say. UUNET is the only ISP that is offering such automatic credits.

frame have the benefit of alerting both the customer and the service provider of a potential problem when the consequences are few and the parties can act in a proactive manner to make adjustments

The frequent sharing of information promotes a sense of partnership between the respective parties. This kind of relationship allows the two parties to focus on problem resolution rather than finger pointing and retribution. Proactive metrics, however, means that there is constant monitoring of the metrics (and of the service itself).

How Many SLAs Do I Need?

Ideally, a single end-to-end SLA covers all aspects of ASP customer service. This guarantees customers efficient access to applications when needed. Sometimes, a customer might work with several service providers and need as many as four SLAs to guarantee service.

Network SLA. Covers the network connection between the customer and the ASP. Here, a network service provider (NSP) agrees on a suitable service level agreement for delivery of IP (Internet Protocol) services to a business customer.

Hosting SLA. Covers the hosting services provided to the ASP. The ASP delivery model often mandates that hardware be hosted or collocated with a third party.

Application SLA. Addresses the measurement of application performance. The ASP delineates the domain of its responsibility, service classes to be offered, and parameters of performance and formulates the calculation of performance and penalties (if deemed necessary) to be imposed for failure to meet agreed-on service levels.

Customer care/help desk SLAs. The terms *customer care* and *help desk* refer to a point of contact for customers who seek point-solution assistance. For an ASP, customer care is emerging as the means by which customers (and often their nontechnical, end-user employees) obtain answers to inquiries about service options and upgrades and otherwise address the nontechnical aspects of customer services. The traditional help desk provides technical support for end users.

Good metrics will be carefully defined and have a goal or target. In addition, the SLA should also specify minimum acceptable levels below which a remedy will be called for.

Remedies

Should a problem arise for which remedy has been specified in the service level agreement, then both parties will understand the appropriate course of action. In some cases, though, remedies are specified that are vague, inappropriate, or based on measures that are difficult to clearly gauge. Thus, if remedies are to be specified in an SLA, the following seven principles should be followed so that both the customer and the service provider will enjoy a better relationship, have faster trouble recovery, and be more mutually beneficial (ASP Industry Consortium 2000).

Objective. All measures and their associated remedies should be based on facts and not perception-based service measurements—for example, surveys and interviews. Any service metric should not be too detailed or too complex. Objective, well-thought-out, easy-to-understand service metrics and remedies remain the goal for both parties.

Visible. A remedy that is visible will attract the attention of project leaders and decision makers on both sides. An effective remedy will address important or constant failures that adversely affect the customer of the service provider. Both sides need to focus on making things better rather than documenting how bad things are.

Necessary. Customers want a service to work as advertised, period. A remedy that the customer does not recognize, appreciate, and demand is not effective and thus is not necessary.

An effective remedy will connect visibility to measurable failures that have a business impact important to the customer. The goal is to have a remedy that is necessary so that both the customer and the service provider can move ahead once the inevitable problem or crisis will arise.

Proportional. Common sense would suggest that an effective remedy would fit the severity of that fault that triggers it. Some service providers employ a "one size fits all" solution to a remedy—for example, one hour of credit for one hour of downtime. This approach falsely assumes that, without the service, the customer simply returns to conducting business in a manual mode or finds other things to do. This ignores the reality that the customer now relies on the service to conduct business.

Continuity. Any remedy must not be so severe that it will discourage the service provider from continuing to provide services to the customer. Remedies must encourage the business relationship to continue after the immediate crisis has passed.

A service provider will typically act as an invisible force to enhance the customer's IT infrastructure. This makes presenting the value of the services offered difficult to convey. If the customer does not understand the value the service provider adds, the customer will want less performance at a lower price. And a customer who attempts to use a remedy as a punishment is not committed to building a lasting relationship.

Creative. Remedies do not have to be financial-based responses. In reality, any remedy should be viewed as a response to infrequent special circumstances. A creative remedy might involve having the service provider company president call his or her counterpart in the customer's organization. Other creative approaches might involve the service provider acknowledging the problem and apologizing, escalating the problem to higher levels within both organizations, involving a trouble shooting team in both organizations, acknowledging that working together collaboratively on system enhancements or new products can be beneficial for both parties, and so forth.

Balance. Finally, any remedy must answer the question, "What remedy is appropriate for a specific fault?" Ensuring that both parties are comfortable with any remedies will ensure that the relationship is one that will endure for a number of years; in other words, it is a win-win relationship.

SLA agreements will generally balance risk with reward, protecting the provider from service failures outside of its control or rewarding it for assuming risk over which it may not have direct control. Generally speaking, an SLA that covers only the services over which the service provider has direct control will be much more cost-effective than one that attempts to make the SP responsible for every eventuality, like acts of God or nuclear annihilation. Service provider customers should seriously consider all points along the service chain and determine those that may result eventually in suspension or invalidation of the SLA. Potential triggers include the following:

- Actions of third parties, like failure or disruption by telecommunication companies or data storage providers, that limit a customer's access to the service provider.
- Outsourced maintenance providers.
- Disruptions in service due to maintenance issues on the customer's network that are serviced by a third-party provider.
- Customer contractors.
- Any disruption in service attributable to any customer or third-party contractor (construction crews, utility crews, and so forth).
- Internal infrastructure failures.
- Any disruption attributable to the customer's IT infrastructure, from system failures to system incapacity to handle traffic and communication requirements, and so forth.
- Customization of software and/or hardware components.

Unless specified in the SLA and service contract, most service providers will not be responsible for service disruptions or problems due to customer's customization of hosted software programs and services.

Dispute Resolution

A contract that clearly outlines the rights and obligations of the parties significantly reduces the scope for disagreement to arise in the course of the parties' business relationship. The source of the largest number of disputes is likely to be the gap between the actual performance by a service provider and the performance expected by the end user/customer, based on the terms of the underlying SLA. Thus, clear, well-negotiated SLAs that are comprehensive and well drafted are fundamental to minimizing the risk of disputes.

Don't assume that hiring an xSP means that you can forget about technology issues. According to Sara Plath, VP of About.com, continued communications between both parties is essential. "People shouldn't think this goes on automatic pilot," she says. "It takes proactive communication to make your needs, schedule, and business priorities understood." (Tweney 2001)

Even the most carefully drafted SLA will not prevent disputes between the parties from arising. There are always unforeseen circumstances or matters on which the parties genuinely cannot agree. In such a case, the parties will need to resort to a dispute resolution mechanism. It is advisable, therefore, to have a separate clause referring to dispute resolution. SLA agreements will generally balance risk with reward, protecting the provider from service failures outside of his or her control or rewarding him or her for assuming risk over which he or she may not have direct control.

Generally speaking, an SLA that covers only the services over which the service provider has direct control will be much more cost effective than one that attempts to make the xSP responsible for every eventuality. xSP customers should seriously consider all points along the service chain and determine which may result in suspension or invalidation of the SLA.

A reality of commercial relationships is that disputes do arise. Because of the one-to-many delivery model, a service provider's exposure to liability may be multiplied several-fold. Particularly, in an international relationship, the commercial and legal risks can increase significantly, as does the potential for conflict due to language barriers, different legal codes, and commercial cultures.

Recognizing this, the ASP Industry Consortium with the assistance of the World Intellectual Property Organization Arbitration and Mediation Center, based in Geneva, Switzerland, prepared a set of dispute avoidance and resolution guidelines specifically tailored to reflect ASP business models. While this initiative will likely not be of immediate benefit to most businesses and organizations, it clearly will assist multinational organizations.

Because most parties to a dispute are interested in a quick and fair resolution, alternatives other than litigation exist, as shown in Table 8.3.

The parties typically choose a method for dispute resolution based on the contractual relationship, the likely amount of conflict, and the identity of the parties. The advantages for using an alternative dispute resolution process include the following:

Table 8.3 Alternative Dispute Resolution Options

LEAST FORMAL		
↑	Negotiation	An informal process where the parties attempt to resolve their differences through direct interaction. A neutral third party may act as a facilitator in some cases.
	Settlement counsel	The parties retain legal counsel who is given a mandate to resolve the dispute. Settlement counsels are typically not permitted to participate in any subsequent legal proceedings if the attempts at settlement fail.
	Mediation	A voluntary, nonbinding, and confidential procedure in which a neutral intermediary assists the parties to reach a settlement. In some cases, the intermediary will provide the two parties with an evaluation of the issues and a recommended settlement.
	Mini-trial	A private, confidential, nonbinding procedure that takes the form of a "mock trial" in which the parties make a presentation to a panel of neutral third parties.
	Early neutral evaluation	Private, confidential, nonbinding voluntary procedures in which the parties submit the issues to a third-party evaluator. The evaluator applies all of the legal principles that would be used in the event of formal litigation.
	Neutral, fact-finding expert	A private, voluntary, nonbinding procedure in which the parties submit specialized issues to an expert for a neutral evaluation of facts.
	Ombudsperson	A fact-finder used to investigate and assist in resolving grievances and complaints. Generally, this individual will make a nonbinding report of the issues and make a recommendation to resolve the issue.
	Dispute review board	A private, voluntary procedure in which an informed standing group of experts can quickly deal with disputes as they arise. This approach is often used in construction and in high-value outsourcing agreements. The findings of the board can be binding or advisory.
	Arbitration	A private, voluntary procedure involving the application of rights, in accordance with applicable law, by one or more arbitrators who have the power to render a decision. The decision can be binding or advisory.
↓	Litigation	Formal, public process for resolving disputes before a court of appropriate legal jurisdiction.
MOST FORMAL		

Adapted from ASP Industry Consortium, 2000.

Speed. In the service provider environment, getting any dispute resolved quickly and amicably is critical because the service provider is providing a service on which the business or organization depends. The premise that both parties have something to gain with a quick resolution will usually mean cooperation to resolve the difficulty and move on. The goal is a timely resolution that both parties can live with—in other words, a win-win solution. Litigation obviously takes time several years in most cases), is expensive, and by its very nature ensures that one of the parties is declared the "loser."

Cost savings. An early settlement will normally result in substantial cost savings for both parties. Even arbitration can often take considerable time and money to reach a conclusion.

Privacy and confidentiality. A private resolution of a dispute is often in the best interests of both parties. And, the lower the dispute's profile, the greater the likelihood that the two parties will be able to resume normal business operations.

Expert decision makers. The issues surrounding a service provider dispute will more than likely involve technology and technical issues. The parties thus have the opportunity to involve an expert neutral party who is knowledgeable about the business, technical, and legal issues that may be involved in the dispute. The involvement of a neutral expert will lead to valuable savings of time and money.

Preservation of business relationships. Because the service provider model is focused on the delivery of a valuable service, quickly resolving any dispute will likely lead to a continued and harmonious relationship between the two parties. An alternative dispute resolution process allows the lines of communication between the two parties to remain open. It would not be very helpful to have one of the parties say "have your lawyer talk to my lawyer and we will see you in court."

Predictability of outcome. With an alternative dispute resolution process, the resolution is based on the willingness of the two parties to compromise, rather than having a solution forced on them. The more formal approach of using litigation or arbitration is typically characterized as an "all-or-nothing" result or having the arbitrator attempting to achieve a "solomonic" decision.

Creative business-driven solutions. Using an alternative dispute resolution process, it is possible to achieve a win-win resolution that might not be available if the more formal process were used. In some cases, the top executives of the two parties will be involved, a factor that encourages more business-based rather than legalistic resolutions.

Procedure flexibility and party control. Both the service provider and customer are free to chose an alternative dispute resolution procedure that is most suitable for meeting their respective business objectives and timeframe. If need be, the parties can refine the process by narrowing the factual and legal issues at hand.

Business disruption. While an alternative dispute resolution process does require senior management resources, the amount of time and staff resources using this approach pales in comparison to the disruptive and time-consuming effect of litigation.

Jurisdiction issues. An alternative dispute resolution procedure can eliminate one of the most significant problems likely to emerge in service provider disputes—that of jurisdiction. It eliminates the possibility that one party may have to defend its interests in potentially inconvenient forums.

If the two parties are really interested in quickly resolving any issue, they will utilize a less formal approach to dispute resolution or perhaps a combination of approaches—for example, direct negotiation between the president of the customer's company and the president of the service provider. If needed, these two individuals could then agree to employ a neutral expert.

Conclusion

Although the service provider industry is facing multiple challenges lately, the SLA is still the best instrument to establish long-lasting win-win relationships between service providers and their customers. All it takes is an environment that is open for suggestions and continuous improvements, an environment that acknowledges its strengths and its weaknesses. Besides this attitude for openness, a solid knowledge base is needed about possibilities and impossibilities regarding the offered and provided levels of services. Both the service provider and the customer can benefit from a high-quality service as agreed on in a clearly written service level agreement that establishes expectations for both parties.

Outsourcing Blunders

Outsourcing mistakes seem to repeat themselves with enough frequency that managers should be alerted (Paul 2001). Among the five top outsourcing blunders are:

1. Don't get entangled in a long-term contract.
2. Don't let your responsibilities collide with those of the outsourcer.
3. Don't neglect to measure success (or failure).
4. Don't be a control freak.
5. Don't bet on a dark horse.

Sample SLA Agreement

Here's a sample of an ISP service level agreement highlighting key areas of mutual concern for the ISP as well as the business customer.

Skipper Internet Services Inc. provides many services to its subscribers through its system including dial-up access to the Internet, World Wide Web page hosting, and USENET discussion groups. Skipper has certain legal and ethical responsibilities regarding the use of its computer network and equipment involved in these services. Skipper does not and cannot control the content, quality, or accuracy of information available through its system or over the Internet in general. These Terms of Service set forth the basic rules, which apply to Skipper's services and use of its system. Skipper may change these Terms of Service in the future upon notice published online or otherwise provided by Skipper.

BY USING SKIPPER'S SERVICES AND SYSTEM, A SUBSCRIBER AGREES TO COMPLY WITH AND TO BE LEGALLY BOUND BY THE TERMS OF SERVICE AS PUBLISHED ONLINE OR OTHERWISE AVAILABLE FROM SKIPPER FROM TIME TO TIME. If the Terms of Service, Skipper's services, system, or pricing is or becomes unacceptable to a subscriber, the subscriber's only right shall be to terminate its account in accordance with the Section labeled "Suspension & Cancellation."

Skipper's general policy is to act as a neutral provider of access to the global Internet in all its diversity. Skipper has specific ethical concerns regarding the use of its computers detailed below. Skipper reserves the right to suspend or cancel a customer's access to any or all services provided by Skipper when Skipper decides, in its sole discretion, that the account has been inappropriately used.

Lawful Use of Service

Skipper's system and services may be used only for lawful purposes and in a manner in which Skipper believes, in its sole discretion, to be consistent with the rights of other Skipper subscribers and third parties. While Skipper is not responsible for the content of hosted Web sites, content on all Skipper-hosted Web sites must comply with all federal, state, and local laws and must not infringe the rights of any third party. Skipper's services and system may be used only for lawful purposes and consistent with all rights of other parties. Without limiting the foregoing, Skipper's services and system shall not be used in a manner that would violate any law or infringe any copyright, trademark, trade secret, right of publicity, privacy right, or any other right of any person or entity or for the purpose of transmitting or storing of material that is obscene, libelous, or defamatory. Use and access to other networks through Skipper's system must comply with the rules for such other networks.

Determination of a violation will be made at the sole discretion of Skipper, and Skipper, in its sole discretion, will determine what action will be taken in response to a violation on a case-by-case basis. Skipper reserves the right to release the usernames of customers involved in violations of the foregoing to system administrators at other providers, in order to assist them in resolving disruptions and security incidents, and to valid law enforcement authorities investigating illegal activities. Subscriber agrees to reimburse Skipper for all legal costs, personnel costs, and processing costs associated with assisting law enforcement in the investigation of illegal activities.

Modifications to Service

The services provided by Skipper and Skipper's system are expected to change from time to time. Skipper reserves the right to change any service offered or the features of any service offered or its system without notice, including changes to access and use procedures, such as idle disconnections, and system hardware and software.

Payment Terms

A subscriber must pay fees per Skipper's rate schedule in effect from time to time as a condition to obtaining access to Skipper's services and system. A subscriber must also pay any sales, use, or like taxes. If the payment method is by credit or debit card and payment is not received by Skipper from the card issuer or its agents, the subscriber agrees to pay all amounts due on demand by Skipper. Rate changes will be effective when published online or otherwise provided to subscribers. All Skipper service charges are due in advance of the service. Payments not received on the due date are considered delinquent and are subject to immediate suspension. Payments not made within 30 days of original billing date are subject to immediate termination without notice. Monthly charges will not be prorated.

Refund Policy

If an account is cancelled within 14 days of the initial sign-up date, the customer is entitled to a refund of some of or the entire amount charged. If payment is by credit card, the customer is entitled to a full refund, consisting of the setup fee and first-month charge, credited to the credit card. If payment is by check or refund by check is requested, the customer is entitled to a full refund, consisting of the setup fee and first-month charge, less a $20 service charge for processing.

Acceptable Use

Skipper recognizes three areas of use: what a Skipper customer does with his or her own computer equipment; what a Skipper customer does with his or her Skipper account; and what a customer does with his or her privileges on Skipper computer equipment (mail server, Web server, and so forth).

Skipper has no authority or desire to determine how someone uses his or her own computer equipment. Skipper has some responsibility for how someone uses his or her Skipper account and significant responsibility for how someone uses Skipper's computers.

Please note, Skipper reserves the right to cancel any account at any time for issues related to:

Connectivity. Each subscriber account is limited to one single dial-up connection at any one time. It is the responsibility of the subscriber to keep the password secure. Legitimate passwords are between six and eight characters in length, in all lowercase, and are not part of any recognizable word found in any dictionary.

Subscriber is allowed unlimited, on-demand access to Skipper's systems or service. Skipper's dial-up connections are not provided on a dedicated basis. Any subscriber that is consistently connected to Skipper's system for periods of eight hours or more shall be subject to having its account placed under suspension and/or terminated.

Subscriber is responsible for all use or misuse, with or without subscriber's knowledge or consent, of the Skipper account.

Email confidentiality. Electronic mail passes through multiple mail servers on the Internet as it passes from source to destination. One can never be guaranteed privacy from every possible mail server; therefore, someone seeking total privacy should use some encryption scheme to render messages unreadable by eavesdroppers.

Skipper treats email messages as private. Exceptions are those permitted by law, including under the Electronic Communications Privacy Act of 1986 (the "ECPA"). The ECPA permits Skipper limited ability to intercept and/or disclose electronic messages, including, for example (i) as necessary to operate the system or protect Skipper's rights or property, (ii) upon legal demand (court orders, warrants, subpoenas) or (iii) where Skipper receives information inadvertently that appears to pertain to the commission of a crime. Users should be aware that electronic messages may be intercepted lawfully or unlawfully outside of Skipper's system. In addition, although Skipper has implemented certain security measures, Skipper cannot guarantee that its system or stored data of a subscriber will be free from unauthorized intrusion or otherwise guaranty the privacy of information of any user.

Limits on disk space usage. Skipper provides as an added benefit to its dial-up users limited access to certain Skipper server computers. This benefit typically consists of email access, World Wide Web page hosting, and telnet access to a wide range of applications. Skipper dial-up users are subject to a limit of 5MB of disk space (10MB for Virtual Host Accounts) for all disk usage, including incoming mail files and personal Web pages. Skipper reserves the right to remove files that exceed this limit. The customer is responsible for keeping backups of customer files stored on Skipper computers.

Transfer refers to the amount of data your Web site sends to the browser. Excess transfer costs are 25 cents per megabyte. We reserve the right either to remove your Web site or to bill for excess data transfer.

Interpretation

These Terms of Service supersede all other written and oral communications or agreements with regard to the subject matter. A waiver or modification of these Terms of Service shall only be effective if in a writing signed by an authorized officer of Skipper. These Terms of Service shall be governed by and construed in accordance with the laws of the state of ___ without regard to choice or conflict of law principles. Any legal action or proceeding arising under or relating to the Agreement shall be brought in the federal or state courts of the state of ___, and the parties hereby consent to personal jurisdiction and venue therein. If any provision of these terms and conditions is found to be unenforceable or invalid, the remaining provisions shall been enforceable and valid to the greatest extent permitted law.

CHAPTER 9

Concerns about Using a Service Provider

A recent survey conducted by the Information Technology Association of America found the actual benefits for using an xSP service were significant. Among these benefits were the following:

- Gaining access to high-end applications
- Alleviating the shortage of IT personnel
- Providing a guaranteed performance/uptime
- Increasing flexibility for the organization
- Reducing initial capital outlay
- Lowering IT costs over time
- Reducing time of implementation
- Improving security (ITAA 2000)

Yet, despite these significant benefits, organizations that are using an xSP, as well as those that are considering using an xSP, typically have a number of concerns. A recent survey of potential xSP customers suggests that these concerns are focused on the topics of quality of service, security, cost, and speed of implementation, as shown in Table 9.1.

Table 9.1 List of Concerns about xSPs

RANK	FACTOR
1	Guaranteed reliable service
2	Security
3	Professional business knowledge
4	Total cost of ownership
5	Predictable fees
6	Scalability to meet business growth
7	Speed of implementation
8	Custom reporting
9	Access to new technology
10	Amount of customization required

Reliable Service

System reliability is often expressed as a percentage of uptime, for example 99.9 percent. Adding one "9" to a guaranteed level of service can add significant dollars to the contract. The importance of recognizing the implications of different levels of system availability will have on a business must be understood prior to starting to negotiate a service level agreement. Yet, the implications of an Internet e-commerce Web site or an application(s) that is unavailable for staff members can not be overemphasized. The consequences of downtime can be reflected in at least four ways:

Lost productivity. If an application or system is unavailable to an organization's staff members, then all or some of them will have their productivity significantly lowered until the service is available again. Consider an organization with 250 staff with an average employee cost of $40 per hour (with benefits). This organization generates some $50 million in annual revenues (revenues per employee would be roughly equivalent to $24,000 per hour). Thus, one hour of system downtime has a financial impact of $10,000 of lost productivity for the organization's staff members. A recent study by The Standish Group found that the average cost for planned downtime for ERP, supply chain, and e-commerce applications was $7,500 per minute. Unplanned outages obviously would cost even more.

Lost revenues. A business might have an Internet site that allows customers to conduct financial transactions—for example, buying and selling shares of stock. Some of these firms have suffered system downtime, and the business press has suggested that lost revenues might be as much as $15 million in a 15-minute period—or $60 million in a one-hour period.

Reduced market capitalization. Should an Internet site experience system downtime, then the financial marketplace might exact a significant price. System reliability problems experienced by Yahoo! and eBay resulted in a sharp reduction in market capitalization in prior years.

Low switching costs. Should a customer attempting to connect to an Internet Web site to conduct business experience problems due to system reliability problems, then the customer can easily ("one click") select a competing Web site to complete the transaction immediately. This will, in turn, result in reduced revenues, as noted previously.

The key to ensuring a scalable Web site that can handle the average and peak volume of transactions in a reliable manner while at the same time ensuring the security of the transaction is to have the necessary computer equipment and software in place to do the job. One of the keys to providing both security and reliability is that the Web site be located in a state-of-the-art data center.

The Data Center

The application software for the xSP service sits on one or more servers located at a data center. xSPs have three options with regard to data centers:

- The xSP provider could build its own.
- The xSP provider could lease space with a hosted service provider, often times called collocation.
- The xSP provider could use a managed service provider for data center services.

One of the advantages with contracting for data center services is that the application software can reside in two or more geographically dispersed locations, for example, on the East and West Coasts of the United States.

There are a number of issues associated with a data center that need to be addressed (see Table 9.2). Aside from the obvious concerns of physical security and environmental controls, it is important to understand that the data center needs to have fiber optic connections to the backbone of the Internet to minimize response times experienced by end users using the xSP service. Typically redundant data communication lines (e.g., OC-3 and/or OC-12 connections) are used to ensure the quickest possible path to the Internet's backbone and provide a backup should a line fail for some reason. The implications for fiber optical connections is to minimize the number of "hops" or links that a transaction must take to move from point A to point B on the

Internet. For the end user, the fewer the hops, the faster the response time he or she will experience.

As the bandwidth increases for every segment of the Internet, whether a connection from a business to an ISP, an ISP to the backbone of the Internet, or the Internet backbone itself, the better the overall performance that will be experienced by the end user. Obviously, applications designed to run over the Internet will perform better than those that are using other technologies. In some cases, the internal networking infrastructure of many small and medium-sized organizations is insufficient to utilize an xSP solution and will thus need to be upgraded.

Third parties that provide data center services include, among others, Exodus, Qwest, Digex, and NaviSite. In some cases, the staff monitoring the performance of the server(s) for an xSP might be staff from the data center provider or they may be part of the xSP's staff.

Table 9.2 Data Center Checklist

ISSUE	FACTORS
Physical Security	Access control (cards, keys, fingerprint scanners, retinal eye scanners, etc.) Human security guards—24 x 7 Internal & external cameras Security logs
Environmental Controls	Internal control, e.g., temperature control, humidity control External control, e.g., stabilized computer racks Flood protection Fire protection sensors & alarms
Electrical Power	Uninterruptible power supply Back-up diesel generators
Internal Data Center Connectivity/ Bandwidth	Minimal bandwidth requirements have been established (e.g., Gigabit Ethernet)
Network Connectivity	Proximity to Network Service Provider Internet backbone Multiple paths to the Internet? Access to multiple Internet backbone providers? Able to connect to dedicated leased lines Does the data center proactively measure and diagnose connectivity and performance issues? How is traffic prioritized and what happens during periods of congestion? Are there escalation procedures for connectivity and performance problems?

Network Infrastructure

An xSP may employ a number of networks and technologies to connect customers to hosted application servers or to the Internet. In some cases, dedicated leased lines and frame relay technology may be used to provide a high degree of security and performance protection/bandwidth guarantees. The Internet is also a popular means of service delivery, as it is ubiquitous and universally accessible, regardless of customer access technology (e.g., dial-up line, cable modem, leased line, frame relay, and so forth).

Because no one-service provider owns the Internet, it is virtually impossible to guarantee transaction response times. Thus, many data centers have fiber optic links to multiple Internet backbone providers (e.g., AT&T, Sprint, MCI, UUNet, among others) to ensure the best possible response times or to route the Internet traffic on the backbone used by an organization's ISP.

Table 9.2 *Continued*

ISSUE	FACTORS
Workspace	Adequate space for racks of servers, disk drives & other associated computer equipment Growth space Storage space Offices/Conference rooms
Server Hardware	Servers, operating systems supported
Network Security	Firewalls installed Antivirus software used Virtual private networks used Intrusion detection and monitoring
Management Services	Installation of operating system upgrades, database management system upgrades, repair or replacement of defective equipment Written policies and procedures Reboot of systems Database backups Disaster recovery plans Background check of employees Security audit regularly performed by an outside 3rd party, authoritative group Results of the security audit shared regularly with all customers
Site Mirroring	If a data center experiences a major problem as is down for an extended period of time, where will customers receive their data center services?

Security Concerns

Security concerns are one of the primary factors preventing IT managers from adopting xSP services. Security cannot be viewed from a single point in time or focus on a single device; rather, it is an ongoing process. Security must be provided at each and every point of connectivity with the WAN, regardless of the technology employed, to prevent unauthorized entry and access to an organization's internal data. Using secure sockets layer (SSL) allows data to be encrypted, but it is just one tool that should be employed to ensure secure transactions via the Internet.

The application software itself should also have security built into it so that each user is able to access only specific modules or selected portions of a module, depending upon his or her job level and responsibilities. This application-specific level of security is sometimes called "sandbox security" because the user is restricted to a specific sandbox in which to play.

The Computer Security Institute conducts an annual "Computer Crime and Security Survey" with the assistance of the Federal Bureau of Investigation. Highlights of the 2001 survey, with a sample size of 538 organizations, primarily large companies and federal government agencies, include the following:

- Eighty-five percent of the respondents detected computer security breaches within the last year.
- Sixty-four percent indicated that they had suffered financial losses as a result of the computer breaches.
- Thirty-five percent of the respondents indicated that the value of their financial losses totals some $377 million. The average value of loss for each type of breach is shown in Figure 9.1.
- The primary loss occurred as a result of the theft of proprietary information, followed by financial fraud.
- Not surprisingly, 70 percent of the respondents indicated their Internet connection as the most frequent point of attack; see Figure 9.2.
- Fifty-eight percent indicated they had experienced 10 or more incidents.
- And, 78 percent of these organizations report denial of service attacks.

You can obtain a free copy of the "2001 Computer Crime and Security Survey" by visiting the Computer Security Institute at http://www.gocsi.com.

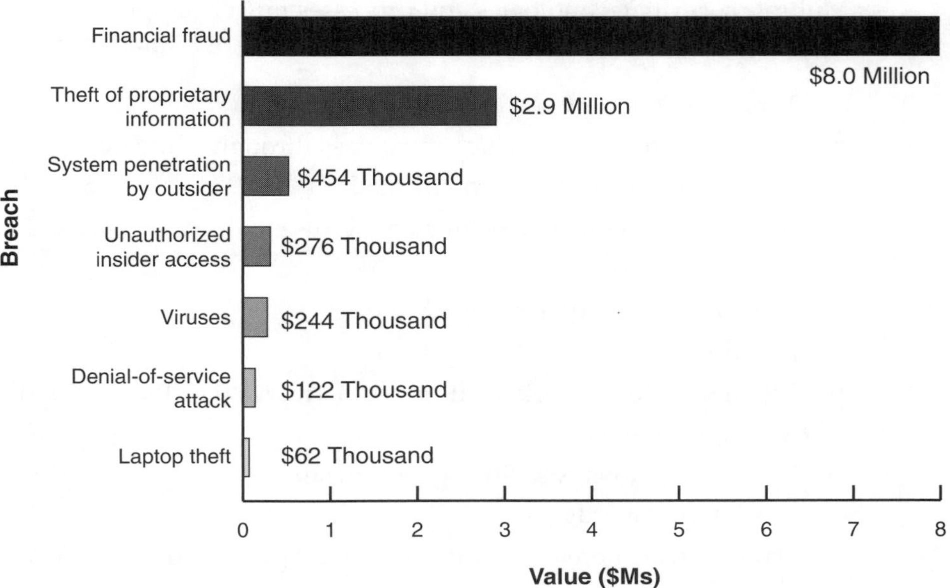

Figure 9.1 Value of security breaches.

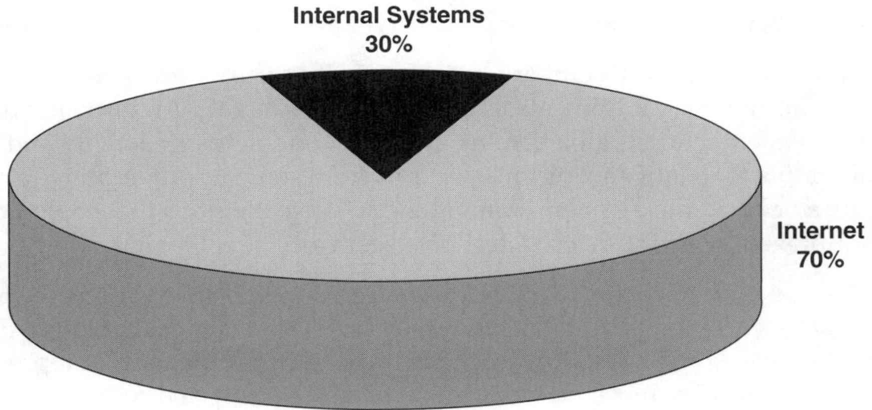

Figure 9.2 Security breach points.

Multiple security technologies and processes must be applied at various points in an xSP network. These include, but are not limited to, the following:

- Data center
- All WAN connections, which must pass through a firewall
- All users, who must be authenticated
- All data, which must be scanned for viruses
- The network
- Frame relays' permanent virtual circuit
- Leased lines
- Virtual private network for IP-based networks (i.e., the Internet)
- Customer premises
- WAN connections pass through a firewall
- User ID/passwords
- Virtual private networks tunnel and encryption initiation/termination

A virtual private network or VPN is a private network, in which the privacy is introduced by some method of virtualization, constructed within the public Internet. Thus, the connected computers behave as a seamless private network. A VPN increases the security between an end user and a remotely located application server using the Internet. In other words, within a larger public data network (the Internet), a smaller private space is carved out, using software that keeps that network's transactions private and secure. A VPN can be established for each session by the end user, or it can be transparent to the end user. A VPN uses a technology called IP tunneling that encrypts the transaction between the two points—the server and the desktop workstation.

Those within an xSP company responsible for security must be constantly monitoring and auditing all security points for threats. An intrusion detection system inspects all incoming and outbound network activity and attempts to identify suspicious patterns from someone attempting to compromise or hack into a system. Among the possible methods that could be employed by an intrusion detection system are the following:

Passive system versus reactive system. A passive system detects the potential security breach, logs it, and issues an alert. On the other hand, a reactive system will detect the security breach, log off the user, or reprogram the firewall to block network traffic from the suspected source.

Misuse detection versus anomaly detection. With misuse detection, the intrusion detection system analyzes the information and compares it to a large database of attack signatures and characteristics. This approach is particularly effective when a specific attack has already been documented, for example, an email virus. Using an anomaly intrusion detection system, the normal state of a network is defined. The anomaly detector monitors the network looking for anomalies.

Network-based versus host-based systems. A network-based intrusion detection system analyzes the individual packets moving within the system, looking for packets that may have been overlooked by the firewall. Using a host-based intrusion detection system means that the activity on each individual computer or server is analyzed.

Some of the big accounting firms have developed a security audit for e-commerce companies and xSPs. Having a security audit performed on a regular basis and posting the results of each audit should be a requirement for each xSP.

Due, in part, to the safeguards noted previously, today millions of financial transactions occur whereby credit card numbers are safely shared. In an increasingly network-centric world, simplistic and naïve fears about network security will, in time, wither away.

The British Standard 7799 (BS7799) is probably one of the most widely recognized security standards. Yet for all of its strengths, the BS7799 standard was not widely embraced because it lacked flexibility and often did not fit well with a number of IT environments.

The BS7799 standard did, however, form the foundation for the ISO 17799 standard, which is starting to gain acceptance within private industry and government agencies as well as in xSPs. Compliance with ISO 17799 allows an organization to demonstrate conformity with security policy development and implementation standards. Should an xSP be in compliance with ISO 17799 then it is helping its customers feel comfortable that their data is safe in a hosted environment.

TIP

Further information about ISO 17799, including the ability to download a copy of the standard itself, a directory of software that will assist in the preparation of an ISO 17799 audit, and other helpful resources can be found at http://www.iso17799software.com/.

Should an xSP comply with or be in the process of complying with the standard, then its customers will have greater confidence in the security of its data and associated transactions. The standard is composed of 10 major sections:

Business Continuity Planning. This section covers how to prevent interruptions to business activities and critical business processes from the effects of a major failure or disaster.

System Access Control. The section assists an organization in controlling access to information, preventing unauthorized access to computer systems, ensuring protection of networked services, and detecting unauthorized activities.

System Development and Maintenance. This section works to ensure that security is built into operational systems, prevent loss and misuse of user data, protect the confidentiality and integrity of information, and maintain the security of application system software and data.

Physical and Environmental Security. The goals of this section are to prevent unauthorized access to information and business premises, prevent the loss or damage of assets and interruption to business activities, and prevent the compromise or theft of information.

Compliance. The objectives of this section are to comply with the provisions of any criminal or civil law, statute, and regulatory or contractual obligation as they pertain to security and to maximize the effectiveness of the system audit process.

Personnel Security. This section focuses on efforts to minimize risks of human error, theft, fraud, or misuse of facilities and to minimize the damage from security incidents and malfunctions.

Security Organization. The objectives of this section are to manage information security within the organization, maintain the security of information assets accessed by third parties, and maintain responsibility when information processing has been outsourced.

Computer & Network Management. The goals of this section are to ensure the correct and secure operation of the information processing facilities, minimize the risk of system failures, protect the integrity of software and information, ensure the safeguarding of information in networks, and prevent the loss or misuse of information exchanged between organizations.

Asset Classification & Control. This section ensures that corporate assets and information assets receive an appropriate level of protection.

Security Policy. This section's objective is to provide management direction and support of information security.

The Center for Internet Security (http://www.cisecurity.org) suggests that there are additional security standards with which an xSP should be familiar and/or be compliant. These include the following:

- Internet Engineering Task Force (IETF) Site Security Handbook. Available at: http://www.ietf.org/rfc/rfc2196.txt?number=2196.
- Information Systems Audit and Control Association (ISACA). Available at: http://www.isaca.org/cobit.htm.

- Federal Information Systems Controls Audit Manual (FISCAM). Available at: http://www.gao.gov/policy/12_9_6.pdf.
- Generally Accepted System Security Principles (GASSP) developed by the International Information Security Foundation. Available at: http://www.auerbach-publications.com/white-papers/gassp.pdf.
- National Institute of Standards and Technology (NIST) Principles and Practices for Securing IT Systems. Available at: http://www.csra.nist.gov/publications/nistpubs/800-14/800-14.pdf.
- SysTrust Principles and Criteria for Systems Reliability. Available at: http://www.aicpa.org/assurance/systrust/edannoun.htm.

Assessing the Risks of Access to Information

Effective security for a business or organization requires a set of policies that specifies what the security policies are, plus a set of procedures and technologies that will implement these policies. Part of a security policy is a periodic review of the potential security risks.

- **Control e-risks by controlling e-content. Establish and enforce policies that govern the creation and content of email and Internet documents.**
- **Consult with your internal or external counsel to determine the best email retention and deletion policy for your company, then implement it consistently. Include an "empty mailbox" policy for employees. Remember, though, it is illegal to begin a document destruction campaign if pending litigation would be affected by it. Put your retention and deletion policies into place before trouble strikes.**
- **Educate your employees. Provide managers and staff with e-scenarios that could affect the well being of the company and the security of employees' jobs. Follow up with actions employees can take to help limit risks.**
- **Keep your eyes open to unusual or suspicious behavior on the part of employees and outsiders. The adage "better safe than sorry" is never truer than when applied to e-risks.**
- **Don't leave e-risk management to chance. Install monitoring and filtering software to control employees' email and Internet activity. Inform them that you are doing so and describe the risks they face for violating company policy.**
- **And remember that security requires vigilance—whether you have your own staff or a managed security service provider ensure this oversight (Flynn 2001).**

Authentication

In the xSP model, it is important to verify not only users of the system, but also the valid applications and network devices in the delivery model.

User identification. Practices used for authenticating users.

- Each user has a unique user identifier.
- Actions are correlated to users.
- All user IDs correlate to currently authorized users.
- Inactive user IDs are disabled.
- Users are required to authenticate.
- Access to the stored authentication data is restricted.
- Authentication data is protected when transmitted.
- Users have a limited number of allowed logon attempts.

Interprocess communication. Programs that interact with other programs, on the same machine or over a network connection, must be able to authenticate the peer. In addition, sessions should be timed out after a certain period of inactivity.

Access Control

Access control is the classification of resources, the separation of duties, and the implementation of a system that defines and enforces a relationship between resources, duties, and the user.

Discretionary access controls. Access is granted based on authorizations granted to a user.

Mandatory access controls. Access is granted based on classifications of data and an overall access policy determined by those classifications. Mandatory access controls are normally preferred over discretionary ones because it is systems administrators who control access and not users.

Location. Access to data or programs may need to be restricted based on physical or logical location.

Integrity

Integrity is the protection of applications and data from unauthorized modifications or interruptions in service. Applications and data must be protected from both malicious and accidental modification.

Viruses/Trojan horses. A Trojan horse is a software program that appears to be an innocent application, but when launched causes damage to your computer system. A virus is a similarly destructive program that has the added danger of being self-replicating. Risks include the following:

- Data files, operating systems, and software are all vulnerable to compromise of integrity by viruses and Trojan horse programs.
- HTML and other documents, such as Word files, can contain macro or script programs. Care must be taken when non-trusted parties can affect the content of these and similar documents.
- Systems should be developed so that data transmission via network, data bus, and so forth cannot be intercepted and passed on in an altered state. Authentication of the transmitter or receiver can help mitigate this risk.
- Implementation of secure network protocols helps protect against man-in-the-middle attacks.

Denial of service. A denial of service (DOS) attack attempts to flood target with thousands of legitimate looking transactions, eventually overwhelming the target computer's ability to cope with the volume of transactions.

Confidentiality. Confidentiality is the protection of applications and data from disclosure to unauthorized persons or programs.

Network monitoring. Network communications should be designed to prevent data and applications from being compromised by network "sniffers" and other passive network monitoring devices and systems.

Covert channels. Applications and operating systems should be designed so that separate business functions have limited visibility of one another. For example, if one user does not have authorization to determine if another user account exists on a system (perhaps read-access to a password file), then the login program should not be able to provide this information.

Object reuse. To the extent possible, disk space, memory, and other temporary storage should be "scrubbed" (that is, cleared) before reuse to guarantee that the previous contents cannot be recovered.

Traffic analysis. The ability to determine the frequency, timing, or amount of data transmitted or other resources may provide confidential information to an unauthorized party. As a general matter, users should not be able to determine how and when other users are in the system.

Nonrepudiation. Nonrepudiation is the ability to prove to a third party that a sender actually sent a message. In the ASP model, it is important to be able to reliably prove that a user of services cannot be denied that use.

Public key algorithms. Public key algorithms can be used to implement digital signatures as well as provide for encryption of message contents, using for example, VeriSign's Global Site Certificate technology. Is 128 bit encryption technology used?

Transaction security. Transactions that cross the Internet should use a variety of means to ensure their security. For example is secure sockets layer (SSL) technology or its equivalent used? Are transactions stored on separate servers from a Web site server?

Referee systems. Independent systems, perhaps those of a third party, should be used to referee transactions and provide nonrepudiation.

Accounting and Audit

Accounting and auditing systems maintain a record of system and user activity.

Accountability. To the extent possible, accounting and audit systems should track the activity of an individual using the application and also should produce tracking reports.

Reconstruction of events. An organization should be able to use the audit trail to determine how, when, and why a system event occurred.

Intrusion detection. Monitoring and management systems should detect anomalous use of system resources or events that occur outside of the designed chain of events.

Problem identification. Audit and accounting data may be used to isolate problems (other than intrusions) as they occur.

Proactive review of accounting and audit data. Logs and reports are normally reviewed proactively for signs of irregular activity.

Availability/Continuity of Operations

xSPs must plan and implement procedures to ensure that operations continue in case of hardware/software failures, natural disasters, or other unforeseen events.

Business impact assessment. This important step forces the xSP to consider all types of disasters and interruptions in service and to determine the business impact of each event.

Business continuity planning. A plan should be developed that outlines the procedures the xSP will use to minimize or remedy operational interruptions identified in the business impact assessment.

Risk mitigation. Systems should be developed to maximize the tolerance for faults. This can be accomplished in part by eliminating single points of failure and designing redundant systems.

Physical threats. The physical environment must be protected from threats such as fire, extreme humidity, emanations, earthquakes, and others.

Alternate power. Electrical conditioning and backup systems should be implemented that allow operation without dependence on the power utility. UPS (uninterruptible power supply) and diverse/redundant power feeds are recommended.

Response and recovery. The planned response of the xSP to a physical or network threat or the response to a physical disaster is crucial to how quickly the xSP can become operational and restore all of its customers back to normal operation. Keep in mind these concerns:

- Arrangements should be made for off-site tape and media storage.
- Critical personnel should be identified.

Physical Security

Physical security is the application of physical barriers and control procedures as preventive measures or counter-measures against threats to resources and sensitive information.

Site location and construction. Data center sites should be selected after considering items such as the local crime rate and whether the location is prone to flooding, earthquakes, and other natural disasters.

Physical access. Prevention of access to facilities should include multi-staged entry with multiple secured doors between public areas, such as a lobby, or any room housing wiring, computers, or network equipment.

Tape and media storage. Production media should be protected from unauthorized access. On-site and off-site backups should be protected from unauthorized access. Sensitive documentation (both hard and soft copies) should be located in a physically secure area. Unauthorized duplication of sensitive documentation is a high-risk exposure and should be prevented.

Professional Business Knowledge

If your service provider, especially an MSP or ASP, has staff with extensive experience and knowledge about your type of business—in other words, industry knowledge—then a customer can expect that the installation will proceed in a much more expeditious manner. In addition, the xSP can also make suggestions that would improve the return on investment.

The key to maximizing the potential returns from using the services of a service provider is to clearly understand the strengths and weaknesses of your organization and then employ the services of an xSP that will minimize or eliminate your identified weaknesses.

E-Security Update

As Internet commerce continues to soar thanks to emerging technologies like ASPs, cyber crime is increasing exponentially. According to a recent survey by research firm Meta Group Inc., 9 out of 10 companies and government organizations reported security breaches over a recent 12-month period. Of the 42 percent willing (or able) to quantify the damages and financial losses, the total ran to $265 million. And these are only the reported cases. Meta Group suggests that at least 50 percent of cyber crimes go unreported due to the potentially adverse publicity, embarrassment, and negative effect such disclosure would have on consumer and investor confidence. As more companies continue to embrace the Internet commerce channel, Meta Group reports that the private sector will see funding increases for information security controls and program costs, increasing by 25 percent to 30 percent by 2003/04 over current spending levels. (Passori 2000)

Total Cost of Ownership

Total cost of ownership (TCO) is a methodology designed to identify and measure components of IT expense beyond the initial cost of implementation. For example, there have been a number of published studies that have identified the total cost of ownership of a personal computer in an office environment. These studies indicate that the initial and recurring costs for maintain a desktop workstation on a network can exceed $10,000 per year. While the initial hardware costs may be less than 15 percent of the total the remaining costs accumulated when the personnel required to acquire, maintain, and update desktop applications and perform maintenance on the local area network are considered.

While TCO can be a useful tool to reduce ongoing costs by improving IT management practices, it will leave out some costs—for example, complexity costs, strategic factors, soft costs—and, more importantly, it totally ignores benefits that will accrue when a project is implemented.

The total cost of ownership approach does not recognize the benefit of volume discounts or the actual costs associated with attempting to support multiple vendors. A preferred approach that recognizes that IT projects have both costs and benefits that result in value for the organization will be presented in the next chapter.

Predictable Fees

Doing business with a service provider, because a long-term agreement is typically put in place, allows the customer to know with a fair degree of certainty what he or she can expect the total cost of ownership to be.

All of the charges are identified and known for some period of time into the future. Adjustments to the levels of service require an adjustment in the service level agreement that is signed by both parties. This predictability of costs is one of the attractive features for a company doing business with an xSP.

Scalability

Some medium-sized and larger businesses and organizations want to make sure that the xSP has the necessary system architecture in place in order to be able to scale or increase the number of users, as needed. Thus, as an application or service is rolled out across geographically dispersed locations within an organization, a scalable system ensures that there will not be a degradation in the quality of the service nor in the speed with which it is adopted by all members of the customer's organization.

Speed of Implementation

One of the strengths of the xSP model is that an organization can quickly begin to use an application. In-house implementation projects typically take five to nine months or longer, while an organization can start using an xSP service in a matter of days or weeks. This shortened implementation cycle is accomplished by providing to the customer a reduced set of decisions or options that he or she can make initially. In addition, the way in which some services are delivered are changed—for example, training is available via the Internet 24 × 7 rather than having employees attend an on-site training session. In most cases, on-site training is available as an optional, added-charge service.

Support Issues

As xSPs take on responsibility for hosting and managing applications, they must also take on the support role for these applications, essentially becoming the IT help desk for that application. Almost all xSPs require that an organization's IT department be responsible for maintaining the local area network and the connection to the ISP for Internet service, as well as resolving any problems related to the Web browser.

The xSP's help desk provides support relating to use of the software application(s). Usually the xSP allows customers to contact help desk personnel using the Internet, email, fax, and telephone. One of the superior features of Internet access to the help desk software, sometimes called customer relationship management software, is that the end user is able to quickly ask a question and the system will provide a response using its problem/resolution database. At this Web site for xSP customers, the user can also determine the status of a previously reported problem, participate in a chat room, and view tips on how to use the application in a more productive manner.

Custom Reporting

In addition to the variety of standard reports that are provided by the xSP, especially an ASP, for each application, the typical xSP may be able to provide custom reports for an additional fee.

Access to New Technology

Embracing the services of an xSP sometimes allows a organization to begin to use a new technology more quickly that has the potential of radically changing the way in which it does business. Given that the Internet has significantly speeded up the requirements for businesses and organizations to introduce new product and services into the marketplace, doing business on the Internet may provide a strategic advantage for the organization.

Amount of Customization Required

Most organizations believe, justifiably or not, that they have a number of unique requirements that will need to be met before they can achieve all of the benefits from outsourcing with an xSP. Customer organizations have two ways in which they can deal with this situation. First, they can note all of their unique requirements but hold any action on requesting the xSP to make changes to the software or levels of services being delivered until after the project has been implemented for a period of time—six months or so. After a period of time of actually using the new service, the customer organization may well decide to ignore some or all of its customized requirements.

Alternatively, the customer can request all of the changes that he or she wishes to have made. This will often drive the costs up significantly and delay the implementation process.

Conclusion

Clearly the Internet has shown that an organization does not need an application on a server or desktop. Yet, most organizations are still hesitant to give up too much too soon, especially mission-critical applications (Kearney 2000). Thus, a number of organizations that are using an xSP are using the service for niche applications—for example, reporting travel-related expenses.

But the reality is that most organizations will find that they will need to rely increasingly on outsourcing to xSPs. The secret is to select xSPs that will become partners in helping your organization succeed with its stated goals.

CHAPTER 10

Selecting Service Providers

Imagine, if you will, a work day that begins like any other. You sail through the morning's ablutions, zip through the comic pages of America's Greatest Newspaper, and attempt a quick email check before heading out. Your employer's email servers seem to be down, however. So, with a shrug, you chalk it up to a little rebooting action somewhere and head off to start the day. Then, suddenly, your pager, cell phone, and every other wired device vibrate with blazing beeps and piercing rings. Forget the reboot theory. Sometime, during the dark of night, your company's Internet service provider went out of business. Bit the dust. Kicked the can. Pulled the big plug.

And you, dear manager, are about to walk into the nightmare of all nightmares: an email-free office that also lacks all high-speed Internet access. Impossible, you say? Stop scoffing. Even if your organization hosts its own Web sites, manages its own email, and sprinkles holy water on the servers twice a month, you still are at risk. Just ask all those thousands of former business customers of NorthPoint Communications, the mega-ISP that ceased operations in March 2001 after declaring bankruptcy the previous January.

Vendor management, formerly known as strategic partner relationships, takes on a new sense of urgency in this ripening era of expense reductions and shrinking provider pools for outsourcing of value chain, supply chain, and customer relationship resources.

Tighter controls over vendors and their subcontractors can lead to optimized costs and leveraged business opportunities that might not have been possible 12 or even 6 months ago. And organizational strategic initiatives that depend on outsourced IT should confirm the viability of those vendors given the bloodied shakedown in the entire Internet industry.

Companies engaging service providers must validate that the agreed-on service levels are met. This may require internal systems or a third party to be engaged because today most service providers do not have sufficient systems to provide complete data.

The application service provider that wants to store your organization's human resources files could very well be reinventing itself into an xSP or a management service provider. Or your DSL provider could call it quits after fighting the good fight on regulatory battlegrounds for far too many months. Truly, the scenarios are endless.

An initial review of contract language for service levels, contingency plans, and future needs in light of current conditions facing all IT service providers would help mitigate risks of service failures, network disruptions, and data security breaches. It could also help protect critical, high-priority Web-enabled applications like email as revised corporate budgets are slashed even deeper.

So How Do You Start?

Create a business case for this service provider diligence that includes internal rate of return on investment as well as identifying all of the tangible and intangible costs. Include all planning, implementing, and managing costs.

Obtain business ownership and management sponsorship for this effort from the chief executive officer, chief operating officer, chief technology officer, or chief information officer, plus funding.

Create a Third-Party Vendor Task Force with representatives from the organization's or division's internal compliance, legal, and technology units as well as line of business contacts who manage the vendor relationship. If there is a small number of IT vendors, it may be extremely beneficial to include their representatives as well.

Prioritize business processes, projects, and initiatives affected by the effort. Set a reasonable schedule for completion with some built-in flexibility.

Develop a Task Force Deliverables Timeline including audit schedule, diligence reports, action plans, and, if necessary, implementation guidelines. Remember that the task force is traditionally a temporary tool and should not be considered a permanent group. Thus, the action plan will also need to consider whether a standing committee, team, or working group is required moving forward.

Create line-of-business awareness of the need to examine and update service provider vendor contracts through formal and informal channels. Emphasize the goals of maintaining customer satisfaction while reducing costs. One of the realities of business, and your service providers know this as well as you do, is that there are always less expensive options out there that may not be better, but they are cheaper.

Implement the project, with special emphasis on maintaining deadlines and budget controls.

Identify gaps and discrepancies in service level agreements, and mitigate risks. Engage all relative parties, but don't even try to include your organization's entire headcount. Respect boundaries as well, but if vendor cooperation levels are less than engaging, be honest about how important this exercise is to the future of the relationship.

Update and revise all contingency plans, including contact information, for possible future service providers and subcontractors, for every level of service disruptions, including vendor failures like that of NorthPoint.

Outline next steps, cognitive of best practices of industry peers and competitor best practices for your organization as well as the vendors participating in this exercise.

Present findings and recommendations to supervisory committees like executive councils or boards of directors. Elicit comments and work feedback into the findings.

Manage expectations on all sides. And there is only one valid and reasonable business expectation: no surprises.

Of course, none of us can prevent surprises. If we could, we would be using our paranormal abilities in other forums outside the workplace. But service providers should not be surprised that organizations expect their vendors to exceed their standards, not just match them with half-hearted lip service. Nor should they be surprised when a task force knocks on their door as part of its due diligence effort.

Service Provider Relationship Cycle

Like everything in business, the service provider relationship is a cyclical one with ups and downs. It has four phases:

Initiation phase. Here's where the service offerings of the service provider are marketed in all their shining glory as the customer's IT needs are examined and assessed. Financial concerns, including time to market and time to deploy as well as actual return on investment, should be key metrics as well as performance, security, and reliability standards. If early due diligence shows that this relationship will not satisfy the business needs or expectation of the end user, then that is the time to reassess the entire conversation. Any service level agreement should have the internal and/or external legal team's review before the contract is finalized (See Chapter 8 for more on service level agreements).

Installation phase. This is where the implementation of new technology standards and services begins. Some internal tasks are handed over to the service provider, and special care must be taken that no crucial processes are lost or damaged during this process. It is extremely important for the end user to demand monitoring and security performances reaching 100 percent reliability as the installation ramps up. It is also very important that the internal IT staff be given clear and explicit training within the new arena.

Execution phase. Here the service provider takes over all management of all services as stated in the SLA and its responsibilities. The internal staff is relieved of any and all support for these services, and it is theoretically free to focus on strategic IT issues. Management should expect regular updates and reports from the service provider on the performance, functionality, and security of the applications as outlined in the SLA. Management should also begin to note increases in time and cost savings as forecasted in its due diligence analysis.

Ending phase. All good things must come to an end. This phase covers the termination of the SLA and the change-over of the service provider responsibilities to the customer or to another service provider. The most important concern here is security matters, ensuring that the former service provider no longer has access to its ex-customer's data and that the data remains intact and safe.

Top 10 Questions to Ask Your Service Provider

As you enter the initiation phase with a service provider, here are 10 questions to ask the service provider before even looking at its service offerings:

1. What areas can you identify as needing improvement within our current IT organization? Be explicit.
2. How will your relationships with existing suppliers support our company's growth? What type of future relationships are you planning with other suppliers?
3. What roles do training and feedback play in your customer support practices?

4. How will you plan to manage SLA disputes and breaches? How will these resolutions be funded?
5. Outline your procedure for incident or problem reports.
6. What are your key performance indicators, effectiveness controls, security standards, and why?
7. What is your staff turnover rate? Future hiring plans?
8. What are the service provider's funding sources? Is the provider profitable?
9. What are the biographies of your top executive team?
10. References. References. And more references!

What to Expect from a Service Provider

Customers will develop high satisfaction levels with their service providers only when their expectation levels meet both IT and business demands. To create a valuable, long-term relationship with a customer, service providers must provide outstanding levels of the following items:

Service. Simply put, this is the consistent delivery of the highest-quality IT services available on the outsourcing market to date. If a customer starts to expect anything less, then it is time to find a new service provider.

Performance. Peer best practices and benchmarking of not only the customer's industry but of the service provider's particular offering should mold performance expectations for the IT services as well as the business process for the outsourced functions. Customers should expect, and indeed demand, to see immediate contributions from the service provider relationship to the business model. Promises of "Next Quarter" don't count. Nor does anything less than the delivery of implementation projects that are on time and within budget.

Customer support. The service provider's help desk must be able to meet not only the daily contractual arrangements, but also the long-term strategic needs of a customer. If a customer's business ramps up at warp speed, the service provider service offering must keep pace with the increase in volume. Clearly documented processes that are consistently followed will help create a stable flow of information on and offline. Retention of current customers due to high levels of satisfied service will do more for a service provider's bottom line than multiple acquisitions of new customers who soon disappear.

Security. Service providers of all species must convince their customers that the SP security exceeds all customer expectations. Remember, these efficient, cost-effective security precautions that support backups and real-time data replication also have to save businesses money in staff and infrastructure. We'll discuss security in greater detail in the individual chapters on service providers, but note that across the board, security is the key hurdle for all service providers to clear before any sale can be made.

Choosing an xSP is an important decision for any organization. This is particularly true because the organization will be dependent on the xSP for providing quality and reliable service. And for some organizations, this dependency is even greater because the organization is using one or more ASP services that provide mission-critical services (e.g., accounting, customer care, enterprise resource planning, and so forth).

The Planning Process

Before focusing on the specifics of selecting an xSP, a business or organization should take a step back and ensure that it has a good understanding of why it is considering using a service provider. The reasons some organizations will want to consider a service provider include the following:

- The organization can't afford a huge IT capital outlay at this time.
- IT isn't a core competency.
- The organization is finding it difficult to attract and retain IT staff.
- The organization needs to deploy applications rapidly.
- The organization needs to migrate from older to newer technology.
- The organization would like to reduce its technology budget.
- A start-up organization does not have the capital resources to make significant IT investments.
- The organization is growing rapidly and needs to scale its IT infrastructure quickly.
- The organization needs a flexible IT infrastructure due to mergers and acquisitions (Dewire 2000).

Some organizations will want to complete a planning process as a prelude to adopting a specific service provider. Whether the planning process is called strategic planning, direction planning or business planning or results in the preparation of a business plan, the end result is that the management team will know what is central or core to the range of services and products required by its customers. The issues that need to be addressed in any planning process include the following:

Service to customers. Should new services be added? Might an existing service or services be dropped? Can existing services be improved?

Products. Is the existing mix of products meeting the needs of our customers? Should we be refocusing our products in the light of a changing competitive arena?

Technology. Is the company's technology state-of-the-art? Is state-of-the-art important? Should the organization consider other technology options such as outsourcing or using a service provider?

Staff development. Are staff members rewarded for keeping their skills current? Is the business and IT department able to attract and retain skilled staff members? Is the compensation package adequate?

Facilities and space. Is existing space well used? Is the layout of space appropriate for staff given the range of services and functions performed? Is additional space needed?

As shown in Figure 10.1, which identifies the typical components of the planning process, the management team will be able to focus on how the library delivers its products and services to its customers. Among the technology options that should be considered to deliver services to its customers would be using an ASP service in lieu of continuing to use an in-house automated system.

A part of this strategic planning process should include a review of the existing state of technology within the organization. Categories should include both initial and ongoing costs:

- Planning and consulting
- Computer hardware and peripheral equipment—servers, workstations, printers
- Application and network software/licensing
- Cabling and telecommunications—wiring, network interface cards, hubs/routers/switches, leased lines, Internet connection
- Third-party software product licensing
- Security—firewall software, password authentication, proxy servers, and software
- Access to external databases and systems
- Training
- Support—staff salaries plus support agreements for software and hardware

With these costs in hand, it is then possible to begin to identify the financial savings that might be realized by using a service provider or switching service providers.

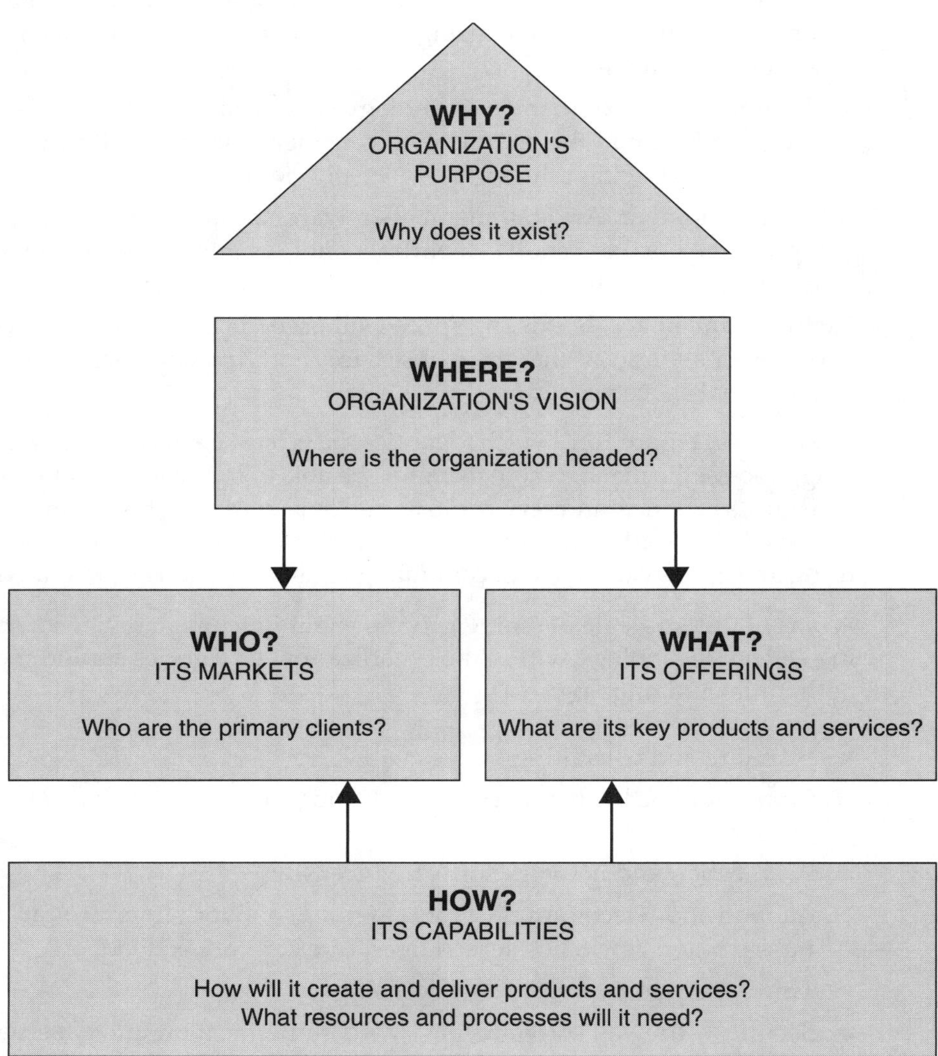

Figure 10.1 Planning framework.
Source: Adapted from Jones 2001

ASP Challenge!

Take the following ASP challenge to determine whether your business or organization might be a candidate for using an application service provider (Hall 2000). If you answer yes to one or more of the following issues, then you are a candidate for ASP services.

1. **Is your organization at a point of discontinuity?**
   a. **Are you facing a new application deployment?**
   b. **Are you trying to determine your e-business go-to-market strategy?**
   c. **How are you tying together your value and supply chains?**
2. **Do you feel managing IT should not be a core competency of your organization?**
3. **Do you need to deploy applications rapidly?**
   a. **Are you undergoing rapid growth?**
   b. **Do you need to scale your IT infrastructure quickly?**
4. **Do you feel your organization cannot afford a large IT capital outlay?**
   a. **Do you need to invest in other parts of your business, outside of IT?**
   b. **Is your organization a start-up that doesn't have cash on hand to make significant IT investments?**
5. **Does your organization need IT flexibility?**
   a. **Is your organization undergoing merger and acquisition activities?**
   b. **Does your organization want the flexibility to switch application environments in the future?**
6. **Does your organization have difficulty attracting and retaining IT staffs?**

Selection Process

An overview of the service provider selection process is shown in Figure 10.2. When considering the choice of a service provider, it is suggested that the business should follow this sequence:

1. *Initiate project.* Those involved in the selection process should be identified, review the selection process with the team members, and set expectations among the team members about the time and effort needed to participate.

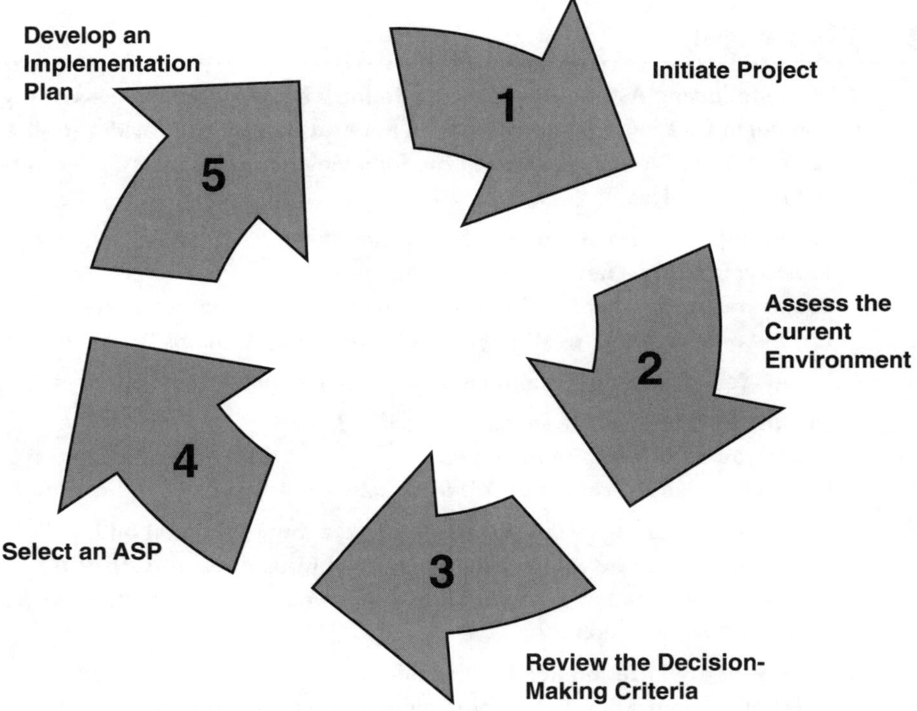

Figure 10.2 xSP solution process.

In some cases, there may be a time constraint that needs to be met by the process. Make sure that key decision makers within the organization are aware of the service provider options and are open to an xSP solution.

2. *Assess the current environment.*

   a. **Determine what service or range of services you could outsource.** These services might be an Internet connection, computer resource services, or applications. The applications could be current applications or new applications that will replace or complement your existing applications.

   Once the organization decides that it should examine the option of using an xSP service, then it will typically prepare a report documenting the analysis of the factors and costs associated with making a decision. This report typically includes a cost/benefit analysis as well as a qualitative analysis. Each of these topics is covered in greater detail at the end of this chapter.

Any investment decision can be categorized in terms of value and risk. Decisions involving a project with very high value and low risk probably do not require a detailed cost/benefit analysis because the decision to proceed is almost a given. Projects with low value and high risk similarly should have little analysis because they will likely be avoided so that resources are not wasted. Projects requiring more analysis are those where the value and the risk are almost evenly matched.

b. **Assess your internal IT capabilities.** What are the strengths and weaknesses of the IT staff and IT infrastructure? Are you trying to implement a new application quickly, reduce or eliminate the IT department to focus on more important aspects of the organization, and so forth.?

3. *Review the decision-making criteria.* Review the selection process plan. Decide whether to issue a formal, but brief, Request for Information or Request for Proposals document. Ask several xSP vendors for a product demonstration. (This usually can be conducted remotely using the Internet. After all, you will likely be using the vendor's service using the Internet as a data communications conduit.)

   Determine what qualities of the application and/or xSP provider are important. Determine what features are most important to you, and choose your xSP based on who has the strongest offering.

   If you are interested in obtaining access to multiple applications, then you will need to determine whether you are willing to do business with multiple xSPs or want to have a single point of accountability for all applications. When an organization uses different xSPs to host specific applications, there is the need to integrate these applications so that data can be shared. This might involve collocating different service provider solutions in the same data center, providing a common communications system among several xSPs, or implementing a message queuing system with geographically dispersed xSPs.

Among the factors that should be considered when making a decision about using an xSP service are these:

4. *Business issues.*

   a. **Expertise.** What are the provider's qualifications? Is the provider a dot-com start-up, or does it have some history as a company? Is it knowledgeable about one particular vertical industry, or is it attempting to appeal to a broad horizontal market? Does it have implementation experience with the applications it is representing (some xSPs are licensing software developed by other third-party vendors)? Obviously, any xSP needs staff that is experienced in implementing and using the application. Is the xSP firm developing its own infrastructure and data center or is this activity subcontracted to another firm? How many employees are employed by the xSP? Any layoffs lately? What is the technology experience and expertise of the xSP's senior management team?

b. **Financial stability.** Is the company large enough, and does it have the necessary financial resources to spend the necessary up-front capital to provide an xSP service to its customers? What is the company's reputation in the industry?

Industry experts have suggested that as many as 60 percent of the more than 1,000 ASPs will either go out of business or be acquired before the end of 2003 (Caulfield 2001). For example, Pandesic, a joint venture of Intel and SAP, announced that it was going out of business a short 18 months after being created, leaving more than 100 customers scrambling for a way off a sinking ship. A number of DSL service providers have also recently shut down without giving their customers too much notice.

c. **References.** Are there existing customers of the xSP service that a prospective customer can talk with to gain an understanding of their experiences?

d. **Termination.** Is there a graceful and relatively painless way to terminate the contract? Is it possible to cancel the agreement with reasonable notice—no more than 90 days?

5. *Software and Hardware.*

a. **Functionality.** Does the xSP service offer all of the software applications I want to rent? Is there a particular function(s) within each application that is crucial for a customer? Are there setup options to customize the application to fit the needs of the customer? Or, does the customer need to pay extra for customizing an application? How can a customer make suggestions for enhancing the software?

b. **Usability.** How easy is it to perform a variety of tasks that will be performed numerous times each day? Is the application using a Web browser user interface for all modules?

c. **Underlying technology.** Is the application stored on a dedicated server or shared on a server that provides access to multiple organizations? Note that dedicated servers cost more. Can the infrastructure grow to handle anticipated growth in the volume of transactions and/or size of the database? How are new software releases handled? How frequently are software releases installed?

6. *Operations.*
   a. **Availability.** Is the xSP service available for use all of the hours the customer is open? In all time zones, should the organization have branch offices on the East and West Coast? Branches in international cities? What happens if service degrades or if there is a system failure? Are there redundant paths from the data center to the Internet? What is the xSP's track record for downtimes? Are there multiple data centers? How physically secure are the data centers? Are there back-up generators in case of electrical brownouts or rolling blackouts?
   b. **Response times.** Will the xSP vendor be able to provide a service with acceptable response times across the Internet? Are leased lines an option? Are response times monitored and reported to the customer on a regular basis (Richter 2000)?
   c. **Ease of deployment.** How quickly can the organization start to use the application? Is training available via the Internet? Is on-site training optionally available? How easy is it to make changes to system set-up parameters? What is required of the customer's staff to get the application up and running? How easy is to import data? Can a business easily export records without asking, "Mother may I" from the service provider?
   d. **Commitment to quality service.** Is the xSP vendor staffed appropriately to respond to problems that will inevitably arise? What are the hours that the help desk is staffed? What happens after hours? Will the help desk staff handle both technical and application-specific questions? Can a customer log on to the Web to report a problem, discover the status of a previously reported problem? Are there any guaranteed times to solve problems? What happens if the Internet connection goes down at the customer's end? At the xSP's end? How does a customer request a software enhancement, and who votes on setting priorities? Clearly an xSP needs to assist the customer in aligning expectations in terms of what is wanted versus what can be delivered. This is usually down with a clear service level agreement.
7. *Service level agreement.*
   a. **SLA agreement.** Is a specified level of customer support identified? Is there a guarantee for system availability? What hours of the day and days of the week is the application available? Is it possible to tailor the SLA to meet the needs of your organization? What happens if the xSP vendor fails to meet one of several guarantees? Note that a small organization will, in most cases, be unable to modify a standard SLA.
   b. **Security.** Some industry observers suggest that security should be an organization's first concern (Wittman 2000). Who owns the data? How

does the xSP ensure the security of the customer's data? Is the data routinely backed up? Is a virtual private network or VPN used to ensure the security of each transaction? Can the customer choose to use a leased line in lieu of using the Internet? Does an outside third party perform a security audit on a regular basis? And the results of each audit should be available for the customer's inspection. What happens in the event of a security breach?

8. *Pricing.*
   a. **Costs.** Are there any one-time startup or setup fees? What are the ongoing per-user (per-seat) per-month/year fees? Are any third-party software licenses included in the base price of the service? Can software be made "rent to own"? Any charges for storing data? What pricing options exist? What is the duration of the agreement (one, three, or five years)?
   b. **Administration.** How is billing done? Do you have a choice for monthly, quarterly, or annual billing? Are a variety of performance reports available? Does the xSP routinely survey its customers? What are the results?
9. *Selecting an xSP.* Determine the xSP service that will best meet your needs. Produce a brief report summarizing the selection process.

   Communicate the decision to the vendor. Schedule a series of telephone and face-to-face meetings to negotiate a service level agreement (probably applicable for medium-sized and larger organizations only).

10. *Develop an implementation plan.* Review the setup options that are available to the organization. The xSP vendor will, typically, provide a series of default setup options. These setup options should not be revised or be only slightly revised until the company has had an opportunity to utilize the software for some period of time. The company will, of course, want to make sure that the setup defaults match its needs. This implementation plan should establish the individual within the organization who is the point of contact with the vendor and who has the authority to act on behalf of the customer. The business should choose a "go live" date that will have minimal impact on its customers.

    The implementation plan should identify all of the parties that will be involved in using the xSP service, for example, the xSP vendor, the company's ISP, and other service providers, so that clear and quick communication can occur when problems arise—as they inevitably will. The success of using an xSP depends on continued communication between both parties.

Ask Before You Jump

As outsourcing becomes a strategy that is adopted by more and more organizations, the issue then becomes how to choose an xSP? Organizations must therefore carefully assess the offerings, experience, and demonstrated capabilities of potential providers. Thus, here are 10 critical questions to ask of any service provider.

1. ***Does the provider have a track record of service commitment?***
   Does the xSP recognize that the heart of its business is "service"? Has the provider been recognized for quality customer support? Is there a regular customer satisfaction survey? What does the service provider do with this data? When you talk to some of its existing customers (of course you will!), how do they characterize the service that they are receiving? How do you gain access to a help desk? Does the service level agreement (SLA) cover customer service standards and have associated financial guarantees?

2. ***How will your account be managed?***
   What is the service provider's account management plan? Who is the primary individual with whom you will be dealing? How frequently will you likely interact with this person? How frequently does he or she return telephone calls, emails, and faxes?

3. ***Does the provider have existing customers and how happy are they?***
   Having candid conversations with a service provider's existing customer is a crucial part of doing due diligence. Ask for the complete customer list and then choose whom to contact. You should speak to a minimum of six or seven customers that have an industry profile similar to your organization's. Strive to ask open-ended questions that will more likely elicit honest answers rather than simple yes/no questions. Have there been problems? What types of problems were experienced? How long did it take to resolve the problems? Was the customer happy with the resolution? How would each customer characterize the strengths and weaknesses of the xSP?

4. ***What is the quality of the provider's infrastructure and management personnel supporting it?***
   While it is likely that each service provider will be using top-of-the-line equipment and software, you still need to understand the architecture of the provider's infrastructure. Who are its equipment and software component partners? Are there multiple links to the Internet backbone (with what providers)? What has been the recent and historical metrics for availability, reliability, and scalability? Is there a quality control process, procedure, and documented methodology? How often does the service provider upgrade its equipment? How much does it plan to spend within the next year?

Continues

Ask Before You Jump *(Continued)*

5. ***What security measures are in place?***
What physical security safeguards are in place to limit access only to authorized individuals? What firewall and intrusion detection software does the service provider have in place? Have there been any security problems? Is a background check routinely run for all internal service provider personnel? Is a qualified outside third-party employee assigned to perform a security audit on a regular basis? What happens to the results of these audits?
6. ***Is a migration plan offered?***
Does the service provider have a plan in place to migrate responsibility for the service from the customer to the xSP? Can the plan be modified to meet the needs of your organization? Does the plan have a test and review before the actual turnover occurs? Are operations overlapped, or is the new service turned on "cold"? What was the experience of existing customers with regard to migration?
7. ***How is the service priced?***
While it is clearly more important to focus on service levels rather than price when making a selection, make sure that you understand how the service is priced. Make sure there are no hidden costs so that a financial surprise can not occur six months after you start a service. What are the financial consequences should a service provider fail to meet an agreed-on service level?
8. ***How experienced is the service provider?***
Aside from the length of time a service provider has been around (obviously an important metric), what are the depth and breadth of its offerings? Does the provider have roots in a different industry or has it always focused on this segment of the IT environment? Has the provider demonstrated particular strengths?
9. ***How much flexibility is offered?***
Is the service provider interested in tailoring its services to meet your needs, or are you dealing with a sales representative who is over-committing the xSP? Have other customers been able to receive some customized services? What has their experience been? Be wary of a service provider who is willing to reinvent its business model (the likelihood of success must be rated very low!).
10. ***Is the provider financially viable?***
Carefully examine all of the financial information about the health of the service provider. If it is a relatively new company, what is its cash flow strength? What is the cash burn rate? What is its Dun and Bradstreet rating?

Of course, the tried and true adage must always be observed: Check. Check. And check again!

To RFP or Not to RFP?

Organizations have used a Request for Proposal (RFP), Request for Quotation (RFQ), or Request for Information (RFI) to acquire computer hardware, software, and turnkey systems for more than 25 years. In general, the RFP process over the last 10 to 15 years has taken on a life of its own. Specifications developed by one organization to reflect its unique needs will "magically" appear in a host of RFP documents that are subsequently prepared as organizations "cut and paste" sections of previously issued documents. It's almost as if businesses have entered a twilight zone with self-replicating specifications.

Once proposals have been received, organizations will typically use a checklist to determine what vendors are responsive to their needs. The check marks are then added to decide the winner without considering that the vast majority of the specifications will have little impact on the daily operating procedures of an organization. An alternative approach would ascertain what are the critical 8 to 10 functions and features of a system and make a selection based, in large part, on such an analysis. For example, the usability of a system, as exemplified by minimizing the number of mouse clicks or keystrokes required to complete a particular task or activity, might be judged to be important.

If an RFP is to be used to select an xSP service, the whole focus of the process must be on the quality of services that the organization will receive. In such an environment, the organization should not care about the database or operating system used to deliver an application. The primary focus should be on the end goals and not the means to the end.

There are a number of Web sites that provide directories that facilitate the process of finding an xSP that may fit the needs of your company. One of the better sites may be found at http://searchxsp.techtarget.com/buyersGuide/0,,sid28,00.html.

Product Demonstrations

Given that the xSP is going to deliver a service via the Internet, it is reasonable to expect that an organization would receive a product demonstration via the Internet rather than having someone come on-site. Such Internet-enabled demonstrations will help vendors keep the price of the xSP service affordable.

Avoiding Outsourcing Mistakes

Buyers, especially those that have never outsourced, may make a mistake because they have little experience to guide them. Here are 12 mistakes to look out for.

Supplier Mistakes

1. **Ignoring the customer's unique needs. Buyers need to make sure that sellers focus on the outcomes and not the sales process itself.**
2. **Ignoring the importance of leverage. Suppliers have several advantages that they can leverage. These include access to scare resources, ability to substitute cheaper resources for expensive ones, process expertise, and access to capital.**
3. **Avoiding accountability. Sales contract and service level agreements (SLAs) often say "trust me" rather than clearly defining what is to be delivered.**
4. **Sending in the "C" team to manage the account. Sending in the untrained and ill-prepared sends a clear message to the customer: You don't count. This leads to dissatisfaction.**

Buyer Mistakes

1. **Relying too heavily on executive contact. It takes more than top-level executives getting together and agreeing on a deal. The devil is in the details.**
2. **Letting the supplier lead the process. If this happens then accountability often gets left at the starting gate.**
3. **Paying by problem resolution. This will only lead to more problems, which means the supplier gets more money.**
4. **Interfering with the process. Buyers sometimes have a hard time letting go.**
5. **Signing a contract with too long a term. Short terms in the Internet era are a necessity.**
6. **Improper governance. From the customer's perspective, the responsibility for interfacing with the supplier should be assigned to someone who is responsible and can provide oversight.**
7. **Lack of accountability. Both parties need to be held accountable.**
8. **Forgetting the supplier is a business asset. Suppliers can add significant value—if they are consulted and not treated as a vendor providing a commodity (Bendor-Samuel 2001).**

Cost/Benefit Analysis

The intent of any cost/benefit analysis is to identify the potential impacts of a decision. Rather than becoming overwhelmed by the details of the process, focus instead on the level of effort in performing the analysis so that it is proportional to the importance of the decision. Thus, if an organization spends $10,000 on automation it should spend significantly less time and effort in preparing an analysis (back of an envelope, perhaps?) than an organization that spends $1 million a year.

Each cost and benefit category should be assessed as to your ability to quantify and predict the category. For example, some categories will have *hard impacts* (a cost for new computer equipment is predictable, and it is easy to determine the exact cost). *Soft impacts*, such as productivity gains and increase in market share, rely on uncontrollable factors and thus are less certain to quantify. *Unquantifiable impacts*, such as improved customer satisfaction, are uncertain and difficult to quantify.

In preparing a cost/benefit analysis, five possible methods are available to make a comparison of alternatives (King and Schrems 1978). These are the following:

- Maximize benefits for a given cost
- Minimize costs for a given level of benefits
- Maximize the ratio of benefits over costs
- Maximize the net benefits (present value of benefits minus the present value of costs)
- Maximize the internal rate of return on the investment

Notice that the criterion often asked for by decision makers, "Maximize benefits for minimum costs," is a contradiction in terms and has no value in a cost/benefit analysis.

The choice of the most appropriate cost/benefit analysis method depends on the situation, and the different approaches can yield different results. A series of examples illustrate this point.

1. If the business only has $10,000 to spend on a project or activity, then the first method is appropriate: *Maximize benefits for a given cost*.
2. If the organization knows exactly the benefits it wishes to achieve and is not interested in additional benefits, even if they are available and cost more, then the second method of analysis is appropriate: *Minimize costs for a given level of benefits*.

3. Often the alternatives present a wide range of costs and a corresponding wide range of benefits. In this case, the third method of analysis should be used: *Maximize the ratio of benefits over costs.*
4. The ratio approach does not recognize that some alternatives will achieve their benefits over a number of years and that these benefits often have different starting points or "benefit streams." In this case, the business should use the fourth method of analysis: *Maximize the net benefits (present value of benefits minus the present value of costs)*. A present value analysis recognizes that a dollar today is worth more than a dollar received at some point in the future.
5. Organizations in the for-profit sector are often asked to use the fifth method of analysis: *Maximize the internal rate of return on the investment*. A recent survey of organizations with experience in outsourcing found that they experienced a range of return on investments, as shown in Figure 10.3.

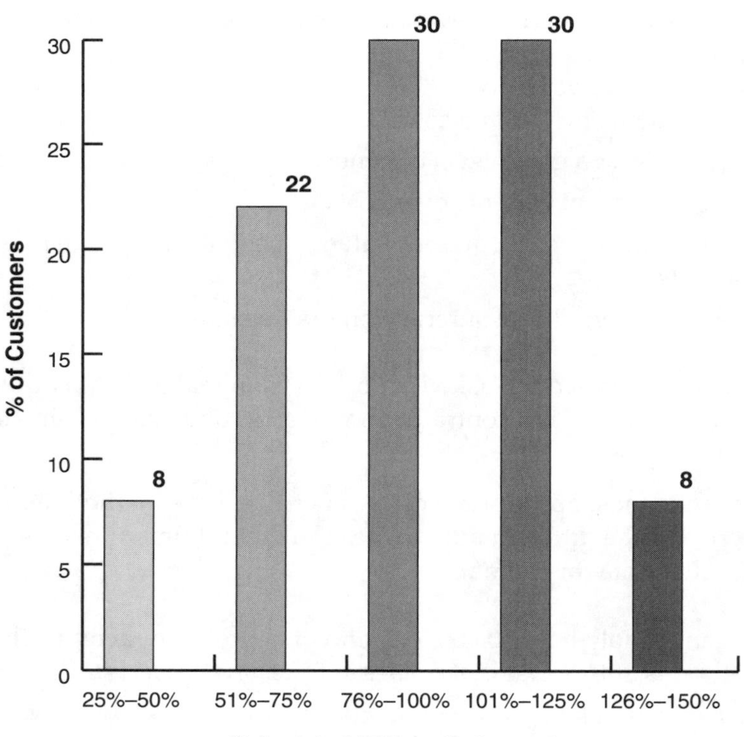

Figure 10.3 Estimated return on outsourcing Investment.

If an organization is considering using an xSP service, it would be reasonable to assume that an in-house system or an xSP-based service will provide roughly the same functionality and thus the analysis should use the second method: *Minimize costs for a given level of benefits.*

Preparing the cost/benefit analysis can be made easier if these suggestions are followed:

1. The most challenging task is to reduce all benefits to quantifiable terms: dollars and cents or, as some cynic's have noted, "dollars and sense." If it can't be quantified, the benefit should not be included in the analysis. Rather, there should be a separate section in the report discussing the analysis performed that identifies all of the qualitative aspects of each alternative.
2. Quantify the benefits and costs of each alternative in terms of dollar benefits and dollar costs.
3. Be conservative in estimating benefits and liberal in assessing costs. In order to obtain better estimates, the following steps are suggested:
   a. Identify and quantify benefits *first*.
   b. Identify all components for each benefit expected to be received as a result of a project or change in how a service is provided. Benefits are defined as "the consequence of an action, that protects, aids, improves, or promotes the well-being of an individual or organization. Benefits take the form of cost savings, cost avoidance, improved operational performance, better allocation of resources, and 'intangibles,' e.g., better understanding of a particular situation." Benefits are centered on customers.
   c. Obtain administrative approval of the value of the benefits for each alternative before proceeding further.
   d. Identify and calculate project costs for each alternative.
   e. This approach assists in preventing benefits from almost always exceeding costs. After all, it is not too often that the phrase "runaway benefits or benefit overruns" is heard to describe the status of a project (King and Kraemer 1981).

      Identify all components for each cost expected to be incurred as a result of undertaking the project. Costs should be identified by the year in which they are expected to occur.
4. Recognize that there are other costs and factors that must be considered. Among these factors may be the following:
   a. **Transition costs.** Are there any one-time costs associated from moving from one system to another? Training costs?
   b. **Complexity costs.** Investing in new technologies means that the organization needs to support multiple technologies and standards.

c. **Technical risk.** How likely is it that things can go wrong? What would be the impacts? Are there any contingency plans? In some organizations, this is referred to as scenario planning.

d. **Flexibility value.** Investing in infrastructure or a new technology may enhance or impede future IT projects. Would a new technology have an impact on the speed of software development or the implementation process?

e. **Commercial factors.** Will the technology vendor be around for awhile? Does the vendor have a proven track record? Is the vendor delivering "best in class" technology?

5. Prepare a brief report documenting the analysis and the recommended approach. Obviously the costs associated with the purchase of a system (software licenses, server, installation and staffing) are estimates, and any organization would need to use either its best estimate or actual dollar figures from its budget. In any analysis, staffing costs should include not only salary but also fringe benefits.

Qualitative Assessment

Generally, organizations have little difficulty in identifying intangible benefits or qualitative factors associated with an alternative. These often include improved customer services, enhanced public image, and better information for making management decisions.

A qualitative assessment of the alternatives should identify those factors that are common across all options as well as the positive and negative attributes of each alternative.

Once the service delivery impacts have been identified for each alternative, an analyst can then prepare the profit-and-loss statement. The ideal alternative will be one that has only desirable features but, unfortunately, rarely do system alternatives achieve the "ideal" status. The selected alternative, using only qualitative factors, is the one with the most desirable features and the fewest undesirable features.

A central issue in this kind of analysis is the amount of influence in the decision-making process that any qualitative analysis should have when compared to the quantitative cost/benefit analysis. In most organizations, greater emphasis is typically placed on the quantitative analysis. It should be noted that it is not unusual to have different rankings of alternatives when comparing the results of the quantitative and qualitative analysis. If there is not substantial agreement between the final decision and the rankings of the cost/benefit analysis, then either the cost/benefit analysis did not take account of some factor(s) or the decision maker is seeking to use the analysis as justification for a decision previously made.

Conclusion

The process for considering the use of an xSP can occur relatively quickly or occupy a considerable period of time depending on the size of the organization and the size of the financial decision. As with most things, the decision ultimately comes down to a matter of trust. Are you comfortable having an important service being outsourced with a third-party company? If you are, then doing business with one of the many xSPs that are in the marketplace will likely lead to some significant benefits for your organization.

Everything in business is a series of trade-offs. The decision of whether to trust IT technology or mission-critical software applications to a service provider is no different—it certainly has its own set of pros and cons. To outsource—that is, trust an outside vendor—clearly introduces risk to your business or organization. But evaluating and managing risks is clearly what today's environment is all about.

So, to ISP, ASP, WSP, MSP, or xSP? That is the question …

APPENDIX

Additional Resources

ISP Web Resources

Web-based Resources

Information about the ISP industry, news, and other resources is available from a number of Web sites.

www.classifieds.internet.com

This is a good resource for finding jobs, ISP equipment, domain names, and more.

www.enewsletters.internet.com

This is the site to visit to sign up for ISP electronic newsletters.

www.internetnews.com/isp-news

This site is a great source for finding out information about the ISP industry, mergers, flameouts, and use of technology, and so forth.

www.isp-lists.com

This is the site to visit for access to current and archive discussion lists about ISPs.

www.isp-planet.com

This site provides current information about the ISP industry.

www.thelist.internet.com

This site allows an individual, organizations, or businesses to find one or more ISPs serving their area. You can search by telephone area code or country code for ISPs located in the United States and Canada.

ASP Resources

Web-based Resources

The following Web sites provide ASP industry information, news, and resources for companies interested in becoming an ASP as well as for organizations or businesses considering the use of an ASP.

www.allaboutasp.org

www.aspindustry.org

www.aspconsortium.org

Any of the above URLs will connect you to the home page of the ASP Industry Consortium. This site provides a wealth of information about ASPs, provides a locator to help end users find an ASP, provides tools for one ASP to partner with another, and generally serves as an advocate for the ASP industry. An extensive FAQ document and an investment and market research report can be downloaded for free by nonmembers. More extensive information resources are available for the nearly 1,000 members of the consortium. The consortium has subcommittees working on best practices, research, education, and membership.

www.Alentis.com

This site claims to provide unbiased descriptions and analysis of more than 1,200 ASP solutions. A visitor can compare specific services offered and rates charged by these providers.

www.ApplicationPlanet.com

This site is a resource center for users of Web-based business services.

www.ASPConnection.com

This site provides current industry news plus a forum to interact with others about the industry.

www.ASP-Directory.com

This site offers a directory service to assist potential customers in finding ASP vendors.

www.aspindustry.com

This site is an information center for application service providers, their delivery partners, and their customers.

www.aspinsights.com

ASP Insights is an editorially focused Web site, covering news and trends related to the application hosting industry. While it represents a valuable resource for anyone with a general market interest, ASP Insights is edited specifically for the ASP executive. ASP Insights offers an analytical look at the latest developments within the ASP space, from mergers and acquisitions to product announcements and partnerships. The content is currently dispersed among seven different sections.

www.aspisland.com

This site, which is aimed at chief information officers and IT professionals, provides news, commentary, industry events, technical forums, and discussions on the ASP industry.

www.ASP-Lists.com

This is an ASP email discussion list community.

www.ASPOutsourcingCenter.com

This site provides ASP industry news, publishes an *ASP Outsourcing Journal*, and provides Outsourcing Exchange to link buyers and sellers of services.

www.aspnews.com

This site delivers global news and industry analysis for application service providers. This site publishes a monthly newsletter in PDF format and is accessible at www.aspnews.com/review.htm.

www.xspRegistry.com

This site is a reference locator to ASP services that also provides access to news and information about ASP products and services.

www.aspstreet.com

This site is probably one of the better sites for the latest industry news. It provides news, reviews, events, resources, and discussion forums on the ASP market place. This comprehensive site provides a quick poll, which helps to understand what is happening in the ASP arena.

www.asp.thelist.com

This site provides a reference locator for end users to find an ASP and for ASPs to find additional partnering opportunities.

www.SearchASP.com

This site is a comprehensive portal with an ASP-focused search engine. This well-organized site assists the visitor in navigating to capture information. An email alert is available to alert you to breaking news.

www.webharbor.com

This site provides a resource locator for end users to find an ASP; it covers news, classified ads, software reviews, and discussion forums for the ASP industry. The site provides a search engine for finding ASPs by functional area. The site also sponsors an industry newsletter called *ASP Industry News*.

www.worldofasp.com

This is a technical Web site for ASPs, VARs, NSPs, and others who provide applications to end users via Citrix, Microsoft Windows Terminal Services, Tarantella, and client-based operating systems.

www.zdnet.com/enterprises/

The ZDNet Web site has a complete section devoted to IT resources, including ASPs. This site provides one of the best resources on the Web for information from a broad cross-section of the computer industry. In addition to news and a directory of ASPs, the user can participate in forums (discussions) on a wide variety of topics and sign up for newsgroups.

Print Resources

a-com. A monthly trade publication that focuses on the ASP industry.

ASP Advisor. A free newsletter offered by International Data Corporation (IDC), an information technology market analysis firm.

ASP News Review. A monthly publication that focuses on the events in the ASP industry.

Wireless SP Resources

Web-based Resources

www.wlana.com

Wireless LAN Association (WLANA) educates and promotes the use of wireless networking technology including personal area networks, local area networks, LAN-to-LAN bridges, and public access.

www.wi-fi.com

Wireless Ethernet Compatibility Alliance certifies the interoperability of IEEE 802.11 products and promotes Wi-Fi as the global wireless LAN standard.

www.wlif.com

Wireless LAN Interoperability forum (WLIF) promotes the OpenAir standard (802.11 FH).

www.pfdm-forum.com

OFDM (Orthogonal Frequency Division Multiplexing) Forum to focus on a single compatible OFDM standard.

www.bluetooth.com

Bluetooth Special Interest Group (Bluetooth SIG) promotes the interoperability of the Bluetooth standard.

www.homerf.com

HomeRF Working Group developed a specification for wireless communication in the home called SWAP (Shared Wireless Access Protocol).

www.hiperlan.com

The HiperLAN Alliance works on the worldwide deployment of HiperLAN systems.

www.grouper.ieee.org/groups/802/11

This the site of the group that is responsible for the development of the IEEE 802.11 standard.

www.grouper.ieee.org/groups/802/15

This is the site of the group that is responsible for the development of the IEEE 802.15 standard.

www.etsi.org/bran

This is the site of the group responsible for the development of the Broadband Radio Access Networks (BRAN) for Europe using a HiperLAN-based standard.

www.w3.org/Mobile/

This site provides W3C mobile access standards.

www.w3.org/tr/note-html40-mobile/

This site provides HTML 4.0 guidelines for mobile access.

Portals and News Sites

www.allnetdevices.com/wireless

This site provides industry news and information.

www.cnet.com/wireless

This site provides CNET Wireless news, industry information, and product reviews.

www.wirelessadvisor.com

This is a general wireless Web site that offers a search engine for wireless, cellular, and digital PCS phone companies serving your area (search by Zip code or city name), a wireless glossary, FAQs, and links to other resources.

www.wireless.internet.com

This is a good site with broad coverage of wireless news, research, and product information.

MSP Resources

Web-based Resources

www.mspassociation.org

This is an industry-sponsored site that provides a search engine to find MSPs that might be suitable for your organization, access to a Buyers Guide, and a list of MSP member companies.

Glossary

3G An International Telecommunications Union (ITU) specification for the third generation of mobile communications technology (analog cellular was the first generation, digital PCS the second). 3G promises increased bandwidth, up to 384 Kbps when a device is stationery or moving at pedestrian speed, 128 Kbps in a car, and 2 Mbps in fixed applications. 3G will work over wireless air interfaces such as GSM, TDMA, and CDMA. The new EDGE (Enhanced Data rates for Global Evolution) interface has been developed specifically to meet the bandwidth needs of 3G.

Acceptable Use Policy A written policy specifying how an employee should use and not abuse network resources.

Access Control The ability to selectively control who can get at a software application or manipulate information in a computer-based system.

Active Server Pages A specification developed by Microsoft for a dynamically created Web page with a .ASP extension that utilizes ActiveX scripting. Active Server Pages run under Microsoft's Internet Information Server on a Microsoft Web server; although referred to with the acronym ASP, it should not be confused with "application service provider."

Active X Microsoft component standard, designed to allow interoperability between common desktop and Web-based applications; Active X's strength lies in its ability to allow development in a wide variety of programming languages, such as Visual Basic, Java, or C++.

ADSL The most common form of DSL. A is short for asymmetrical, indicating that the service is faster for downloads than uploads.

Agent Software applications that carry out preprogrammed functions on behalf of a user, operating within specific, tailored boundaries. For example: an "intelligent" email filter used to eliminate spam or scan for viruses or a shopping device that can search the Web and transact a purchase under predetermined price parameters

Aggregator Within the application service provider industry, aggregators collect software products from multiple ASPs and combine them into a single product offering, permitting an aggregator to offer best-of-breed solutions, entailing the delivery of application suites composed of products chosen from among assorted vendors

American National Standards Institute (ANSI) ANSI, pronounced "antsy," is the U.S.-based organization dedicated to developing industry-wide standards for technology. ANSI is a member of the International Organization for Standardization (ISO).

AMPS Analog Mobile Phone Service is the standard for analog cellular phone service used in the United States and other countries. It is the most widely deployed cellular system in the United States and the rest of the world. AMPS is gradually being phased out, to be replaced by either CDMA or D-AMPS.

Analog The distinguishing feature of analog representations is that they are continuous (e.g., the human voice). In contrast, digital representations consist of values measured at discrete intervals.

Antivirus Software used to detect viruses and stop them from infecting a computer or network.

API An acronym for Application Programming Interface, a set of routines, protocols, and tools for building software applications. A good API makes it easier to develop a program by providing all the building blocks and links. A programmer puts these blocks together.

Most operating environments, such as MS-Windows, provide an API set so programmers can write applications consistent with the operating environment. Although APIs are designed for programmers, they are ultimately good for users because they guarantee that all programs using a common API will have similar interfaces. This makes it easier for users to learn new programs.

Applet A program designed to be executed from within another program. Because applets have small file sizes, are cross-platform compatible, and can't be used to gain access to a user's hard drive, applets are ideal for small Internet applications accessible from a browser. Applets are often embedded in Web pages.

AppleTalk A local area network architecture built into all Macintosh computers and Apple laser printers.

Application Short for "application program," sometimes abbreviated to "app," an application is a software program that performs a specific task such as word processing, spreadsheets, accounting, etc.

Application Logic The computational aspects or business rules that tell a software application how to operate.

Application Service Provider (ASP) An ASP deploys, hosts, and manages access to a packaged software application to multiple parties from a centrally managed facility. The applications are delivered over networks on a subscription basis.

ATM An acronym for Asynchronous Transmission Mode, an information transfer standard for routing high-speed, high-bandwidth traffic such as real-time voice and video, as well as data bits.

Attenuation The decrease in a signal's power from transmission to reception. The received signal is lower in power because of such factors as line resistance, distance, and network configuration.

Authentication The process for identifying an individual, usually based on a user name and password. Authentication is distinct from authorization, which is the process of giving individuals access to system components based on their identity.

Availability The portion of time that a system can be used for productive work, expressed as a percentage. Sometimes call uptime.

Backbone A backbone is a network that has other networks attached to it, instead of user devices like PCs and servers. This allows backbones to operate at much faster speeds than local networks.

Backsourcing The process of pulling a function back in-house as an outsourcing contract expires.

Bandwidth The speed or transmission or the number of bits of information that can move through a communications medium in a given amount of time; the capacity of a telecommunications circuit/network to carry voice, data, and video information. Typically measured in Kbps and Mbps.

Benchmarking A tool for performance measurement that compares the activities within one organization with a number of other comparable organizations.

Best-of-breed The best application software available as compared to analogous applications based on a set of common criteria.

Bit Error Rate The number of transmitted bits expected to be corrupted when two computers have been communicating for a given period of time.

Bloatware Software programs that require large amounts of disk space and RAM (random access memory), effectively consuming valuable computer resources.

Bluetooth A computing and telecommunications specification that describes how mobile phones, computers, and personal digital assistants can interconnect with one another using a short-range wireless connection.

Bots Bots, from robots, are smart software programs that run in the background of a computer, performing specific repetitive tasks. A bot can search the Internet, comparison shop, clip news articles, etc. Hotbots, search bots, shopping bots, and spiders are among the species of bots. They are sometimes called intelligent agents.

BPO Short for Business Process Outsourcing.

bps An acronym for bits per second, a measure of data transfer rates. Faster is better, and the bigger the number the faster the rate.

Browser Software that is used to view various Internet resources and is capable of viewing text, images, and various other file formats as well as playing sound and showing videos.

Burst Information Rate or **BIR** The Burst Information Rate is the speed or rate of information that the customer may need over and above the CIR. A burst is typically a short duration transmission that can relieve momentary congestion in the LAN or provide additional throughput for interactive data applications.

Cache Information saved in computer memory for later use. For example, Web browsers save recently viewed pages in a cache so the exact pages are not downloaded again should the user request them. This feature thus saves the Internet resources and time.

Capacity The ability for a network to provide sufficient transmitting capabilities among its available transmission media and respond to customer demand for communications transport, especially at peak times.

CDMA Code division multiple access is a digital cellular technology that uses spread-spectrum techniques. Unlike competing systems, such as GSM, that use time division multiplexing (TDM), CDMA does not assign a specific frequency to each user. Instead, every channel uses the full available spectrum. Individual conversations are encoded with a pseudo-random digital sequence. CDMA is a military technology first used during World War II by the English allies to foil German attempts at jamming transmissions. Qualcomm Inc. became the first company to commercialize CDMA.

CDPD Short for Cellular Digital Packet Data. This is a specification for supporting wireless access to the Internet and other packet-switched networks at speeds of up to 19.2 Kbps.

Cellular Refers to communications systems, especially the Advance Mobile Phone Service (AMPS), that divides a geographic region into sections, called cells. The purpose of this division is to make the most use out of a limited number of transmission frequencies. Each connection, or conversation, requires its own dedicated frequency, and the total number of available frequencies is about 1,000. To support more than 1,000 simultaneous conversations, cellular systems allocate a set number of frequencies for each cell. Two cells can use the same frequency for different conversations as long as the cells are not adjacent to each other. For digital communications, several competing cellular systems exist, including GSM and CDMA.

CGI Abbreviation of Common Gateway Interface, a specification for transferring information between a World Wide Web server and a CGI program. A CGI program is any program designed to accept and return data that conforms to the CGI specification. The program could be written in any programming language, including C, Perl, Java, or Visual Basic. One problem with CGI is that each time a CGI script is executed, a new process is started. For busy Web sites, this can slow down the server noticeably.

Challenge-Handshake Authentication Protocol (CHAP) A secure procedure for validating a network connection request. The server sends a challenge request message to the requestor, who responds with encrypted authentication information—the user name and password.

Channel A broad term referring to the pathway between two locations on a voice or data network.

Chat A real-time conversation, typically using text, among multiple online users. Chat rooms have discussions focused on a particular topic.

CIR Short for Committed Information Rate, a specified amount of guaranteed bandwidth (measured in bits per second) on a frame relay service. The frame relay network vendor guarantees that frames not exceeding this level will be delivered. It's possible that additional traffic may also be delivered, but it's not guaranteed. Some frame relay vendors offer inexpensive services with a CIR equal to zero. This essentially means that the network will deliver as many frames as it can, but it doesn't *guarantee* any bandwidth level.

Circuit A line that connects devices.

CLEC Acronym for competitive local exchange carrier. Any LEC that competes with the incumbent local exchange carrier (ILEC) in a given market. A company may be the ILEC in one market and CLEC in another.

Click-stream Information collected about where a Web user has been on the Web.

Client/Device Hardware that retrieves information from a server.

Client/Server Client/server replaced mainframe computing as the dominant system for business information architecture in the late 1980s; clients (see "client-side") are typically less powerful, graphically enabled software platforms that "request" computation from a server; the server is typically a more powerful processing platform that "serves" requested data or tasks back to the requesting clients; Web browsers have emerged in the 1990s as a universal client able to access multiple applications, fueling the movement away from the client/server to the ASP business.

Client side The side of an application that resides on the user end of a network; the PC or terminal where the end user works would be the client side of the client/server model; the client side of an ASP application would be the browser.

Clustering Group of independent systems working together as a single system. Clustering technology allows groups of servers to access a single disk array containing applications and data.

CO Acronym for central office. Also called central switch or telephone exchange. A telephone company facility serving a specific area. One or more phone lines run from a subscriber's home or office to a CO.

Collocation The placement of one company's computer/network equipment on the premises of another company.

Comma-delimited A data format in which each piece of data is separated by a comma. This is a popular format for transferring data from one application to another because most database systems are able to import and export comma-delimited data.

Competitive Access Provider (CAP) A telecommunications company that provides an alternative to a Local Exchange Carrier or LEC for local transport and special access telecommunications services.

COM Short for Component Object Model, COM is a binary code developed by Microsoft. Both OLE (Object Linking and Embedding) and ActiveX are based on COM.

Competitive Access Provider (CAP) A telecommunications company that provides an alternative to an LEC for local transport and special access telecommunications services.

Cookie While browsing certain Web pages, small files are downloaded to your computer that hold information that can be retrieved by other Web pages on that site. Cookies contain information that identifies each user: login or registration information, specified preferences, passwords, shopping cart information, and so on. The user revisits the Web site; his or her computer will automatically distribute the cookie, establishing the user's identity.

CORBA Short for Common Object Request Broker Architecture, which is an architecture that enables a software program, called objects, to communicate with one another regardless of the programming language in which the object is written. Two competing models are Microsoft's COM and Sun's RMI.

Cracker Someone who intentionally breaches the security of a computer system, usually with the intent of stealing information or disabling the system.

CRM An acronym for customer relationship management, an application that manages crucial customer relationships by automating customer-related services (e.g., order processing, sales, marketing, and help desk assistance).

Crosstalk Interference on analog lines created by cables that are too close together. Crosstalk may produce static, buzzing, or multiple conversations on one line.

CSU/DSU An acronym for channel server unit/digital server unit. A device used to terminate telephone company equipment and prepare data for the router interface.

Cyberfraud The most common crime using the Internet is online credit card theft. Typically someone will order goods over the Internet using stolen credit cards. Another form of cyberfraud is nondelivery of merchandise or software bought online.

D-AMPS Digital advanced mobile phone service is a second-generation digital version of the first-generation analog AMPS standard. D-AMPS is currently the most widely used digital wireless standard in the Americas and Asia. D-AMPS was designed to use existing bandwidth and channels more efficiently. It uses the same 30 kHz spacing as AMPS, but uses TDMA (time division multiple access) as opposed to FDMA (frequency division multiple access) or CDMA (code division multiple access) to allow serial use of individual channels by multiple users, similar to how telegraph lines were used 100 years ago. D-AMPS uses digital TDMA, but it also must be compatible with installed AMPS base station networks.

Data Center A centralized computer facility for remote access by customer end users.

Datagram A packet of information sent to the receiving computer. It is conceptually similar to a telegram in that the message can arrive any time, without notice.

Data Mining An analytic process that examines large sets of information for hidden patterns and relationships.

Data Warehouse A database containing copious amounts of information, organized to aid decision making in an organization. Data warehouses receive batch updates and are configured for fast online queries to produce succinct summaries of data.

DCE Short for Data Communications Equipment; term used for a modem-to-modem connection.

Dedicated Line A point-to-point, hard-wired connection between two service locations.

Demarcation Line The point at which the local operating company's responsibility for the local loop ends. Beyond the demarcation point (also known as the network interface), the customer is responsible for installing and maintaining all equipment and wiring.

Denial of service (DOS) attack An attack by a hacker who generates so many messages to a Web site that regular users can not get through or the site shuts down.

DHCP Acronym for Dynamic Host Configuration Protocol. It allows computers using the TCP/IP protocol to be assigned an IP address automatically rather than requiring that a fixed IP address be assigned to the computer.

Digital Data is represented by 0 (off or low) and 1 (on or high). Computers must use an analog modem to convert digital data into analog form for transmission over ordinary telephone lines.

Digital loop carrier Equipment used to concentrate many local-loop pairs onto a few high-speed digital pairs or one fiber optic pair for transport back to the central office. DLC systems reduce wiring cost.

Digital Subscriber Line (DSL) A technology designed for the Internet that brings high-speed, digital data to a home or office over ordinary copper telephone lines. It comes in various "flavors" of varying bandwidth and simplicity for installers and users. Asymmetric Digital Subscriber Line or ADSL supports data rates from 1.5 to 9 Mbps when receiving data. Symmetric Digital Subscriber Line or SDSL supports data rates up to 3 Mbps.

DNS Short for Domain Name System (or Service), an Internet service that translates domain names into IP addresses. Because domain names are alphabetic, they're easier to remember. Every time a domain name is used, a DNS service must translate the name into the corresponding IP address. For example, the domain name www.example.com might translate to 128.105.732.14.

DoCoMo DoCoMo means "anywhere" in Japanese. It is the name of an NTT subsidiary and Japan's biggest mobile service provider, with over 31 million subscribers as of June 2000. In February 2000 NTT DoCoMo launched its i-mode service. DoCoMo's i-mode is the only network in the world that now allows subscribers continuous access to the Internet via mobile telephone. The service lets users send and receive email, exchange photographs, do online shopping and banking, download personalized ringing melodies for their phones, and navigate among more than 7,000 specially formatted Web sites. The current i-mode data transmission speed is just 9.6 Kbps; its next-generation mobile system, based on Wideband CDMA (WCDMA), can support speeds of 384 Kbps or faster, making mobile multimedia possible.

DOCSIS Short for Data Over Cable Service Interface Specification. A relatively new industry standard defining how cable modems communicate over cable TV lines. Any DOCSIS modem will work on any DOCSIS-compatible cable data network.

Domain name A name of a service, Web site, or computer in a hierarchical system of delegated authority—the Domain Name System.

Download To receive data from a remote computer.

Downstream The direction data flows from a remote computer to your computer.

Downtime When your computer, computer network, access to the Internet, or an Internet-based service provider isn't working. The opposite of uptime.

DS-1 Data communications circuit capable of transmitting data at 1.5 Mbps. Currently DS-1 or T-1 lines are in widespread use by organizations for video, voice, and data applications.

DS-3 A data communications circuit capable of transmitting data at 45 Mbps. A DS-3 or T-3 line has the equivalent data capacity of 28 T-1s. Currently used only by organizations and carriers for high-end applications.

DSL See Digital Subscriber Line.

Dynamic HTML New HTML extensions that enable a Web page to react to user input without sending requests to the Web server. Both Microsoft and Netscape have submitted proposals to the W3C, which is developing a final specification.

Dynamic IP address An IP address that is assigned by a device acting as an HDCP server. A dynamic IP can be different each time you turn on your computer.

EDGE Short for enhanced data rate for GSM evolution. EDGE defines protocols that will carry data as fast as 384 Kbps.

ELEC Short for enterprise local exchange carrier. A corporation operating as its own LEC to obtain better carrier rates. An ELEC may sell services to other carriers from a separate profit center.

Electronic Data Interchange (EDI) The electronic communication of the business transactions (orders, confirmations, invoices, etc.) of organizations with differing platforms. Third parties provide EDI services that enable the connection of organizations with incompatible equipment.

Encryption The translation of data into a secret code. To read an encrypted file, you must have access to a secret key or password that enables you to decrypt it. Encrypted data is sometimes called cipher text.

Enterprise Resource Planning (ERP) An information system or process integrating all manufacturing and related applications for an entire enterprise. ERP systems permit organizations to manage resources across the enterprise and completely integrate manufacturing systems.

Ethernet A local area network used to connect computers, printers, workstations, and other devices within the same building. Ethernet operates over twisted wire and coaxial cable.

Extranet An intranet that is partially accessible to authorized outsiders using a user name and password. Typically, suppliers and important customers are able to access an Extranet.

Facilities Management A type of outsourcing that typically transfers ownership of a customer's data center equipment, software licenses, and IT staff to an outsourcing organization.

Fast Ethernet A LAN transmission standard that supports data transmission rates up to 100 megabits per second (Mbps). Fast Ethernet is 10 times faster than standard Ethernet and is sometimes called 100BaseT.

Fat Client A computer that includes an operating system, RAM, ROM, a powerful processor, and a wide range of installed software applications that can execute either on the desktop or on the server to which it is connected. Fat clients can operate in a server-based computing environment or in a stand-alone fashion.

Fault Tolerance A design method that incorporates redundant system elements to ensure continued systems operation in the event of the failure of any individual element.

FDDI An acronym for Fiber Distributed Data Interface. A standard for transmitting data on optical-fiber cables at a rate of about 100 Mbps.

FDMA Short for frequency division multiple access. A method for allocating bandwidth to PCS service based on the division of available bandwidth into a series of channels, each of which is assigned to a call with a cell. It is the basis for the AMPS system.

FH Short for frequency hopping, a practice used in several communications systems to avoid interference that is restricted to particular frequencies.

Fiber optic Fiber optic technology—made possible by photonic science—uses glass, plastic, or fused silica threads to transmit data. A fiber optic cable consists of a bundle of super-thin threads that are capable of transmitting data via pulses of light. Key advantages of these laser-powered cables include vastly higher-speed data transmission over longer distances and less data loss.

Firewall A system designed to prevent unauthorized access to or from a private network. All messages entering or leaving the intranet pass through the firewall, which examines each message and blocks those that do not meet the specified security criteria.

Frame The basic logical unit in which bit-oriented data is transmitted. The frame consists of the data bits surrounded by a flag at each end that indicates the beginning and end of the frame. A primary rate can be thought of as an endless sequence of frames.

Frame Relay A high-speed packet switching protocol popular in networks, including WANs, LANs, and LAN-to-LAN connections across vast distances.

FTP An acronym for File Transfer Protocol, the protocol used on the Internet for transferring or sending files.

Gbps An acronym for Gigabits per second, a measurement of data transmission speed expressed in billions of bits per second.

G.Lite An ITU standard for DSL technology that delivers 1.5 Mbps downstream. Pronounced "gee-dot-lite."

GPRS General Packet Radio Systems, a standard for wireless communications that runs at speeds up to 150 kilobits per second, compared with current GSM (Global System for Mobile Communications) systems' 9.6 kilobits. GPRS, which supports a wide range of bandwidths, is an efficient use of limited bandwidth and is particularly suited for sending and receiving small bursts of data, such as email and Web browsing, as well as large volumes of data.

GSM Global System for Mobile Communications is one of the leading digital cellular systems. GSM uses narrow-band TDMA, which allows eight simultaneous calls on the same radio frequency. GSM was first introduced in 1991. As of the end of 1997, GSM service was available in more than 100 countries and has become the de facto standard in Europe and Asia.

Groupware A class of software that helps groups of colleagues, sometimes called workgroups, organize their activities. Groupware supports scheduling of meetings, email, preparation of documents, file distribution, and electronic newsletters.

Handheld computer This is a portable computer that is small enough to be held in one's hand. Although extremely convenient to carry, handheld computers have not replaced notebook computers because of their small keyboards and screens. The most popular handheld computers are those that are specifically designed to provide PIM (personal information manager) functions, such as a calendar and address book. Some manufacturers are trying to solve the small keyboard problem by replacing the keyboard with an electronic pen; however, these pen-based devices rely on handwriting recognition technologies, which are still in their infancy.

HDML Handheld Device Markup Language is used to format content for Web-enabled mobile phones. HDML is phone.com's (formerly known as Unwired Planet) proprietary language, which can be viewed only on mobile phones that use phone.com browsers. HDML came before the WAP standard was created. HDML and the phone.com gateway are most popular throughout North America. In Europe, WML and the Nokia WAP gateway and browser are the emerging standard. Some versions of phone.com browsers do interpret basic WML.

HDSL Short for high-bit-rate digital subscriber line. A flavor of DSL that delivers up to 1.544 Mbps of data symmetrically over two copper twisted-pair lines. The range of HDSL is limited to 12,000 feet; signal repeaters extend the service farther from the CO.

Head end The cable company's main signal reception and distribution facility. The head end is the cable TV equivalent of a phone company CO, and all TV cables for a given area route back to a single head end.

Hop An intermediate connection in a string of connections linking two network devices. The more hops, the longer it takes for data to go from source to destination.

Host Any computer on a network that is a repository for services available to other computers on the network.

Hosted Outsourcing Complete outsourcing of a company's information technology applications and associated hardware systems to a company.

Hostname The name given to an individual computer or server attached to a network or to the Internet.

HTML Short for Hypertext Markup Language, the authoring language to create documents on the World Wide Web. HTML defines the structure and layout of a Web document by using a variety of tags and attributes.

HTTP Short for Hypertext Transfer Protocol, the underlying protocol used by the World Wide Web. HTTP defines how messages are formatted and transmitted and describes what action Web servers and browsers should take in response to various commands.

Hyperlink Text that contains a word or phrase that can be clicked on to cause another document, record, or Web site to be retrieved and displayed.

Hypertext Documents that contain links to other documents. When a user selects a link the second document is automatically displayed.

IDSL Short for ISDN digital subscriber line. A form of DSL providing a symmetrical speed of 144 Kbps over the copper wire provisioned for ISDN. Repeaters enable service up to 35,000 feet from the CO.

IEEE 802.11 A family of specifications developed by a working group of the Institute of Electrical and Electronic Engineers (IEEE). There are three specifications in the family: 802.11, 802.11a, and 802.11b.

The 802.11 and 802.11b specifications apply to wireless Ethernet LANs and operate at frequencies in the 2.4 GHz region of the radio spectrum with data speeds of 1–2 Mbps for 802.11 and 5.5–11 Mbps for 802.11b.

ILEC Acronym for incumbent local exchange carrier. Any LEC (telephone company) dominating the local market.

Independent Software Vendor (ISV) Generally a firm that develops software applications that is not associated with a computer systems manufacturer.

Instant Messaging Instant messaging provides the ability to identify someone who is online and send and receive messages with that person in near real time.

Integrated Services Digital Network (ISDN) An information transfer standard for transmitting digital voice and data over telephone lines at speeds up to 128 Kbps.

Inter-Exchange Carrier (IXC) A telecommunications company that provides telecommunication services between local exchanges on an interstate or intrastate basis.

Internet A global network connecting hundreds of thousands of networks that connect millions of computers. Each Internet computer, called a host, is independent.

Internet Business Service An ASP that has built its business from the ground up with applications developed initially to be run only over the Web.

Internet Message Access Protocol (IMAP) A standard format for retrieving email messages. IMAP uses simple mail transfer protocol (SMTP) for communication between the email recipient and the server.

Internet Protocol (IP) The protocol that governs how computers send packets of data across the Internet. It allows a packet to traverse multiple networks on the way to its final destination.

Internet Service Provider (ISP) Company that provides access for users and businesses to the Internet.

Internetworking Sharing data and resources from one network to another.

Interoperability The ability of systems or products that adhere to standards to work together automatically. Examples of such standards include HTTP and TCP/IP.

Intranet A network belonging to an organization, accessible only by the organization's members, employees, or others with appropriate authorization.

IP See Internet Protocol.

IP address A numerical identifier for a device on a TCP/IP network. The IP address format is a string of four numbers, each from 0 to 255, separated by periods.

IPX Short for Internetwork Packet Exchange, a Novell NetWare networking protocol. IPX is used for connectionless communications.

ISDN Short for Integrated Services Digital Network, a digital telephone service that handles voice and data simultaneously. Increasingly going out of favor as faster technologies, such as DSL, become more widely deployed.

Java A high-level programming language developed by Sun Microsystems. Java is an object-oriented language similar to C++, but simplified to eliminate language features that cause common programming errors.

Java 2 Enterprise Edition (J2EE) A Java platform designed for mainframe-scale computing that provides an environment for developing and deploying enterprise applications. J2EE simplifies development and decreases programming by utilizing modular components and allowing the middle tier to handle much of the programming automatically.

JavaBeans A Sun specification that defines how Java objects interact. JavaBeans are similar to Microsoft's ActiveX controls except they can run on any platform.

Jini Based on Java, this is a Sun system for connecting any type of device, including a Net device, to a network.

Key In security systems, a password needed to decipher encoded data.

Kilobits Per Second (Kbps) A data transmission rate of 1,000 bits per second.

Latency In networking, the amount of time it takes a packet to travel from source to destination. Together, latency and bandwidth define the speed and capacity of a network.

LDAP An acronym for Lightweight Directory Access Protocol, a set of protocols for accessing information directories. LDAP should eventually make it possible for almost any application running on virtually any network to obtain directory information, such as email addresses and public keys.

Leased Line A telecommunications line dedicated to a particular customer along predetermined routers.

LEC Short for local exchange carrier. A local telephone company.

Legacy application or system Computer systems that remain in use after more modern technology has been installed. Organizations are often reluctant to cease using legacy applications because they represent a significant investment in time and money.

Linux An open-source, multitasking operating system written in the C programming language that is a variant of Unix and named after the developer of the kernel, Linus Torvalds of Finland.

Local Area Network (LAN) A network of workstations that are linked together. Each node in the LAN can communicate with each other, by sending email or engaging in chat sessions.

Local Access Transport Area (LATA) One of approximately 164 geographical areas within which local operating companies connect all local calls and route all long-distance calls to the customer's interexchange carrier.

Local Exchange Carrier (LEC) A telecommunications company that provides telecommunication services in a defined geographic area.

Local Loop The wires that connect an individual subscriber's telephone or data connection to the telephone company central office or other local terminating point.

Location-based A sort of mobile *push* system, where companies find users rather than users having to make a request. The ability to auto-locate mobile users was initiated by a 1996 FCC initiative aimed at making it easier for emergency workers to locate wireless 911 calls. The FCC required that by October 2001, mobile service systems be able to trace emergency calls to within 125 meters (roughly 400 feet) of their location. By 2005, this location service must be available to all mobile customers. Networks can use the cell ID assigned to each active cell phone to obtain very rough estimates of users' locations. GPS (Global-Positioning System) technology will allow much more accurate tracking.

MAC Address Short for Media Access Control address.

Megabits Per Second (Mbps) A transmission rate where one megabit equals 1,024 kilobits.

Middleware Software that connects two otherwise separate applications. Middleware is the "plumbing" that passes data from one application to another.

MIME Short for Multimedia Internet Mail Extensions. A protocol that defines a number of content types, which allow programs like Web browsers to recognize different kinds of files and deal with them appropriately.

Modem A device for converting digital (data) signals to analog and vice versa, for data transmission over an analog telephone line.

Multiplexing The combining of multiple data channels onto a single transmission medium. Sharing a circuit—normally dedicated to a single user—between multiple users.

Multiuser The ability for multiple concurrent users to log on and run applications from a single server.

Name server A computer that matches Web site names to IP addresses. Also sometimes called a DNS server.

Net-centric Software Ready-to-use software solutions that can be downloaded or delivered via the Internet rather than out-of-the-box from a retailer or e-tailer.

Network Access Point (NAP) A location where ISPs exchange each other's traffic.

Network-Attached Storage (NAS) Network-attached storage uses a single server connected to an Ethernet LAN (Local Area Network) with its own Internet protocol address to handle the data storage and access on the network and relieve the pressure on the application or enterprise (business) server. NAS is easier and less expensive to implement than the alternatives and uses proven technology to do the job. Even better, network-attached storage solutions allow faster data access and can be deployed rapidly.

Network Computer (NC) A "thin" client hardware device that executes applications locally by downloading them from the network. NCs adhere to a specification jointly developed by Sun, IBM, Oracle, Apple, and Netscape. They typically run Java applets within a Java browser or Java applications within the Java Virtual Machine.

Network Computing Architecture A computing architecture in which components are dynamically downloaded from the network onto the client device for execution by the client. The Java programming language is at the core of network computing.

Network packets Data transmitted over a network is subdivided into packets.

NFS Short for Network File System. A set of protocols that allows use of files located on other computers as if they were located locally.

Offsite Storage A Web-based service that rents computer disk space for the storage of documents and files to individuals and companies. Access is available 24 hours a day, 7 days a week.

Online Analytical Processing (OLAP) Software that enables decision support via rapid queries to large databases that store corporate data in multidimensional hierarchies and views.

Online Profiling Using cookies and personal information obtained from other sources, a Web site will create a profile of a customer's buying and browsing habits.

Open Source Source code or "source" are the instructions created by programmers to develop software. Most source code is proprietary for obvious reasons, for example, Microsoft's Windows. Advocates of open source projects such as Linux and the Mozilla browser claim that other can quickly and easily enhance a product that then can be shared by others. Opponents point to the incompatible product versions that are available.

Outsourcing The transfer of components or large segments of an organization's internal IT infrastructure, staff, processes, or applications to an external resource such as an application service provider.

Packaged Software Application A computer program developed for sale to consumers or businesses generally designed to appeal to more than a single customer. While some tailoring of the program may be possible, it is not intended to be custom-designed for each user or organization.

Packet A bundle of data organized for transmission, containing control information (destination, length, origin, etc.) the data itself and error detection and correction bits. In IP networks, packets are often called *datagrams.*

Packet Switching A network in which messages are transmitted as packets over any available route rather than as sequential messages over switched or dedicated facilities.

Password A secret series of characters that enables a user to access a file, computer or program. The password helps ensure that unauthorized individuals do not access the computer.

Password Authentication Procedure A procedure for validating a network connection request. The requestor sends the network server a user name and password. The server can validate and acknowledge the request.

PCS Short for personal communications service, a form of digital cellular service used in the United States that operates in the 1,900 MHz frequency range.

PDA Short for personal digital assistant, a handheld device that combines computing, telephone/fax, and networking features. Most PDAs use a stylus rather than a keyboard for input. John Sculley, former CEO of Apple, first used the term PDA in 1992.

Peering The commercial practice under which nationwide ISPs exchange each other's traffic without the payment of settlement charges.

Performance A major factor in determining the overall productivity of a system, performance is primarily tied to availability, throughput, and response time.

Permanent Virtual Circuit (PVC) A PVC is what connects the customer's port connections, nodes, locations, and branches to each other. All customer ports can be connected to each other, resembling a mesh, but PVCs usually run between the host and branch locations.

PIM Short for personal information manager, a type of software application designed to help users organize random bits of information. Although the category is fuzzy, most PIMs enable you to enter various kinds of textual notes—reminders, lists, and dates—and to link these bits of information together in useful ways. Many PIMs also include calendar, scheduling, and calculator programs.

Point of Presence (POP) A dial-in location so that you can connect to the Internet. To the user, a POP is a local telephone number.

POTS Short for plain old telephone service. Standard telephony for placing and receiving calls.

POP Short for post office protocol, a mail protocol that allows a remote mail client to read mail from a server.

PPP Short for point-to-point protocol. This protocol allows a computer to use the TCP/IP protocols with a standard telephone line and a high-speed modem.

PPPOE Short for point-to-point protocol over ethernet. A protocol that allows DSL providers to meter connection time and to acquire a smaller, cheaper block of IP addresses. PPPOE changes DSL from an always-on to an on-demand service and lets providers reduce the size and cost of their Internet connection infrastructures.

Pretty Good Privacy (PGP) A technique for encrypting messages on the Internet. PGP is free and is based on the public-key encryption method, which uses two keys—one is a public key that you disseminate to anyone. The other is a private key that you use to decrypt messages that you receive.

Privacy The right to freedom from unauthorized intrusion. Proliferating use of a number of technologies has made it easier to gather volumes of information about individuals and companies. Some concerned citizens are calling for legislative protection.

Protocol A definition of how a computer will act when talking to other computers. Standard protocols allow computers from different manufacturers to communicate.

PSTN Short for public switched telephone network; same as POTS.

Public-Key Encryption A cryptographic system that uses two keys—a public key known to everyone and a private or secret key known only to the recipient of the message. Only the public key can be used to encrypt the message, and only the private key can be used to decrypt the message. What's needed is a global registry of public keys, which is one of the promises of LDAP technology.

Quality of Service (QoS) A collective measure of the level of service a provider delivers to its customers. QoS can be characterized by several basic performance criteria, including availability (low downtime), error performance, response time and throughput, lost calls or transmissions due to network congestion, connection setup time, etc.

RAID Short for redundant array of inexpensive disks, a category of disk drives that employ two or more drives in combination for fault tolerance and improved performance. There are number of different RAID levels. The three most common are 0, 3, and 5:

Level 0: Provides *data striping* (spreading out blocks of each file across multiple disks) but no redundancy. This improves performance but does not deliver fault tolerance.

Level 1: Provides disk mirroring (two sets of disks to store two copies of the data).

Level 3: Same as Level 0, but also reserves one dedicated disk for error correction data. It provides good performance and some level of fault tolerance.

Level 5: Provides data striping at the byte level and also stripe error correction information. This results in excellent performance and good fault tolerance.

Regional Bell Operating Company (RBOC) Pronounced "R-bock," the seven Baby Bells were created with the 1983 breakup of AT&T or Ma Bell. The seven include Ameritech, Bell Atlantic, Bell South, NYEX, Pacific Bell, Southwestern Bell, and US West.

Remote Access The hookup of a remote-computing device via communications lines such as ordinary phone lines or wide area networks to access distant network applications and information.

Remote Presentation Services Protocol A set of rules and procedures for exchanging data between computers on a network, enabling the user interface, keystrokes, and mouse movements to be transferred between a server and client.

Router A communications device between networks that determines the best path between them for optimal performance. Routers are used in complex networks of networks such as enterprise-wide networks and the Internet.

Scalability Ability to expand the number of users or increase the capabilities of a computing solution without making major changes to the systems or application software.

SDMA Space division multiple access is a variation of TDMA and CDMA that potentially will be used in high-bandwidth, third-generation wireless products.

SDSL Short for symmetric digital subscriber line. A form of DSL that transfers data upstream and downstream at the same speed (up to 2.3 Mbps) over a single copper twisted-pair line.

Secure Electronic Transaction (SET) A security standard that ensures privacy and protection for conducting credit card transactions over the Internet. Rather than a credit card number, a digital signature is employed.

Security Software Computer software installed on a computer network or individual workstation that protects it from a hacker attack. Typically the software includes firewall and antivirus software.

Server The computer on a local area network that often acts as a data and application repository and that controls an application's access to workstations, printers, and other parts of the network.

Server-based Computing A server-based approach to delivering business-critical applications to end-user devices, whereby an application's logic executes on the server and only the user interface is transmitted across a network to the client. Its benefits include single-point management, universal application access, bandwidth-independent performance, and improved security for business applications.

Service Level Agreement (SLA) A binding contract or agreement between an end-user organization and an ASP. It details the specifics of the partnership, including customer service and data security.

Servlet An applet that runs on a Web server. A servlet is persistent—it stays in memory and can fulfill multiple requests.

SGML An acronym for Standard Generalized Markup Language. SGML is an international standard and is the basis for HTML and a precursor to XML.

Short Message Service (SMS) A service for sending text messages of up to 160 characters to mobile phones that use global system for mobile (GSM). The cell phone can receive the message even if the phone is being used.

Simple Mail Transfer Protocol (SMTP) A TCP/IP-based standard for sending email messages between servers on the Internet. Once received, the messages are stored using either Internet message access protocol (IMAP) or point of presence (POP).

Single-Point Control One of the benefits of the ASP model, single-point control helps reduce the total cost of application ownership by enabling widely used applications and data to be deployed, managed, and supported at one location. Single-point control enables application installations, updates, and additions to be made once, on the server, which are then instantly available to users anywhere.

SLIP Short for Serial Line IP, allows a computer to connect to the Internet using a telephone line and a high-speed modem. SLIP is being superseded by the PPP protocol.

SNR Short for signal-to-noise ratio, an engineering measure of the amount of information that can be extracted from a transmitted signal.

SOAP Short for Simple Object Access Protocol, a common format for exchanging data stored in diverse formats and databases. Approved by the World Wide Web

Consortium, SOAP uses XML and HTTP to define a component interoperability standard on the Web. Microsoft's implementation of SOAP is called BizTalk, and IBM's is WebSphere.

Spider A simple software program used by a search engine to scan the Web. Spiders are bots that crawl from link to link searching for new sites.

SSL Short for secure sockets layer, a protocol for transmitting private documents via the Internet. SSL works by using a private key to encrypt data that transferred over the SSL connection. Most Web browsers support SSL.

Static IP address An IP address that never changes and is typically used in businesses rather than with consumers.

Storage Area Network (SAN) SANs allow users to store large amounts of data off their crowded corporate networks at potentially lower cost. SANs make use of the same type of fiber optics that revolutionized long-distance tele/data communications. Essentially, SANs combine data management with physical connections and optical infrastructure so that data can be housed off-site and still be easily accessible to users within a corporate network via servers. SANs will soon provide any-to-any connections, which means they allow any kind of client computing device (PDAs, notebooks, wireless phone) to connect to information on any type of storage computer.

Streaming The end user sees video or hears an audio file as a continuous steam as it arrives rather than waiting for the entire file to be received.

T-1 Data communications circuit capable of transmitting data at 1.5 Mbps.

T-3 A digital carrier facility used for transmitting data through the telephone system at 45 Mbps (equivalent to 28 T-1s put together).

TCP Short for Transmission Control Protocol. TCP is the Internet protocol that facilitates a connection-oriented reliable link to the network.

TDMA Short for time division multiple access. This approach divides each frequency into a series of timeslots. Each user is assigned a series of timeslots during which they can broadcast.

Telephony The technology associated with the electronic transmission of voice, fax, or other information between two parties historically associated with the telephone. A telephony application programming interface that assists in providing these services. Using the Internet, three new services are now available:

Ability to make a normal telephone call
Ability to send fax transmissions
Ability to send voice messages along with text email

Thin Client A low-cost computing device that accesses applications and and/or data from a central server over a network. Categories of thin clients include Windows-based terminals (which make up the largest segment), X-terminals, and network computers (NC).

Total Cost of Ownership (TCO) Model that helps IT professionals understand and manage the budgeted (direct) and unbudgeted (indirect) costs incurred for acquiring, maintaining, and using an application or a computing system. TCO normally includes training, upgrades, and administration as well as the purchase price.

Total Security Architecture (TSA) A comprehensive, end-to-end architecture that protects the network from security threats.

TP Monitor Short for transaction processing monitor, a software program that monitors a transaction to ensure that the transaction processes completely. A TP monitor can also be used to assist in load balancing of servers.

Transmission Control Protocol (TCP) The transport layer protocol built on top of the Internet Protocol (IP) in a TCP/IP network. The IP deals only with moving packets of information; TCP enables servers to establish a connection and exchange data streams. It guarantees that the data packets will be delivered and in the same order in which they were sent.

Transmission Control Protocol/Internet Protocol (TCP/IP) A suite of network protocols that allow computers with different architectures and operating system software to communicate with other computers on the Internet. It is the de facto standard for communicating data over the Internet.

Tunneling A technology that enables one network to send its data via another network's connections. Sometimes called IP tunneling.

UDDI Short for Universal Description, Discovery, and Integration, a DNS-like distributed Web directory that would enable services to discover each other and define how they can interact and share information. The end result is expected to be a standards-based Internet directory of business information.

UMTS Universal Mobile Telecommunications System is a third-generation (3G) mobile technology that will deliver broadband information at speeds up to 2Mbits. Besides voice and data, UMTS will deliver audio and video to wireless devices anywhere in the world through fixed, wireless, and satellite systems. UMTS services will launch commercially sometime in the year 2001.

Uptime The amount of time your system is working; the ideal is 100 percent of the time.

URI An acronym for universal resource identifier. The string (often starting with http://) that is used to identify anything on the Web.

URL Short for uniform resource locator. A term used sometimes for certain URIs to indicate that they might change. The URL appears in the address line in the Web browser window, for example, http://www.wiley.com.

User Interface The part of an application that the end user sees on the screen and works with to operate the application, such as menus, forms and buttons.

User Name A name used to gain access to a computer system. In most systems, users can choose their own user names and passwords.

VAN Short for value added network.

VDSL Short for very high data rate digital subscriber line. An evolving form of DSL that can deliver data at a rate of 13 to 52 Mbps downstream and 1.5 to 2.3 Mbps upstream over a single copper twisted-pair line. The operating range of VDSL is up to 4,500 feet from the CO.

Virtual Private Network (VPN) A secure, encrypted private Internet connection. Data is encrypted before being sent and decrypted at the receiving end to maintain privacy and security. A set of communication rules has been created called point-to-point tunneling protocol (PPTP) to create VPNs.

Virus A software program that is loaded onto your computer without your knowledge and runs against your wishes. Most viruses can also replicate themselves. A simple virus that can make a copy of itself over and over again is dangerous because it will quickly use all available memory and bring the system to a halt. An even more dangerous type of virus is one capable of transmitting itself across networks and bypassing security systems. Anti-virus programs periodically check your computer for the best-known viruses.

Voice Over Internet Protocol (VoIP) The delivery of voice information in the language of the Internet, that is, as digital packets instead of the current circuit protocols of the copper-based phone networks. In VoIP systems, analog voice messages are digitized and transmitted as a stream of data (not sound) packets that are reassembled and converted back into a voice signal at their destination. The killer idea is that VoIP allows telephony users to bypass long distance carrier charges by transporting those data packets just like other Internet information. With VoIP, your PC becomes your phone and you can call anywhere in the world for the cost of a local call.

W3C Short for the World Wide Web Consortium, an entity composed of many organizations that work on developing common standards for the evolution of the Web.

WAP Short for Wireless Applications Protocol. WAP is a specification that allows wireless devices to access interactive information services and applications from screens of mobile phones.

WASP Short for wireless application service provider.

WCDMA Wideband code division multiple access is a third-generation mobile communication protocol similar to GSM that is expected to provide enough bandwidth for wireless multimedia applications.

Web Refers to the World Wide Web (www) and is what the Internet became with the introduction of HTML.

Web Browser A software application used to locate and display Web pages. The two most popular browsers are Netscape Navigator and Microsoft Internet Explorer.

Web Hosting Placing an organization's Web page or Web site on a server that belongs to another company and can be accessed via the Internet.

Wide Area Network Local area networks linked together across a large geographic area.

Windows-Based Terminal Thin clients with the lowest cost of ownership, as there are no local applications running on the device. See also network computer.

WLL Short for wireless local loop. A broadband connection system that uses high-frequency radio links to deliver voice and data without the problems of gaining right-of-way for a fiber optic cable installation or finding adequate copper connections for DSL. Also known as fixed-point wireless.

WML Wireless Markup Language is an XML language used to specify content and user interface for WAP devices; the WAP forum provides a DTD for WML. Almost every mobile phone browser around the world supports WML. WML pages are requested and served in the same way as HDML pages. For Web servers to serve WML pages, they must contain the text, .vnd, .wap, or .wml MIME type file extensions.

xDSL This term refers to the assorted flavors of the DSL connections including, but not limited to, ADSL (Asymmetric Digital Subscriber Line), HDSL (High bit-rate DSL), and RADSL (Rate adaptive Asymmetric Digital Subscriber Line).

XML Short for Extensible Markup Language, a version of the Standardized General Markup Language (SGML) designed especially for the Web.

WSP Short for Wireless Service Provider.

References

Allen, Leilani. "ASP selection." *Mortgage Banking*, 60 (9) 2000: 121–122.

Andress, Mandy. "Internal SLAs benefit the entire company." *InfoWorld*, 23 (18), April 30, 2001, 52.

ASP Industry Consortium. *An Overview of Dispute Avoidance and Resolution Best Practices in the ASP Industry White Paper.* Wakefield, MA: ASP Industry Consortium, 2000. Available at: www.allaboutasp.com.

Bannan, Karen J. "How upstarts are changing Web hosting." *Internet World*, 6 (20), October 15, 2000, 76–88.

Bhaskar Neil and Wendell Jones. "Formula for ASP success." *Software Magazine*, 20 (4), August/September 2000, 18–20.

Bendor-Samuel, Peter. "The Dirty dozen: 12 Outsourcing mistakes and how to avoid them." *OutsourcingJournal.com*, June 2001. Available at: www.outsourcingcenter.com.

Bhattacharjee, Debashish. "The devil is in the details." *Intelligent Enterprise*, 4 (2), January 30, 2001, 12–15.

Bianchi, Allessandra. "Software on the Web: ASPs are coming ASAP." *Inc.*, 22 (5), April 2000, 29–32.

Broadbeam Corporation. *Beginner's Guide to Implementing a Successful Wireless Solution*. A White Paper. Princeton, NJ: Broadbeam Corporation, 2000. Available at: www.broadbeam.com.

Caulfield, Brian. "Cover Your ASP." *eCompany*, 2 (1), January/February 2001, 138–40.

Chappell. Laura. 1999. *Introduction to Network Analysis*. New York: Podbooks.

Cherry Tree. *Application Service Providers (ASP): Spotlight Report*. Edina, MN: Cherry Tree & Co., 1999.

Cherry Tree. 2nd *Generation ASPs: Spotlight Report*. Edina, MN: Cherry Tree & Co., 2000.

Converged Networks Case Studies. 1998. Santa Clara, CA: 3Com Corporation.

Danziger, James N. "Computers, Local Government, and the Litany to EDP." *Public Administration Review*, 37 (1), January/February 1977, 28–37.

Dewire, Dawna. "Applications Service Providers." *Information Systems Management*, 17 (4), Fall 2000, 14–19.

DeZoysa, Sanjima. "Can ASPs bite back?" *Telecommunications*, 35 (4), April 2001, 30–4.

Drier, Troy. "Making Content Work." *Intranet Journal Unwired*, March 2001. Available at: www.intranetjournal.com/articles/200010/uw_10_04_00a.html.

Erlanger, Leo. "Storage as universal dial tone." *Internet World*, (16), August 1, 2001, 30–35.

eTForecasts. *Internet Users Forecast by Country*. Buffalo Grove, IL: eTForecasts, July 2001. Available at: www.etforecasts.com.

Ewens, Peter, Simon Landless, and Stagg Newman. "Showing some backbone." *McKinsey Quarterly*, Number 1, 2001. Available at: www.mckinseyquarterly.com/article_page.asp?tk=334090:996:22&ar=996&L2=22&L3=77.

Flanagan, E. B.(A) "Solution providers in the spotlight." *VARBusiness*, 17 (5), March 5, 2001, 56.

Flanagan, E. B.(B) "Adding to the confusion: A tale of two acronyms." *Computer Reseller News*, 35, March 15, 2001, 7.

Flynn, Nancy. L. *The E Policy Handbook*. New York, NY: AMACOM Books. 2001.

Geier, Jim. "Saving lives with roving LANs—Swedish ambulance becomes a true mobile platform." *Network World*, February 5, 2001. Available at: www.nwfusion.com/reviews/2001/0205bgside.html.

Gerwig, Kate. "Service-level disagreement." *Tele.com*, 6 (11), May 28, 2001, 43–50.

Gilbert, Alorie and Jennifer Mateyaschuk. "A Question of convenience: Hosted ERP applications can be quicker, cheaper, and less risky than conventional implementations." *Information Week*, No. 774, February 21, 2000, 34–36.

Goldman, Chris. "Wireless Java's rich future." *Wireless Review*, March 1, 2001. Available at: www.telecomclick.com/magazinearticle.asp?magazineid =9&releaseid=5569&magazinearticleid=65180.

Girard, Kim. "DSL has the right price." *ComputerWorld*, 35 (20), May 19, 2001, 45–6.

Hall, Mark. "The Case for ASPs." *ComputerWorld*, 34 (24), June 12, 2000, 58–59. Available at: www.computerworld.com/cwi/story/ 0,1199,NAV47_STO45795,00.html.

Hamm, Steve. "Oracle: Why it's cool again." *Business Week*, No. 3680, May 8, 2000, 114–26.

Heim, Sarah J. "Report: Growth in wireless still slow but steady." *Brandweek*, 42 (11), March 12, 2001, 34.

Hogan, Hank. "No strings attached." *Electronic Business*, 27 (7), July 2001, 117–9.

Holden, Greg. "ISP Buyers Guide." *CNET*, August 21, 2000. Available at: http://cnet.com/internet/0-3762-7-2518426.html.

Interactive Week A. "Internet Service Providers." *Interactive Week*, 8 (22), June 4, 2001, S-28–S-32.

Interactive Week B. "Fixed Wireless Providers." *Interactive Week*, 8 (22), June 4, 2001, S-46–S-47.

Interactive Week C. "Mobile Wireless Providers." *Interactive Week*, 8 (22), June 4, 2001, S-48–S-50.

ITAA 2000. *The ITAA ASP Customer Demand Survey*. Washington, DC: The Information Technology Association of America, May 22, 2000. Available at: www.itaa.org.

Jaruzelski, Barry, Frank Ribeiro and Randy Lake. *ASP 101: Understanding the Application Service Provider Model*. A White Paper. New York: Booz-Allen & Hamilton, 2001.

Kane, M. "Enter NAS and SAN." *The McKinsey Quarterly*, 1, 2000, 42–51. Available at: www.mckinseyquarterly.com/article_page .asp?tk=334090:373:4&ar=373&L2=4&L3=42#box1.

Kapoor, Atul. 1999. *Total cost of application ownership (TCA)*. A White Paper, No. 199503. Manasquan, NJ: The Tolly Group. Available at: www.tolly.com.

Kearney, Tim. "Why OUTsourcing is IN: Application Service Providers (ASP) are making it easier for companies to use outside services again." *Strategic Finance*, 81 (7), January 2000, 34–38.

Kemp, Ted. "Sales Reps to Try Wireless CRM." *Internet Week*, August 28, 2000, 22. Available at: www.internetweek.com/ebizapps/ebiz082800-1.htm.

King, Elliot. "Windows remains the OS of choice for application service provider (ASP) access." . *Windows 2000*. Available at: www.win2000mag.com/articles/print.cfm?ArticleID=20112.

King, John L. and Kenneth L. Kraemer. "Cost as a social impact of information technology." In N. L. Moss (Ed.), *Telecommunication and Productivity*. Reading, MA: Addison-Wesley, 1981.

King, John L. and Edward L. Schrems. "Cost-benefit analysis of information systems development and operation." *Computing Surveys*, 10 (1), March 1978, 22–34.

Kolstad, Rob. *Becoming an ISPI*. Berkeley Software Design, Inc., December 5, 2000.

Lake, Matthew. "Top 5 ISP Review." *CNET*, March 6, 2001.

Lawson, Steven. "Bluetooth offers flood of in-building services." *Electronic Engineering Times*. December 19, 2000, 40+.

Lawton, Michael. BIA fn ISP Survey. Chantilly, VA: *BIA Financial Network*, June 2000.

Liebmann, Lenny. "It's New: Baby Sitters." *InternetWeek*, April 2, 2001, 39–41. Available at: www.internetweek.com/indepth01/indepth032801.htm.

Locke, Christopher, Rich Levine, Doc Searls, and David Weinberger. 2000. *The Cluetrain Manifesto: The end of business as usual*. New York: Perseus Books.

Martin, Michael. "NorthPoint fiasco sours small business to DSL." *Network World*, 18 (15), April 9, 2001, 25–26.

McWhirter, Douglas. "Stop! Thief! Are you comfortable in turning over your customer information to strangers?" *CRM customer relationship management*, January 2001, 40–46.

Medford, Cassimir. "Pipe dreams." *PC Magazine*, February 6, 2001. Available at: www.pcmag.com/article/0,2997,a%253D4623,00.asp.

Metzler, Jim. *Defining Today's ASP Supply Chain*. A White Paper. Newton, MA: Ashton, Metzler & Associates, November 2000. Available at: www.ashton-metzler.com.

Moore, Geoffrey. 1999. *Crossing the Chasm: Marketing and selling high-tech products to mainstream customers*. New York: HarperBusiness.

Navarrete, Angela. "Fast Forward: Future Internet." *PC World*, 17 (4), April, 2000, 84+.

Octon Technologies. 2001. *Outsourcing*. Stamford, CT: Octon Technologies. Available at: www.octon.com.

Pappalardo, Denise. "Genuity betting on better SLAs." *Network World*, 18 (19), May 7, 2001, 39–40.

Passori, Alfred L. "Risk shift." *Software Magazine*, 20 (3), June 2000, 18+.

Paul, Lauren Gibbons. "Classic Outsourcing Blunders." *Darwin*, 1 (11), August 2001, 49–56.

Pender, Lee and Lorraine Cosgrove Ware. "Decidedly not gee whiz." *CIO Magazine*, March 15, 2001. Available at: www.cio.com/archive/031501/geewhiz.html.

Raths, David. "The honeymoon is over: When the relationship with your outsourcer falls apart, should you get counseling or call it quits?" *InfoWorld*, April 30, 2001, 41–44.

Richter, Randy. "Getting to know your ASP." *Association Management*, 52 (6), June 2000, 19–20.

Rosa, Jerry. "Happily ever after." *Smart Partner*, 4 (25), August 20, 2001, 18–22.

Schactmann, Noah. "IT pros find job-hopping pays." *Information Week*, Issue 843, June 26, 2001, 217–24.

Seybold, Andrew M. "A Wireless Primer—Part I." *PocketPC Magazine*, July 2000. Available at: www.pocketpcmag.com/July00/seybold.htm.

Seybold, Andrew M. "A Wireless Primer—Part II." *PocketPC Magazine*, November 2000. Available at: www.pocketpcmag.com/Nov00/seybold.ptII.htm.

Smetannikov, Max. "Fevered Pitch: Data Centers, MSPs fight over customers." *Interactive Week*, March 19, 2001, 13–15.

Software and Information Industry Association (SIIA). 2000. *New Corporate IT Manager Survey Reveals Growing Interest in ASP Model*. Washington, DC: SIIA. Available at: www.siia.net.

SPEX. "Representative enterprise resource management tools." *Software Magazine*, 20 (6), December 2000, 33–39.

Spring, Tom. "Net phone service revised, revamped." *Network World*, 18 (33). August 15, 2001, 24–25.

Stevenson, Douglas W. NMS: *Network Management White Paper—What it is and what it isn't*. April 1995. Available at: http://netman.cit.buffalo.edu/doc/dstevenson/

TrendsReport 2000. *Software*. Available at: wwwtrendsreport.net/software/3.html.

Tsin, E. "Showdown at the Wireless ISP Corral." *CNET*, September 7, 2000.

Tweney, Dylan. "The Web's new plumbers." *Ecompany.com*, 2 (1), March 2001, 126–28.

Voth, Danna. "ASP Ascendant." *CRM customer relationship management*, January 2001, 34–38.

Walker, Meg. "Small Businesses sold on wireless LANs." *VARBusiness*, 17 (4). February 14, 2001.

Wetzel, Rebecca. BIA Financial Services ISP survey. *BIA Financial Network*, September 18, 2000. Available at: www.bia.com/industryreps.htm.

Wexler, Joanie. "ASPs: Helpful or hype-ful?" *Business Communications Review*, 30 (9), September 2000, 32–8.

Wireless Internet Applications Case Study. Miami FL: Dataforce Corp. February 1, 2001

Wittmann, Art. "Is there an ASP in your future?" *Information Week*, No. 791, June 19, 2000, 75–80.

Zona Research. *Application Service Providers and the Evolution of the Internet Integrated Enterprise*. Redwood City, CA: Zona Research, September 1999.

Zona Research. *The Zona Enterprise Usage Study (ZEUS) Application Service Provider Report, Q2 2000*. Report prepared in conjunction with the Best Practices Committee of the ASP Industry Consortium. Redwood City, CA: Zona Research, August 2000.

Zona Research. *The Zona Enterprise Usage Study (ZEUS) Application Service Provider Report, Q1 2001*. Report prepared in conjunction with the Best Practices Committee of the ASP Industry Consortium. Redwood City, CA: Zona Research, February 2001.

Index

T